THE MILITARY OCCUPATION
of the
TERRITORY OF NEW MEXICO
from
1846 to 1851

THE MILITARY OCCUPATION
of the
TERRITORY OF NEW MEXICO
from
1846 to 1851

Facsimile of Original 1909 Edition
by
Ralph Emerson Twitchell

New Foreword
by
Richard Melzer, Ph.D.

SANTA FE

New Material © 2007 by Sunstone Press. All Rights Reserved.

No part of this book may be reproduced in any form or by any electronic or mechanical means including information storage and retrieval systems without permission in writing from the publisher, except by a reviewer who may quote brief passages in a review.

Sunstone books may be purchased for educational, business, or sales promotional use. For information please write: Special Markets Department, Sunstone Press, P.O. Box 2321, Santa Fe, New Mexico 87504-2321.

Library of Congress Cataloging-in-Publication Data

Twitchell, Ralph Emerson, 1859-1925.
 The military occupation of the territory of New Mexico from 1846 to 1851 : fascsimile of original 1909 edition / by Ralph Emerson Twitchell ; new foreword by Richard Melzer.
   p.cm. -- (Southwest heritage series)
 Originally published in 1909 by Smith-Brooks Co., Denver, Colo., under the title: The history of the military occupation of the territory of New Mexico from 1846 to 1851 by the government of the United States.
  ISBN: 978-0-86534-575-1 (softcover : alk. paper)
 1. New Mexico--History--19th century. 2. Mexican War, 1846-1848--Campaigns. 3. New Mexico--Biography. I. Twitchell, Ralph Emerson, 1859-1925. History of the military occupation of the territory of New Mexico from 1846 to 1851 by the government of the United States. II. Title.

F801.T974 2007
78.9'049--dc22

2007061708

WWW.SUNSTONEPRESS.COM
SUNSTONE PRESS / POST OFFICE BOX 2321 / SANTA FE, NM 87504-2321 /USA
(505) 988-4418 / ORDERS ONLY (800) 243-5644 / FAX (505) 988-1025

The Southwest Heritage Series is dedicated to Jody Ellis and Marcia Muth Miller, the founders of Sunstone Press, whose original purpose and vision continues to inspire and motivate our publications.

CONTENTS

THE SOUTHWEST HERITAGE SERIES / I

FOREWORD TO THIS EDITION / II

FACSIMILE OF 1909 EDITION / III

I

THE SOUTHWEST HERITAGE SERIES

The history of the United States is written in hundreds of regional histories and literary works. Those letters, essays, memoirs, biographies and even collections of fiction are often first-hand accounts by people who wanted to memorialize an event, a person or simply record for posterity the concerns and issues of the times. Many of these accounts have been lost, destroyed or overlooked. Some are in private or public collections but deemed to be in too fragile condition to permit handling by contemporary readers and researchers.

However, now with the application of twenty-first century technology, nineteenth and twentieth century material can be reprinted and made accessible to the general public. These early writings are the DNA of our history and culture and are essential to understanding the present in terms of the past.

The Southwest Heritage Series is a form of literary preservation. Heritage by definition implies legacy and these early works are our legacy from those who have gone before us. To properly present and preserve that legacy, no changes in style or contents have been made. The material reprinted stands on its own as it first appeared. The point of view is that of the author and the era in which he or she lived. We would not expect photographs of people from the past to be re-imaged with modern clothes, hair styles and backgrounds. We should not, therefore, expect their ideas and personal philosophies to reflect our modern concepts.

Remember, reading their words and sharing their thoughts is a passport back into understanding how the past was shaped and how it influenced today's world.

Our hope is that new access to these older books will provide readers with a challenging and exciting experience.

II

FOREWORD TO THIS EDITION
by
Richard Melzer, Ph.D.

Historians have long admired Ralph Emerson Twitchell's *The Leading Facts of New Mexican History*, considered the first major history of the state. Put succinctly by former State Historian Robert J. Tórrez, Twitchell's five-volume work has "become the standard by which all subsequent books on New Mexico history are measured."[1] As Twitchell wrote in the preface of his first volume, his goal in writing *The Leading Facts* was to respond to the "pressing need" for a history of New Mexico with a commitment to "accuracy of statement, simplicity of style, and impartiality of treatment." Twitchell added that he sought to make his work "available to the person of moderate means," a truly ironic goal as copies of the first edition of *The Leading Facts* sell for well over $500 on the current rare book market, if one can find them.[2]

Less well known is *The Military Occupation of New Mexico*, published in 1909, and *Old Santa Fe*, published in 1925.

Ralph Emerson Twitchell was born in Ann Arbor, Michigan, on November 29, 1859. According to a fifty-seven page genealogy he prepared and published privately, the Twitchells (or Twichels or Twichells) date back to the time of William the Conqueror in English history. The earliest Twitchell to emigrate to the American colonies arrived in Massachusetts in 1630, "imbued with the spirit of the Puritans," in Twitchell's words. Twitchell's great grandfather fought on the rebel side in the American Revolutionary battles of Lexington and Bunker Hill.[3]

Twitchell earned his LL.B. degree from the University of Michigan in 1882. By December of that year the twenty-three year old had arrived in Santa Fe to serve as a law clerk to Henry L. Waldo, solicitor of the Atchison, Topeka and Santa Fe Railroad in New Mexico.[4] Upon his arrival, the *Santa Fe New Mexican* described Twitchell as "a pleasant young gentleman of excellent social qualities and fine legal attainments."[5] Twitchell worked for the Santa Fe in increasingly important roles for the balance of his legal career.

Twitchell was involved in political and civic activities from his earliest days in New Mexico. In 1885 he helped organize a new territorial militia in Santa Fe and saw active duty in western New Mexico. Later appointed judge advocate of the Territorial Militia, he attained the rank of colonel, a title he was proud to use for the rest of his life. By 1893 he was elected the mayor of Santa Fe and, thereafter, district attorney of Santa Fe County. He was, in fact, one of the capital city's greatest boosters, supporting the use of traditional Southwest architecture, serving as the president of the local chamber of commerce, and acting as director of the Santa Fe Fiesta when it was rejuvenated shortly after World War I.

Twitchell probably promoted New Mexico as much as any single New Mexican of his generation. An avid supporter of New Mexico statehood, he argued the territory's case for elevated political status, celebrated its final victory in 1912, and even designed New Mexico's first state flag in 1915. He served on the management team of New Mexico's prize-winning state exhibit at the Panama-California Exposition in San Diego and was responsible for suggesting the exhibit's unique design, a replica of a Spanish colonial mission church, which later became the design of Santa Fe's new Museum of Fine Arts. Twitchell served on the board of regents at the Museum of New Mexico and, briefly, on the board of regents at New Mexico A&M (now New Mexico State University).

Active in seemingly countless organizations, from New Mexico's Good Roads Club to the National Irrigation Congress, Twitchell consistently rose to leadership roles in each group he joined. In the Republican Party, he chaired the party's central committee in New Mexico from 1902 to 1903. A life member of the Historical Society of New Mexico, he served as the society's vice president from 1910 to 1924 and its president in 1924.[6] Twitchell was even credited with rescuing the Spanish and Mexican archives when the territorial capitol burned in May 1892. Many of his contemporaries must have reiterated the question that former governor L. Bradford Prince posed in a personal letter to Twitchell in 1919: "How [do you] do it?"[7]

No person could have served so long and have done so much

without controversy; Twitchell was no exception. As early as the 1890s he had joined other Republican leaders in the Knights of Liberty, a secret society often identified with the Santa Fe Ring.[8] Twitchell split with several key leaders of his own party, including Max Frost, the editor of the *Santa Fe New Mexican*, whom Twitchell described as "a lying scoundrel,"[9] and Thomas Catron, the most powerful Republican in the territory in the late nineteenth century. In 1892 Catron went so far as to accuse Twitchell of being "under the influence of whiskey and frequenting a very low dive," among other things, at the territorial fair in Albuquerque.[10] Such behavior would have been unusual for Twitchell, if it happened at all, but Catron's charges illustrate the degree of animosity that had developed between the two men within a decade of Twitchell's arrival on the scene.

Twitchell could more accurately be accused of being overly zealous and, as a result, sometimes offensive. In 1901, for example, he wrote to the editor of the *Albuquerque Evening Citizen* with the assertion that any businessman who did not publicly support New Mexico statehood should be "smoke[d] out," implying that those who opposed statehood should no longer be welcomed in the territory.[11] As a result of such statements and poor relations with top Republican leaders like Catron, Twitchell was not included as a delegate to the state constitutional convention of 1910, an affront that undoubtedly bruised his considerable ego.

Twitchell was also involved in two serious controversies regarding Native American rights. In the first of these confrontations, Twitchell had overseen the filming of the sacred Corn Dance, banned to the general public at Taos Pueblo. Without obtaining permission, Twitchell included images of the dance in a movie shown to thousands of visitors to the New Mexico exhibit at the Panama-California Exposition. Convinced that these public showings had caused illness among Indians employed at the exposition, someone broke into the New Mexico building and confiscated the ill-gotten film. Despite an investigation by Pinkerton detectives, the thief was never found. Far worse, Twitchell showed no remorse for betraying the Indians' trust. In fact, he wired Santa Fe for another copy of the film (stored at the Museum of New Mexico), showed the second copy, and blatantly exploited the incident to promote New Mexico and its exhibit at the exposition.[12]

Twitchell became embroiled in a far wider Indian controversy when he served as one of the principal authors of the infamous Bursum Bill in the early 1920s. Introduced by New Mexico's Senator H.O. Bursum, the bill gravely threatened pueblo water rights and considerable portions of Indian lands. Although Twitchell was appointed special assistant to the U.S. Attorney General and traveled to Washington, D.C., to testify before House and Senate committees, the legislation was defeated by the combined effort of pueblo leaders, organized as the All-Pueblo Council, and agitated artists and authors of the Taos and Santa Fe art colonies.[13]

Fortunately for Twitchell, he is less remembered for his involvement in such controversies than for his magnum opus, *The Leading Facts of New Mexican History*. Relying on his own extensive library, the libraries of many colleagues, and every document that might "throw light upon the occurrences of the past," Twitchell created a work in which he "tried to be accurate and fair."[14]

While many contemporaries praised Twitchell's accuracy and fairness, others wondered how fair he could be if one of his major goals, as stated on the first page of his first volume, was to "impress upon the reader's mind the fortitude, the courage, the suffering, and the martyrdom of those who first brought to New Mexico the banner of Christianity and civilization."[15]

Native Americans might well take exception to the idea that only those representing the Catholic faith and Spanish culture displayed fortitude, courage, suffering, and martyrdom in the Spanish colonial period. Spanish newspaper editors also took exception to Twitchell's devotion to English as the preferred language in schools and businesses, at the risk of losing *'el idioma de Cervantes'* and, hence, a major part of their Hispanic culture.[16] Others, like the Hispanic historian Benjamin M. Read, questioned how well Anglo authors like Twitchell could translate Spanish documents and how much accurate historical information was literally lost in their ethnocentric translations.[17] Finally, some questioned Twitchell's objectivity when it was rumored that "the amount of space allocated to contemporaries [in *The Leading Facts*] was weighed by the amount of their subscriptions to help pay for [publication costs]" of at least volumes three, four, and five.[18]

There is no indication that Twitchell heeded this criticism, especially given the near universal acclaim his books received among

Anglo peers in New Mexico and across the country.[19] Inspired by this success and truly devoted to the study of history, Twitchell became the most prolific historian of his era, writing several additional histories of the Southwest, making frequent historical addresses, and founding, financing, and editing an ambitious, but short-lived, periodical called, *Old Santa Fe: A Magazine of History, Archaeology, Genealogy, and Biography*.[20]

But *The Leading Facts* remained Twitchell's major contribution to New Mexico history. Limited to fifteen hundred copies in its first edition, *The Leading Facts* had become a rare book by the 1960s when its first two volumes were reissued by Horn and Wallace in 1963. A rare book again by the late twentieth century, a new, affordable edition is long overdue and quite timely. Just as Twitchell's first edition in 1911 helped celebrate New Mexico's entry into statehood in 1912, the newest edition serves as a tribute to the state's centennial celebration of 2012.

Colonel Twitchell would have wanted it that way; boosting New Mexico, its resources and citizens was, after all, the central purpose of Twitchell's long life and productive career. In the apt words of an editorial in the *Santa Fe New Mexican* at the time of Twitchell's death in 1925: "As press agent for the best things of New Mexico, her traditions, history, beauty, glamour, scenery, archaeology, and material resources, he was indefatigable and efficient."[21]

NOTES

1   Robert J. Tórrez, *UFOs Over Galisteo and Other Stories of New Mexico's History* (Albuquerque: University of New Mexico Press, 2004): 131. Also see Howard Robert Lamar, *The Far Southwest* (Albuquerque: University of New Mexico Press, 2000): 457.

2   Ralph Emerson Twitchell, *The Leading Facts of New Mexican History* (Cedar Rapids, Iowa: The Torch Press, 1911): I:ix.

3   Ralph Emerson Twitchell, *Genealogy of the Twitchell Family* (n.c.: privately printed, 1929). A rare copy of Twitchell's genealogy can be found in the Ralph Emerson Twitchell Papers, Box 1, Folder 4, Fray Angélico Chávez Library, Museum of New Mexico, Santa Fe, New Mexico; hereafter sited as the Twitchell Papers. General biographical works on Twitchell include Myra Ellen Jenkins, "Ralph Emerson Twitchell," *Arizona and the West*, vol. 8 (Summer 1966): 102-06; J. Michael Pattison, "Four 'Gentlemen' Historians of New

Mexico" (Unpublished M.A. thesis, New Mexico Highlands University, 1992): 43-9.

4   Twitchell so admired Waldo that he named his first and only son after his supervisor. The boy's mother, Twitchell's first wife Margaret, died on January 29, 1900. Twitchell dedicated *The Leading Facts* in Margaret's memory. He married his second wife, Estelle Bennett (1872-1952), in 1916. Twitchell, *Genealogy*, 446.

5   Quoted in the *Santa Fe New Mexican*, August 15, 1999.

6   Appropriately, the Historical Society of New Mexico's annual Ralph Emerson Twitchell Award is given "for significant contributions to the field of history by individuals, organizations, or institutions."

7   L. Bradford Prince to Ralph Emerson Twitchell, Flushing, New York, September 10, 1919, Ralph Emerson Twitchell Collection, New Mexico State Records Center and Archives, Santa Fe, New Mexico; hereafter cited as the NMSRCA.

8   Victor Westphall, *Thomas Benton Catron and His Era* (Tucson: University of Arizona Press, 1973): 208-09.

9   Quoted in ibid, 390n.

10 Quoted in ibid., 261. Twitchell and Catron also argued about a loan Catron had made to Twitchell near the turn of the century. Ibid., 390.

11 *Albuquerque Evening Citizen*, April 25, 1901, quoted in Robert W. Larson, *New Mexico's Quest for Statehood, 1846-1912* (Albuquerque: University of New Mexico Press, 1968): 200.

12 Matthew F. Bokovoy, *The San Diego World Fairs and Southwestern Memory, 1880-1940* (Albuquerque: University of New Mexico Press, 2005): 132-34.

13 The best description of Twitchell's role in drafting and defending the Bursum Bill is found in Lawrence C. Kelly, *The Assault on Assimilation: John Collier and the Origins of Indian Policy Reform* (Albuquerque: University of New Mexico Press, 1983): 203-54. According to Kelly, Twitchell's defense of the bill "crumbled and his composure wilted" under close examination before a Senate committee. "By the time [Twitchell] completed his presentation, there was little doubt that the original Bursum Bill was indeed a dead letter." Ibid., 239. On the *Santa Fe New Mexican's* coverage of the bill and its fate, see Oliver LaFarge, *Santa Fe* (Norman: University of Oklahoma Press, 1959): 274-81.

14 Twitchell, *The Leading Facts*, I:viii.

15 Ibid.

16 Doris Meyer, *Speaking for Themselves: Neomexicano Cultural Identity and the Spanish Language Press, 1880-1920* (Albuquerque: University of New Mexico Press, 1996): 119-20.

17 Ibid., 200-01. For Twitchell's strong feelings regarding the teaching of English, see *The Leading Facts*, II:508-09, and his address, "The Public School," delivered at high school commencement in Raton, New Mexico, on May 24, 1899. Ralph Emerson Twitchell, Vertical File, Fray Angélico Chávez Library, Museum of New Mexico, Santa Fe, New Mexico.

18 Beatrice Chauvent, *Hewett and Friends: A Biography of Santa Fe's Vibrant Era* (Santa Fe: Museum of New Mexico Press, 1983): 104. For a sample prepublication subscription card for volumes one and two of *The Leading Facts*, see the Twitchell Papers, Box 2, Folder 7, Twitchell Papers.

19 For a sample of this praise for *The Leading Facts*, see a promotional brochure produced by its publisher, the Torch Press, found in the L. Bradford Prince Collection, NMSRCA.

20 Twitchell's other histories include *Spanish Archives of New Mexico*, 2 vols. (Cedar Rapids, Iowa: The Torch Press, 1914) and *Old Santa Fe: The Story of New Mexico's Ancient Capital* (Santa Fe: Santa Fe New Mexican, 1925). The periodical, *Old Santa Fe*, served as the Historical Society of New Mexico's official bulletin from its inception in 1913 till its demise three years later.

21 Editorial, *Santa Fe New Mexican*, August 26, 1925. Twitchell died at the Clara Barton Hospital in Los Angeles, California, of a paralytic stroke and heart failure on August 26, 1925. He was sixty-five. His last wish, to be buried below the Cross of the Martyrs in Santa Fe, was unanimously approved by the Santa Fe city council, but he was temporarily buried at Fairview Cemetery until a site below the cross could be identified. His funeral was one of the largest in Santa Fe history, with leading members of both major political parties present and a line of cars stretching half a mile. His temporary burial site at Fairview has become permanent and his last wish was never fulfilled. *Santa Fe New Mexican*, August 26-29 and 31, 1925; Paul A.F. Walter, "Obituary: Ralph Emerson Twitchell," *New Mexico Historical Review*, Vol. 1 (January 1926): 78-85; Richard Melzer, *Buried Treasures: Famous and Unusual Gravesites in New Mexico History* (Santa Fe: Sunstone Press).

III

FACSIMILE OF 1909 EDITION

THE HISTORY

OF THE

Military Occupation

OF THE

Territory of New Mexico

FROM 1846 TO 1851

BY THE

GOVERNMENT OF THE UNITED STATES

TOGETHER WITH

Biographical Sketches of Men Prominent in the Conduct of the Government During that Period

BY

RALPH EMERSON TWITCHELL

Vice-President New Mexico Historical Society

DENVER, COLORADO
THE SMITH-BROOKS COMPANY, PUBLISHERS
1909

Copyright, 1909
By Ralph Emerson Twitchell

General Stephen Watts Kearny.

To the memory of Lawrence L. Waldo, who lost his life by the assassin's bullet, at Mora, New Mexico, on the first day of the Mexican uprising, January 19, 1847, this volume is inscribed.

He was a pioneer upon the old Santa Fé-Chihuahua Trail, and, in all his business and social relations, was the true concept of a gentleman.

Although a non-combatant, he was a martyr to the march of American progress and civilization.

CONTENTS

	Page.
CHAPTER I..	17

1. The War with Mexico. 2. Causes and Leading Events. 3. Position Claimed by Mexico. 4. The United States and Its Claims. 5. Annexation of Texas No Just Cause for the War. 6. Mexico Begins Hostilities. 7. Congress Declares Existence of War.

CHAPTER II... 38

1. Organization of the Army of the West, Under General S. W. Kearny. 2. March Across the Plains and Concentration at Bent's Fort. 3. The Army Invades New Mexico and Crosses the Raton Mountains. 4. The Army Reaches Las Vegas and General Kearny Makes Address. 5. The Army Moves on the Capital by Way of San Miguel and the Apache Pass. 6. General Manuel Armijo Masses Mexican Forces at Apache Pass. 7. General Kearny Receives Word that Armijo Has Fled and Army Dispersed. 8. Army Proceeds to Santa Fé. 9. General Kearny Takes Possession of Capital and Hoists the American Flag. 10. Proclamation Issued, Claiming New Mexico for the United States. 11. Kearny, with a Substantial Force, Marches Down the Valley of the Rio Grande and Returns to Santa Fé. 12. Kearny, with Portion of the Army, Leaves for California, Colonel Doniphan Remaining in Command at Santa Fé.

CHAPTER III.. 95

1. The March to Chihuahua. 2. Colonel Doniphan Ordered Against the Navajo Indians. 3. Treaty with the Navajo Indians by Doniphan. 4. Colonel Doniphan Proceeds Down the Valley of the Rio Grande. 5. Battle of the Brazito. 6. Colonel Doniphan Occupies El Paso. 7. Marches on the City of Chihuahua. 8. The Battle of Sacramento. 9. Occupation of the City of Chihuahua. 10. Departure of Army for Saltillo and Monterey. 11. Return of the Army to the United States.

	Page.
CHAPTER IV	122

1. General Sterling Price in Command at Santa Fé. 2. The Archuleta Conspiracy. 3. The Taos Revolution. 4. The Killing of Governor Charles Bent. 5. The Battles of La Cañada, Embudo, Taos and Mora. 6. The Leaders Are Tried by Court Martial and Hanged. 7. Fight with Indians at Red River Canon. 8. Fight at Las Vegas and Destruction of the Town. 9. Fight at Arroyo Hondo. 10. Fr. Antonio Jose Martinez. 11. Legislative Assembly Under Military Rule. 12. Differences Between Military and Civil Authorities. 13. Formation of the Territory of New Mexico.

BIOGRAPHICAL SKETCHES.

1. General Stephen Watts Kearny	203
2. Governor Donaciano Vigil	207
3. Willard P. Hall	230
4. Diego Archuleta	238
5. Thomas H. Benton	250
6. Carlos Beaubien	267
7. Christopher (Kit) Carson	271
8. Manuel Antonio Chaves	285
9. Nicolas Pino	310
10. David Waldo	323
11. William Gilpin	337
12. John W. Reid	346
13. Francis P. Blair, Jr.	368
14. General Sterling Price	358
15. Henry Connelly	365
16. James Magoffin	376
17. Antonio Jose Otero	361
18. Richard Hanson Weightman	381

ILLUSTRATIONS

Subject.	Page.
Portrait of General Stephen Watts Kearny	3
Portrait of General A. W. Doniphan	18
Government Scout—He Led the Way	22
The Army of the West Crossing the Great Plains	25
Old Fort Bent	27
A Valuable Aid to the Commissary Department	30
The Army Crossing the Sapello	34
General Kearny Addressing the People of Las Vegas	37
The Army Leaving Las Vegas for Santa Fé	39
Ruins of Pecos Pueblo—Ancient Aztec Kiva	42
Ruins of Old Catholic Church at Pecos Pueblo	44
Alcalde of Pecos Announcing Flight of General Armijo	47
The Army at Apache Pass	51
Portrait of General Manuel Armijo	55
Fac-Simile of Proclamation of General Armijo	58-59
Raising American Flag Over Old Palace	66
Old Palace, 1909	68
Proclamation of General Kearny at Santa Fé	70-71
Fac-Simile of Oath of Allegiance of Juan Bautista Vigil y Alarid	76-77
Plan of Santa Fé and Its Environs	81
Portrait of Governor Charles Bent	85
Fac-Simile of Page of Stamped Paper	88
General Kearny and Command on the Gila, En Route to California	90
Santo Domingo Indians Entertaining Kearny and Staff	92
Fac-Simile of Page of Kearny Code	94
Portrait of General Doniphan at Seventy Years of Age	97
Portrait of General Sterling Price, 1846	99
General Doniphan Concluding Treaty with Navajo Indians	101
General Doniphan's Command Crossing the Jornada del Muerto	103
Plan of the Battle of Brazito	104
Fac-Simile of Black Flag Carried by Mexicans at Battle of Brazito	106
The Battle of Brazito	108

Subject.	Page.
Cannon Captured at Battle of Sacramento	110
Plan of the Battle of Sacramento	112
Charge of Captain Reid at Sacramento	114
The Missouri Mounted Volunteer	117
Old Church at Taos	126
Battle of Taos—Death of Captain Burgwin	130
Portrait of Fr. Antonio Jose Martinez	135
Battle of Mora	137
Fight at Las Vegas	143
Monument to General Doniphan at Liberty, Missouri	189
Portrait of Gen. S. W. Kearny	202
Portrait of Donaciano Vigil	206
Portrait of Willard P. Hall	229
Portrait of Don Diego Archuleta	238
Fac-Simile of Certificate of Decoration of Cross of Honor to Archuleta by Mexican Government	241
Don Diego Archuleta in Plaza, 1884	245
Fac-Simile of Brigadier General's Commission to Archuleta by Governor Connelly	246
Portrait of Thomas H. Benton	249
Portrait of Carlos Beaubien	266
Portrait of Christopher (Kit) Carson	270
West Pueblo at Taos	273
Old Home of Carson at Taos	276
Grave of Carson at Taos	281
Portrait of Manuel Antonio Chaves	284
Portrait of Nicolas Pino	309
Portrait of David Waldo	322
Portrait of William Gilpin	336
Portrait of John W. Reid	345
Portrait of General Sterling Price	357
Portrait of Governor Henry Connelly	364
Portrait of Frank P. Blair	367
Portrait of James Magoffin	375
Portrait of Richard Hanson Weightman	380

INTRODUCTION.

A comprehensive history of New Mexico remains to be written. Many books and pamphlets, covering various periods in its history, have been published but no one of them is entirely free from errors and inaccuracies.

The general lack of knowledge of the events which have transpired in this portion of our country, even during so brief and recent a period of our history as that covered by this volume, displayed by the average citizen in casual conversation, has prompted and induced its preparation. While making no special pretense as an historical writer, the author has attempted to record, with reasonable accuracy, the events of the American Occupation period. For more than a quarter of a century a citizen of New Mexico, he has always been interested in securing all the information possible relative to its past. No opportunity was lost by way of inquiry of the old residents of the City of Santa Fé and elsewhere during the first years of his residence in the Territory. Almost all of the old men, who were personally cognizant of the affairs of New Mexico during the war with Mexico, have passed away, but in many note books has been faithfully recorded every statement of consequence, bearing upon the history of New Mexico as communicated by them to the author. Old documents, pictures and books and letters have been collected and preserved with scrupulous care.

While yet very young and living in Jackson county, Missouri, the author met and was well acquainted with General Doniphan and Colonel John W.

Reid, who had been a captain in Doniphan's regiment. On many occasions he has listened to a recital of the events transpiring during the great march from the Missouri river to Chihuahua. General Doniphan was always willing to tell of his experiences. Colonel Reid often told of the battles of Brazito and Sacramento. It was he who actually led a charge of cavalry up the hill at Sacramento, against an enemy entrenched and resisting with heavy artillery the assault of the gallant Missouri volunteers. From him was learned the story of the battle of Brazito, how the black flag waved from the lance of the Mexican officer who demanded the surrender of Doniphan, the flight of Ponce de Leon, the Mexican general, the defeat of the enemy at Sacramento, the occupation of Chihuahua, its evacuation and the army's march to join General Zachary Taylor. These stories made great impressions; the pictures formed of battles, of fights with Indians, the hunting of buffalo, the treaty with the Navajos and the descriptions of localities and individuals, have never been eradicated and are as vivid and as realistic as though of yesterday.

New Mexico, in its more than three centuries of Spanish, Mexican and American control, has been the theatre of much historic drama. Here is presented to the student a wonderful field of historic research. The American Occupation period has been chosen as the one most easily described, and, at the same time, one of the most interesting in the history of the American people, containing, as it does, the deeds of men who won the West, men whose courage, devotion to country and true citizenship enabled them to "accomplish the greatest military achievement of modern times, a single regiment of citizen soldiers, marching nearly six thousand miles through five states of a foreign nation, living off the resources of the invaded country, almost annihilating a powerful army, conquering and treating with powerful Indian tribes, and, returning home, graced with the trophies of victory, all with the loss of less than a hundred men."

Such deeds should appeal to every loyal American and should find portrayal in every school house throughout the land, thereby inspiring and instilling the lessons of patriotism, honor, valor and love of country.

In the preparation of this volume occasion has been had to consult the following authorities:

Kendall's Santa Fé Expedition.
Gregg's Commerce of the Prairies.
Marcy's Prairie Traveller.
Bartlett's Explorations in New Mexico.
Reports of Operations of the Army of the West—Emory, Abert, Cooke and Johnston.
Hughes' Doniphan Expedition.
The Doniphan Exposition—Connelley.
Campaigning with Doniphan, Edwards.
Reports of Wheeler and Powell.
Messages of the Presidents, Jackson, Polk and Taylor.
History of New Mexico—Prince.
Letters on The Mexican War—Ex. Document Number 60.
The Vigil Papers—N. M. Historical Society Library.
New Mexican Archives at Washington, D. C.
Court Records—Santa Fé and Taos.
New Mexico Historical Society Library.

The portraits and illustrations are copies of old prints, oil paintings, documents, books and many steel engravings and wood cuts and lithographs. These have been faithfully and artistically reproduced. A number of the illustrations are by K. M. Chapman, an artist of Las Vegas, N. M., drawn from combinations of old pictures and, with the use of historical data and present physical conditions, all are authentic and reliable.

RALPH E. TWITCHELL.

Las Vegas, New Mexico, January 1, 1909.

The Military Occupation
OF THE
Territory of New Mexico
FROM 1846 TO 1851

THE MILITARY OCCUPATION OF NEW MEXICO, 1846-1851.

CHAPTER I.

1. The War with Mexico. 2. Causes and Leading Events. 3. Position Claimed by Mexico. 4. The United States and Its Claims. 5. Annexation of Texas No Just Cause. 6. Mexico Begins Hostilities. 7. Congress Declares Existence of War.

Accuracy of knowledge, intimate acquaintance with facts, mastery of the sources of evidence and of statements, are the necessary fundamental factors in historical writing. Great diligence and patience are important adjuncts.

In the presentation of many related truths, the historical writer often finds it most difficult to convey an impression which is itself a composite truth. In the review of some period of the military history of our country a faithful presentation does not necessarily consist in recording every fact and omitting none. Modes of presentation oftentimes give impressions which are contradictory. Facts, it matters not how exhaustively acquired, are merely the stone and mortar of the writer of history. One does not have to be an artist that he may properly examine and read archives, but some thought and study are required for the making of truthful comment as to the significance of their contents.

Proper conclusions demand great research. To obtain them, the facts demand analytical study. The leading features must be grasped. Their relations

Reprint of Portrait in Hughes' Doniphan Expedition.

must be understood, and, with this material in hand, a presentation will be logical.

The true historian delights in sharing the emotions of a great general whose place in history has been fixed by some conspicuous deed of valor.

The writer of history, in his presentation of events occurring during a given period, may be compared to the lawyer in the preparation and presentation of a case. The lawyer first acquaints himself with the facts. He then applies the law and forms his conclusions. The writer of history digests all the accounts of any series of events. From these, varied though they may be, he draws a conclusion. The lawyer, as he brings out the facts for the consideration of a jury, is engaged in preparing the mind of the juror for the formation of a conclusion. Later, in his capacity of advocate, he does not recite to the jury what the witnesses have said verbatim, but, in a logical presentation of the principal facts, endeavors to assist the juror in the formation of a conclusion similar to the one he has himself drawn from a study and investigation of the weight which should attach to each.

So the historical writer should not be merely a narrator, a chronicler. He should not be the witness giving testimony. He should be the lawyer, the advocate, the painter, the artist evolving an historical picture for the mind and creating impressions which result in conclusions.

We have all read historical narrative which, by the superabundance of details and occurrences, even though one read as carefully and as intelligently as is possible, produces a generality of impression, which may be likened to the viewing of a moving picture film; here and there, as the film unwinds, an incident catches the attention and probably is retained by memory, but of the whole we have nothing but a rapidly moving succession of images to which there is little but beginning and end.

There have been many accounts of the events occurring during the war with Mexico. The gallant deeds of Doniphan and his men have been sung in song and story. There have been criticisms of the policy of our government for its prosecution of the war. During and immediately succeeding the war many narratives and memoirs found way into print. The debates in congress, the reports of commanding officers, the messages of President Polk, the multitude of letters and proclamations, all bear witness, when digested after the lapse of more than half a century, that the dignity and honor of the American people, as voiced by the great majority of the congress of the United States in the Act of May 13, 1846, wherein it was declared that "by the act of the Republic of Mexico, a state of war exists between that government and the United States," demanded that all differences between our country and Mexico existing at that time must be settled by the god of war.

"The world had twice witnessed the extraordinary spectacle of a government, in violation of its own express agreement, rejecting a minister of peace from the United States, clothed with full powers for the amicable adjustment of existing differences," said President Polk. Modern history presents no case in which, in time of peace, one nation has refused to even hear propositions from another for the termination of existing difficulties between the two. This was the state of affairs when the Act of May 13, 1846, was passed.

It was manifest destiny that the American Republic must sooner or later become the possessor of its present area.

Nine years before the actual commencement of hostilities, President Andrew Jackson was of the opinion that the treatment of American citizens by our sister republic had become intolerable and should be no longer endured. In a message to congress in February, 1837, he said that "the length of time since some of these injuries have been committed, the repeated and unavailing applications for redress, the wanton character of some of the outrages upon the property and persons of our citizens, upon the officers and flag of the United States, independent of recent insults to this government and people by the late extraordinary Mexican minister, would justify, in the eyes of all nations, immediate war." But in a spirit of kindness and forbearance, in a matter of such national concern, unlooked for in a man like Andrew Jackson, he further declared that war should not be used as a remedy "by just and generous nations, confiding in their strength for injuries committed, if it can honorably be avoided," and added, "it has occurred to me that, considering the present embarrassed condition of that country, we should act with both wisdom and moderation by giving to Mexico one more opportunity to atone for the past before we take redress into our own hands, and to avoid all misconception on the part of Mexico, as well as to protect our own national character from reproach, this opportunity should be given with the avowed design and full preparation to take immediate

He Led the Way—Government Scout.

satisfaction, if it should not be obtained on a repetition of the demand for it."

Committees of both houses of congress, to which this message of President Jackson was referred, fully sustained his views of the character of the wrongs which we had suffered from Mexico. In fact, no difference of opinion upon the subject is believed to have existed in congress at that time. Both the executive and the legislative branches of our government concurred, and yet, such was the forbearance and desire to preserve peace, that the wrongs of which our country complained and which gave rise to these solemn proceedings in congress, not only remained unredressed but additional causes of complaint of an aggravated character were constantly accumulating.

POSITION OF MEXICO.

The government of Mexico claimed that the United States was overwhelmed with a desire to extend its territory at the expense of that of Mexico, and that so far as Texas was concerned, it had been the firm and certain determination that the Texas Republic should become a part of the United States. That the American government had connived at it and that this fact created an imperious necessity that Mexico, for her own honor, should repel it with proper firmness and dignity. It was declared by the supreme government of Mexico that it would look upon the annexation of Texas as a *casus belli;* and, as a consequence, negotiation was by its very nature at an end, and war was the only recourse of the Mexican government.

Mexico declared that agents of the United States had been active in the Republic of Texas, promoting the cause of annexation, and, availing themselves of the *statu quo* of Mexico, had so prepared and directed affairs that annexation was hastened and effected by means of violence and fraud.

Her statesmen beheld with amazement, at such an enlightened and refined epoch, a powerful and well consolidated state, availing itself of the internal dissensions of a neighboring nation, putting its vigilance to sleep by protestations of friendship, setting in action all manner of springs and artifices, alternately plying intrigue and violence, and seizing a moment to despoil her of a precious territory, regardless of the incontrovertible rights of the most unquestioned ownership and the most uninterrupted possession.

[1]The Mexican Minister of Foreign Relations stated that "if war should finally become inevitable, and if, in consequence of this war, the peace of the civilized world should be disturbed, the responsibility will not fall upon Mexico. It will all rest upon the United States; not upon Mexico, who, with a generosity unequalled, admitted the United States citizens who wished to colonize in Texas, but upon the United States, who, bent upon possessing themselves, early or late, of that territory, encouraged emigration thither with that view, in order that, in due time, its inhabitants, converting themselves from colonists into its masters, should claim the country as their own, for the purpose of transferring it to the United States. Not upon Mexico, who, having in due season protested against so enormous a transgression, wished to remove all cause for controversy and hostilities, but upon the United States, who, to the scandal of the world, and in manifest violation of treaties, gave protection and

---

[1]Correspondence between Don J. M. de Castillo y Lanzas and John Slidell, March 12, 1846.

Kearny's Army Crossing the Great Plains—1846.

aid to those guilty of a rebellion so iniquitous. Finally, not upon Mexico, who, putting out of view her own dearest interests, through her deference for peace, has entertained as long as was wished, the propositions which, with this view, might be made to her, but upon the United States, who, by frivolous pretexts, evade the conclusions of such an arrangement, proposing peace at the very moment when they are causing their squadrons and their troops to advance upon the ports and frontiers of Mexico, exacting a humiliation impossible to be submitted to, in order to find a pretext, if no reason can be found, which may occasion the breaking out of hostilities."

POSITION TAKEN BY THE UNITED STATES.

In response to the declarations made by the Mexican Minister on Foreign Relations, Honorable John Slidell, Special Envoy of the United States, declared that, in the face of incontrovertible evidence, Mexico had abandoned all intention or even hope of ever reestablishing her authority over any portion of Texas, and that the statement that "Texas had been an integral part of Mexico, not only during the long period of Spanish dominion, but since its emancipation, without any interruption whatever during so long a period," came as a great surprise to him, and to learn that "the United States had despoiled Mexico of a valuable portion of her territory, regardless of the incontrovertible rights of the most unquestionable property and of the most constant possession," was not sustained, and that from the time of the battle of San Jacinto, in April, 1836, to the moment of writing, Texas had sustained and exhibited the same external signs of national independence as Mexico herself, and

Old Fort Bent.
Reprint from Hughes' Doniphan Expedition.

with quite as much stability of government; and, quoting from Mr. Daniel Webster, Secretary of State, "practically free and independent; acknowledged as a political sovereignty by the principal powers of the world; no hostile foot finding rest within her territory for six or seven years, and Mexico herself refraining for all that period from any further attempt to reestablish her own authority over the territory." "How weak," said Mr. Slidell, "must be the cause which can only be sustained by assertions so inconsistent with facts that are notorious to all the world; and how unfounded are all these vehement declarations against the usurpations and thirst for territorial aggrandizement of the United States! The independence of Texas, then, being a fact conceded by Mexico herself, she has no right to prescribe restrictions as to the form of government Texas might choose to assume, nor can she justly complain that Texas, with a wise appreciation of her true interests, has thought proper to merge her sovereignty in that of the United States."

"The Mexican government can not shift the responsibility of war upon the United States by assuming that they are the aggressors. With what reason does Mexico attribute to the United States the desire of finding a pretext to commence hostilities? The appearance of a few ships of war on the Mexican coasts, and the advance of a small military force to the frontier of Texas are cited as evidence that the declarations of desire to preserve the peace are insincere. Surely it can not be necessary to remind your excellency that the menaces of war have all proceeded from Mexico."

"With these avowed intentions on the part of Mexico, and, so far as words can constitute war, that state actually existing, with what fairness can she complain of precautions having been taken by the United States to guard against the attacks with which they have been menaced."

On the day following the sending of the letter from which the foregoing extracts have been taken, the 18th day of March, at Matamoras, more than twelve hundred miles from the seat of the Mexican government, General Francisco Mejia, in command of the Mexican forces in that department, delivered an address to the inhabitants of his district and to his soldiers, among other things, declaring:

[2]"Fellow Countrymen:—With an enemy which respects not its own laws, which shamelessly derides the very principles invoked by it previously, in order to excuse its ambitious views, we have no other resource than arms. We are fortunately always prepared to take them up with glory in defense of our country; little do we regard the blood in our veins, when we are called upon to shed it in vindication of our honor, to assure our nationality and independence. If, to the torrent of devastation which threatens us, it is necessary to oppose a dike of steel, our swords will form it; and on their sharp points will the enemy receive the fruits of his anticipated conquest. If the banks of the Panuco have been immortalized by the defeat of an enemy, respectable and worthy of the valor of Mexico, those of the Bravo shall witness the ignominy of the proud sons of the North, and its deep waters shall serve as the sepulchre of those who dare to approach it. The flame of patriotism which burns in our hearts will receive new fuel from the odious pres-

---
[2]Address of General Mejia—Letters on the Mexican War—Ex. Doc. No. 60, page 128.

A Valuable Aid to the Commissary Department.

ence of the conquerors; and the cry of Dolores and Iguala shall be re-echoed with harmony to our ears when we take up our march to oppose our naked breasts to the rifles of the hunters of the Mississippi."

This address was delivered nearly one month prior to the commencement of hostilities and is abundant evidence of the preparations then making by Mexico for a conflict which she evidently courted.

It was also claimed by the American congress and the President of the United States that Mexico, by evasion and the interposition of many forms of difficulty and delay, had twice violated the faith of treaties, by failing and refusing to carry into effect the sixth article of the Convention of January, 1843. That convention declared, upon its face, that the arrangement between the two countries was entered into for the accommodation of Mexico. Awards for claims against Mexico, for losses sustained by American citizens at the hands of citizens of our sister republic, amounting to several millions of dollars, made by a duly constituted commission appointed by both governments, Mexico was unable to liquidate.

The United States was asked to postpone the time of payment and the request of Mexico was promptly complied with. Again Mexico failed to comply with the terms of the convention, which provided for an indemnity to our citizens for acknowledged acts of outrage and wrong, and refused to make payment. The policy of our government toward Mexico was one of kindness, consideration and forbearance. In addition to her failure to comply with her solemn obligations, as declared by treaty, she was constantly giving cause for new complaints and new demands for indemnity to that extent that, while the citizens of the United States were conducting a lawful commerce with Mexico under the guaranty of a treaty of "amity, commerce and navigation," many suffered all the injuries which would have resulted from open war. The treaties, instead of affording protection to American citizens, were the means of inviting them into the ports of Mexico, that they might be plundered of their property and deprived of their personal liberty, if they dared insist upon their rights.[3]

It was believed by the American people and so declared upon the floors of congress, that, [4]"in so long suffering Mexico to violate her most solemn treaty obligations, plunder our citizens of their property and imprison their persons without affording them any redress, we have failed to perform one of the first and highest duties which every government owes to its citizens" and that "the proud name of American citizen, which ought to protect all who bear it from insult and injury throughout the world, has afforded no such protection to our citizens in Mexico." In a message to congress, President Polk declared: "We had ample cause of war against Mexico long before the breaking out of hostilities; but even then we forebore to take redress into our own hands until Mexico herself became the aggressor by invading our soil in hostile array and shedding the blood of our citizens."

The annexation of Texas to the United States was no just cause for offense to Mexico. It was pretended that such was the case, but the contention is wholly inconsistent with the well-known facts connected with the revolution by which Texas became independent of

---
[3]Debates in Congress—1846.
[4]Message of President Polk, December 8, 1846.

Mexico. Texas had declared her independence and maintained it for more than nine years. She had an organized government in successful operation during that period. Her separate existence, as an independent state, had not only been recognized by the United States, but by the principal European powers as well. Treaties of commerce and navigation had been concluded with her by different nations, and it had become manifest that any further attempt on the part of Mexico to conquer Texas would be vain. Mexico, herself, had become satisfied of this fact, for, while the question of annexation to the United States was pending before the people of Texas, the Mexican government, by formal act, agreed to recognize the independence of Texas, provided she would not annex herself to any other power. This formal agreement, whether or not the proviso was carried out, was conclusive against Mexico.

Meanwhile the President of the United States had declared that our relations with Mexico were in a very unsettled condition; that a revolution had occurred in Mexico by which the government had passed into the hands of new rulers.[5]

The minister of the United States had not been received by the existing authorities. Demonstrations of a character hostile to the United States continued to be made in Mexico and nearly two-thirds of the army of the United States was concentrated on the southwestern frontier. This action had become necessary to meet a threatened invasion of Texas by the Mexican forces. This invasion was threatened solely because Texas had determined, in accordance with a

---

[5]Message of President Polk to the Senate of the United States, March 24, 1846.

The Army Crossing the Rio Sapello.

resolution of our own government, to become a part of the American Union, and claimed the Rio Bravo on the south, instead of the Rio Neuces, as its boundary with Mexico; and, under these circumstances, it was plainly the duty of the United States to extend American protection over her citizens and soil. The American forces were concentrated at Corpus Christi. The commanding general was under positive instructions to abstain from any aggressive act toward Mexico or her citizens and to regard the relations between that Republic and the United States as peaceful, unless she should declare war or commit acts of hostility indicative of a state of war.

The Mexican forces at Matamoras assumed a belligerent attitude but no open act of hostility was committed until April 24, 1846, on which day General Atrista communicated to General Zachary Taylor that "he considered hostilities commenced and should prosecute them."[6] On the same day, a party of dragoons sent out by General Taylor, became engaged with a superior force of the Mexican army in which some sixteen Americans were killed and the balance captured.

MEXICO BEGINS HOSTILITIES.

Thus actually began the war with Mexico. On the 13th day of May following, a proclamation by the President of the United States, announcing the existence of war between our country and Mexico, was promulgated. General Taylor, already authorized by the President, by way of precaution, accepted regiments of volunteers, not from the state of Texas alone,

---

[6]Letter of General Zachary Taylor, April 26, 1846, to the Adjutant General of the Army, Washington, D. C.—Ex. Doc. No. 60, page 288.

but from the states of Louisiana, Alabama, Mississippi, Tennessee, Missouri and Kentucky. These volunteers were called out by the governors of the several states. President Polk asked congress for authority to call for troops and for means to carry on the war.[7]

[7]Message of President Polk to the Senate of the United States, May 11, 1846.

General Kearny Delivering Proclamation at Las Vegas, N. M., August 15, 1846.

CHAPTER II.

1. Organization of the Army of the West, under General S. W. Kearny. 2. March Across the Plains and Concentrate at Bent's Fort. 3. The Army Invades New Mexico, Crosses the Raton Mountains. 4. The Army Reaches Las Vegas and General Kearny Makes Address. 5. The Army Moves on the Capital by Way of San Miguel and the Apache Pass. 6. General Armijo Masses Mexican Forces at Pass. 7. General Kearny Receives Word that General Armijo Has Fled and Army Dispersed. 8. Army Proceeds on Way to Santa Fe. 9. Kearny Takes Possession of Capital and Hoists American Flag. 10. Proclamation Issued Claiming New Mexico for United States. 11. Kearny with Substantial Force Goes into Valley of the Rio Grande and Returns to Santa Fé. 12. Kearny with Portion of the Army Leaves for California, Leaving Colonel Doniphan in Command.

The government of the United States immediately began the formation of plans for the organization of an expedition to invade the northern provinces of Mexico. This expedition was known as the "Army of the West" and its command was given to Colonel, afterwards Brigadier General, Stephen W. Kearny. It was destined, particularly, for the conquest of New Mexico and California. The command consisted of two batteries of artillery, under the command of Major Clark, three squadrons of dragoons, under Major Sumner, the 1st Regiment of Missouri Cavalry, under Colonel A. W. Doniphan, and two companies of infantry under Captain Angney. Colonel Kearny commenced his march from Ft. Leavenworth, on the Missouri River, in the latter part of June, 1846. The entire command when concentrated upon the Arkansas River, consisted of 1,558 men and sixteen pieces of ordnance. The army was detached in different columns

The Army Leaving Las Vegas, August 15, 1846.

from Ft. Leavenworth and reunited on the Arkansas River, near Bent's Fort, on the 1st day of August, 1846. The exact point of concentration is not known, but it is said to have been at a place nearly nine miles below the fort, about twelve miles northeast of Las Animas, Colorado.

It was at this point that the expedition was joined by Frank P Blair, Jr., of Missouri, who was a health-seeker at Bent's Fort at the time.[8]

Bent's Fort is described as having been a structure built of adobe bricks. It was 180 feet long and 135 feet wide. The walls were 15 feet in height and four feet thick and it was the strongest post at that time west of Ft. Leavenworth.

The construction of this fort was commenced in 1828, the first fort erected by William Bent, at a point on the Arkansas, somewhere between the present cities of Pueblo and Canyon City, having been disadvantageously located. Four years were required in which to complete the structure. On the northwest and southeast corners were hexagonal bastions, in which were mounted a number of cannon. The walls of the fort served as walls of the rooms, all of which faced inwardly on a court or plaza. The walls were loopholed for musketry, and the entrance was through large wooden gates of very heavy timbers. Forty-five years ago the old walls were standing and the entire structure was in a fair state of preservation, but to-day not a vestige remains, except possibly mounds of earth resulting from the disintegrating adobe bricks of which the walls were built.

---

[8]Emory's Notes of a Military Reconnoisance from Ft. Leavenworth to San Diego—Senate Doc. 30th Cong., 1st Session.

It was near this fort that the first irrigating ditch, constructed by Americans in Colorado, was built. The lands irrigated were between the fort and the ford of the river. It was constructed under the supervision of William Bent.

At this point Kearny despatched Lieutenant De-Courcey, with twenty men, to the Taos valley, for the purpose of ascertaining the disposition of the inhabitants in that portion of New Mexico, and to inform himself as to other matters of importance, germane to the expedition, and report to the general somewhere *en route*. This officer rejoined the column on August 11th, on the Ponil, in what is now Colfax county, New Mexico, bringing in a number of Mexican prisoners, who gave exaggerated reports of the Utes and other Indians joining the Mexicans for the purpose of opposing the advance of the American army, at some point between Las Vegas and the Capital at Santa Fé.

On the 2nd, Captain Cooke was sent in advance, under a flag of truce, to Santa Fé, carrying with him a proclamation issued by General Kearny on the 31st day of July. On the 9th day of August, Cooke reached Las Vegas, where he met the Alcalde, Don Juan de Dios Maes, and was a recipient of his hospitality. The Alcalde, however, immediately despatched a swift messenger across the mountains, by a short trail, carrying a copy of Kearny's proclamation and notifying Governor Armijo of Cooke's arrival at Las Vegas. Captain Cooke, on the following day, proceeded on his journey, passing through San Miguel, where the inhabitants turned out en masse to see him, and on the 12th arrived in Santa Fé. Here all was excitement. The city was filled with soldiers and citizens gathered for the

Old Pecos Ruin—Pueblo of Cicuye.
Reprint from Emory's Account.

MILITARY OCCUPATION OF NEW MEXICO. 43

organization of a force to resist the American advance. Captain Cooke and his party, among whom was James Magoffin of Chihuahua, proceeded to the Old Palace, the seat of government, and were met by the Mayor of the city, Captain Ortiz, who conveyed the news to Governor Armijo, to whose presence Captain Cooke was shortly conducted. The governor was informed by Cooke that he had been sent by General Kearny, commanding the American army, bearing a letter which he would present at the pleasure of his Excellency, and a later hour was set for the official reception of the communication. In the evening Cooke presented the letter and afterwards his call was returned by Governor Armijo, who said he would send a commissioner to meet General Kearny, and declared further that he, himself, would lead a force of six thousand men to meet the Army of the West.

A most excellent understanding prevailed at all times during the progress of this expedition between the regulars and volunteers. The latter, though but recently accustomed to the ease and comforts of smiling home, bore up against fatigue, hunger and the vicissitudes of a long and tedious march through unexplored regions with a zeal, courage and devotion that would have graced time-worn veterans and reflected the highest credit on their conduct as soldiers.

There was a noble emulation in the conduct of both, which, in no small degree, benefited the service, at the same time promoting that cordiality of intercourse which, in after life, both in the civil and the military, made their meetings most cordial and gladsome.[9]

---
[9]Report of Gen. S. W. Kearny—Ex. Doc. No. 60.

Old Pecos Church (Catholic).
Reprint from Emory's Account.

The manner in which the volunteer soldiery of the United States conducted itself during the war with Mexico was a great demonstration, at that time, of the real military strength of the country. Before that war, European and other foreign powers had but imperfect ideas of our physical strength and our ability to prosecute a war, and particularly one waged beyond the confines of the United States. The foreign powers saw that, on a peace footing, we only had 10,000 fighting men. Themselves accustomed to the maintenance in times of peace of great standing armies, for the protection of thrones against their own subjects, as well as against foreign foes, they could not believe it possible for a nation without such an army, well disciplined and of long service, to wage war successfully. They held in low repute our militia, and were far from regarding them as an effective military force. The war demonstrated that, upon the breaking out of hostilities not anticipated, a volunteer army of citizen soldiers, equal to veteran troops, had been brought into the field.

The First Missouri Volunteers, commanded by Colonel Doniphan, made the march to Santa Fé like veterans. In the ranks of that regiment were soldiers, men of birth and position, who afterwards became celebrated in many of the walks of civil life. Dozens of these soldiers who marched to Santa Fé and Chihuahua could be enumerated—men like Willard P. Hall, afterwards governor of the state of Missouri; William Gilpin, afterwards governor of Colorado; Waldo P. Johnson, Richard Hanson Weightman and John W. Reid, leading men in the West after the war had closed.

The regiment was composed indiscriminately of all professions and pursuits — of farmers, lawyers, physicians, merchants, manufacturers, mechanics and laborers—and this not only among the officers, but the enlisted men as well. From their youth, the men in this regiment had been accustomed to the use of firearms, and many of them were expert marksmen. They were men who had reputations to maintain at home by their good conduct in the field. They were intelligent, and there was an individuality of character in the First Missouri Cavalry found in the ranks of few armies which ever went into battle.

The citizen soldier of our country finds no parallel anywhere in the world. The civil war demonstrated this; the war with Spain proved conclusively that with the growth of the country no change had come over our citizenship in the way of fighting men, and all because the American citizen in battle, be he officer or enlisted man, fights not only for his country, but for glory and distinction among his fellow citizens when he shall return to civil life, and, without any reflection upon many living distinguished Americans, it may be added, he fights for office as well.

On the 2d day of August, Kearny's column left the Arkansas, proceeded down the river a short distance, and, turning to the left, marched to a point on the Timpas not far from the present station of that name on the Atchison, Topeka and Santa Fé Railway. Three days later the army reached the Purgatoire, near the present city of Trinidad. Within the next four days the Raton Mountains had been crossed, and, on the 10th, General Kearny arrived at the crossing of the Cimarron River, and a day later had crossed the Ocate. At this time quite a number of native citizens were captured by Kearny's men, and upon their persons was

Alcalde of Pecos Announcing the Flight of General Armijo.

found a proclamation by the prefect of Taos, based upon one already issued by Governor Armijo, calling the citizens to arms to repel "the Americans who were coming to invade their soil and destroy their property and liberties."

On the 13th the column halted at the Sapello River, and the general was advised by an American gentleman named Spry, who had come from Santa Fé, that the Mexican forces were assembling at Apache Canyon, about fifteen miles from the city of Santa Fé; that the pass was being fortified, and advising Kearny to go around it.

The following day General Kearny received his first official message from Governor Armijo, which was as follows: "You have notified me that you intend to take possession of the country I govern. The people of the country have risen *en masse* in my defense. If you take the country, it will be because you prove the strongest in battle. I suggest to you to stop at the Sapello and I will march to the Vegas. We will meet and negotiate on the plains between them." [10]

This message was delivered by an officer of lancers, accompanied by a sergeant and two privates. On the 15th the column was joined by Major Swords, Lieutenant Gilmer and Captain Weightman, who had come from Ft. Leavenworth, bringing and presenting to Colonel Kearny a commission as brigadier general in the army of the United States. These gallant officers had heard that a battle was to be fought the following day near Las Vegas and had ridden sixty miles in order to participate in the engagement.

---

[10] Lt. Emory, page 25.

KEARNY ENTERS LAS VEGAS AND DELIVERS PROCLAMATION
TO THE PEOPLE.

On the morning of the 15th, precisely at eight o'clock, General Kearny and staff galloped into the plaza of Las Vegas, where he was met by the alcalde, Don Juan de Dios Maes, and a large concourse of people. Pointing to the top of an adobe building, one story in height, and located on the north side of the plaza, General Kearny suggested to the alcalde that if he would go to the top of the building, he and his staff would follow, and from that point, where all could see and hear, he would speak to them, which he did, as follows:[11]

"Mr Alcalde and people of New Mexico: I have come amongst you by the orders of my government, to take possession of your country and extend over it the laws of the United States. We consider it, and have done so for some time, a part of the territory of the United States. We come amongst you as friends, not as enemies; as protectors, not as conquerors. We come among you for your benefit, not for your injury."

"Henceforth I absolve you from all allegiance to the Mexican government, and from all obedience to General Armijo. He is no longer your governor (great sensation in the plaza); I am your governor. I shall not expect you to take up arms and follow me to fight your own people who may oppose me: but I now tell you, that those who remain peaceably at home, attending to their crops, and their herds, shall be protected by me in their property, their persons and their religion; and not a pepper, not an onion, shall be disturbed or taken by my troops without pay, or by the

---

[11]Lt. Emory, page 27.

consent of the owner. But listen! He who promises to be quiet and is found in arms against me, I will hang."

"From the Mexican government, you have never received protection. The Apaches and the Navajos come down from the mountains and carry off your sheep, and even your women, whenever they please. My government will correct all this. It will keep off the Indians, protect you in your persons and property; and, I repeat, will protect you in your religion. I know you are all great Catholics; that some of your priests have told you all sorts of stories; that we would ill-treat your women and brand them on the cheek, as you do your mules on the hip. It is all false. My government respects your religion as much as the Protestant religion and allows each man to worship his Creator as his heart tells him is best. Its laws protect the Catholic as well as the Protestant; the weak as well as the strong, the poor as well as the rich. I am not a Catholic myself; I was not brought up in that faith, but at least one third of my army are Catholics and I respect a good Catholic as much as a good Protestant."

"There goes my army; you see but a small portion of it; there are many more behind; resistance is useless."

"Mr. Alcalde, and you two captains of militia! the laws of my country require that all men who hold office under it shall take the oath of allegiance. I do not wish for the present, until affairs become more settled, to disturb your form of government. If you are prepared to take oaths of allegiance, I shall continue you in office and support your authority."

The Army at Apache Pass.

Beyond all question the alcalde and the two captains did not fully appreciate the situation in which they found themselves. The captains did not protest, but looked with down-cast eyes upon the earthen roof upon which they were standing. Noticing his attitude, General Kearny said to one of them, in the hearing of all the people: "Captain, look me in the face, while you repeat the oath of office!" The oath was administered, and General Kearny, attended by his staff, descended, mounted and galloped away to the head of the column. The sun was shining brightly; for the first time since leaving the Missouri River, the guidons and colors of each squadron, battalion and regiment were unfurled. The trumpeters sounded "to horse" with spirit and the rocky hills to the west multiplied and re-echoed the call.

The army moved forward briskly to meet a force of six hundred Mexicans, which it had been said, was in waiting at a gorge in the hills about two miles distant. The gorge was reached and passed, but not a soul was seen. One by one the guidons were furled. Onward marched the army to Tecolote, thence to San Miguel, at both of which places General Kearny reenacted the drama which had occurred at Las Vegas.

Reports now reached General Kearny at every step that the people were rising and that General Armijo was collecting a formidable force to oppose him at the Apache Pass, near Canyoncito, about 15 miles from Santa Fé. The Army of the West proceeded on its way, over a portion of the Santa Fé Trail and, on the 17th of August, captured the son of Damasio Salazar, a citizen of San Miguel, the individual who had so nearly accomplished the death of a few members of the Texas

Santa Fé Expedition a few years before, and whose efforts in that behalf were frustrated through the influence of Don Gregorio Vigil, a man of prominence in that community.

THE PUEBLO OF PECOS; FLIGHT OF GENERAL ARMIJO.

As the command reached the ancient town of Pecos, about one mile beyond the present station of Rowe, on the line of the Atchison, Topeka and Santa Fé Railway, the General was notified, by a Mexican coming from the direction of Glorieta, that General Armijo and his force of two thousand men, which had been assembled at the Apache Pass to oppose the onward march of the American army, had quarreled among themselves and, that General Armijo, taking advantage of the dissension, with his artillery and dragoons, had fled southward.

It was well known that General Armijo was averse to a conflict, but his life had been threatened by some of his own people if he refused to fight. He saw, however, what they failed to realize, the absolute hopelessness of resistance.

The ancient town of Pecos, at which this news was communicated to General Kearny by the Mexican, who, it was afterwards learned, was the alcalde of the district, was once a fortified town. When Francisco Vasquez de Coronado visited the place, accompanied by an army of Spanish soldiers of fortune, in search of gold and conquest, nearly three hundred years before, the pueblo was known as Cicuye and was a place of great strength. It maintained a standing army, and, within its walls, lived the greatest number of people at that time inhabiting any one locality within what is now the United States.[12]

Here, within the estufa of the pueblo, for centuries had burned the eternal fires of Montezuma, and these had ceased to be kept alive up to a time only seven years prior to the coming of General Kearny.

The illustrations are taken from drawings made by the topographical engineer who accompanied the Army of the West, and show the old pueblo and the church as they stood in 1846. Today nothing is left of the pueblo and only a portion of the walls of the old church is still standing. The church was built some time in the middle of the 16th century by Fr. Juan de Padilla, who accompanied the Coronado expedition, but remained at the pueblo after Coronado returned to the City of Mexico.

The remains of the architecture, as shown by the drawings, which are unquestionably authentic, exhibit, in a most prominent manner, the engrafting of the Catholic church upon the ancient religion of the country.

At one end of the small oval hill, upon which stood the pueblo, were the remains of the estufa of the Indians, with all its parts distinct; the other, the ruins of the Catholic church, both showing the marks and emblems of the two religions. The fires from the estufa burned and sent their incense through the air where the fire-worshipping Indian performed his pagan rites, while only a few yards distant stood the church from the altars of which he listened to the teachings of Christ.

---

[12]Castaneda's Account of Coronado Expedition—Vol. 14, Bureau Eth. Reps.

General Manuel Armijo.
From a Picture in the Possession of Don Luis Baca, Socorro, New Mexico.

A very short period before the coming of the American army the tribe became almost extinct and the few remaining went over the mountains to the Pueblo of Jemez, where, it is said, a few of their descendants are still living and keep the sacred fires from the ancient estufa of the pueblo of Cicuye alive and burning.

Lieutenant Emory, whose assistant, a Mr. Stanly, made the drawings from which the illustrations are taken, says: "The architecture of the Indian portion of the ruins presents peculiarities worthy of notice. Both are constructed of the same materials; the walls of sun-dried bricks, the rafters of well-hewn timber which never could have been shaped by the miserable little axes now used by the Mexicans, which resemble, in shape and size, the wedges used by our farmers for splitting rails. The cornices and drops of the architrave in the church are elaborately carved with a knife."[13]

On the morning of the 18th of August General Kearny had reached a point 29 miles from Santa Fé. Not a hostile arrow or rifle was now between the Army of the West and the ancient capital of New Mexico. The general determined to make the march in one day and raise the American colors over the ancient palace before sundown. Fifteen miles from Santa Fé the column reached the point deserted by General Armijo. It is a gateway, which, in the hands of a competent engineer and one hundred resolute men, would have proved a second Thermopylae. Had the position been defended with spirit and ability, General Kearny would have been compelled to turn it by taking the

---

[13]Emory's Account, page 30.

road running to Ojo de Baca (Cow Springs) and Galisteo.

On the way to Santa Fé General Kearny was met by the acting secretary, who brought a letter from Vigil, the lieutenant governor, which informed the general officially of the flight of Armijo, and of his readiness to receive him in Santa Fé, with the hospitalities of the city.

GENERAL MANUEL ARMIJO.

General Armijo was not unlike others of his nation and time. He was not to the purple born and was of low extraction. He finally managed to obtain a foothold in the official circles at Santa Fé and was made collector of customs. Later he became governor, and again, after the murder of Governor Perez, was made governor of the state. He was essentially a cruel man, not only to foreigners, but to his own people. He undoubtedly entertained the same ideas of the American occupation and the causes for the war with Mexico as other state executives and military commanders of the Mexican Republic.

At the City of Mexico, and, in all the newspapers of the Republic, great attempts had been made to exasperate the minds of the people against the Americans. The war was represented to be one for national existence, and that it was the wish of the United States to destroy the Mexican nation. It was declared to be a war of rapine and plunder, many generals, in their proclamations to the people and to the soldiery, declaring that the United States intended to oppress them, to rob their churches and desecrate their altars. General Armijo knew the falsity of these accusations and the injustice and absurdity of such imputations;

Fac-simile of First Page of Proclamation of Governor Armijo, August 8, 1846.

Last Page of Proclamation of Governor Armijo, August 8, 1846.

nevertheless these statements were systematically propagated throughout the country and found many believers in localities where ignorance was great and the means of truth circulation small.

General Armijo had been most active in his endeavors to rouse the people and had made statements which were very effective in some localities. He was very much concerned personally, knowing as he did, the power of the advancing army, and lost no opportunity to bring to bear every pressure possible in the raising of a force sufficient to repel the American advance.

ARMIJO'S PROCLAMATION.

Before General Kearny had entered Mexican territory Armijo knew of the coming of the Army of the West, and Kearny's proclamation, made at Bent's Fort, had also reached him. Armijo had received from St. Louis, Mo., a large amount of ammunition and supplies, which had been brought to Santa Fé in a caravan from Independence. Armijo issued a proclamation to his people, the exact language of which has only lately come to light. In this it was proclaimed:[14]

"The Governor and Commanding General of New Mexico to its Inhabitants:—

Fellow Countrymen:—At last the moment has arrived when our country requires of her children a decision without limit, a sacrifice without reserve, under circumstances which claim all for our salvation.

Questions with the United States of America which have been treated with dignity and decorum by the supreme magistrate of the Republic, remain unde-

---

[14]Vigil Papers—New Mexico Historical Society—Santa Fe, N. M.

termined as claimed as unquestionable rights of Mexico over the usurped Territory of Texas, and on account of this it has been impossible to assume diplomatic relations with the government of North America, whose minister extraordinary has not been received; but the forces of that government are advancing in this department; they have crossed the northern frontier and at present are near the Colorado river.

Hear, then, fellow citizens and countrymen, the signal of alarm which must prepare us for battle!

The eagle that made us equal under our national standard, making of us one family, calls upon you today, in the name of the supreme government and under the Chief of the Department, to defend the strongest and most sacred of all causes. Then you knew how, by your noble efforts and heroic patriotism, without foreign help, to maintain the independence of our nation.

Today that sacred independence, the fruit of so many and costly sacrifices, is threatened, for if we are not capable of maintaining the integrity of our territory, it will all soon be the prey of the avarice and enterprise of our neighbors from the north, and nothing will remain but a sad recollection of our political existence.

But thanks be to the Almighty, it will not be so! The Mexicans of today are the same as those of 1810, who, although divided and without a country, subdued the power and pride of a foreign nation.

With the army and people united in defense of our threatened independence, our outraged national honor and the rights of our vilified country, they form an invincible union.

Fellow citizens and countrymen, united with the regular army, you will strengthen the sentiments of loyalty among your defenders. Now to the call! Let us be comrades in arms and, with honest union, we shall lead to victory.

Remember that the author and conserver of society inscribed in the golden book the following truthful words: "A country divided within itself shall be destroyed." Do not permit these words to escape you; do not separate your personal interests from the common cause, and, with union, resources, public spirit and true patriotism, I assure you that the Mexican Republic will command the respect of its enemies and will demonstrate to the civilized world that she is entitled to be numbered among the free and enlightened nations of the earth.

We are fortunate to have at the head of our su preme government an illustrious, honorable and patriotic general, who in the past has sustained with dignity and energy the sacred rights of our country; one who will lead us to a glorious victory. Let us now be prepared for the coming conflict which is forced upon us. Let us not belittle the power of our enemy nor the size of the obstacles we must surmount.

The God of Armies is also the protector of the justice of nations and, with his powerful help, we will add another brilliant page to the history of Mexico, and demonstrate to the world, if possible, for impossibilities are not expected, that our beloved country is entitled to be known as a free and independent republic. Relative to the defense of this department on account of this invasion, your governor depends entirely upon your own pecuniary resources, your determination, your convictions, all founded in reason, justice, equity and public convenience. Rest assured that your governor is willing and ready to sacrifice his life and all his interests in the defense of his country. This you will see demonstrated by your chief, fellow-countryman and friend,

MANUEL ARMIJO (Rubric.)

Santa Fé, Saturday, the 8th day of August, 1846.

The American general, under the instructions from his government, was charged with the duty of counteracting the injurious imputations, and, in the light of the orders issued by the Secretary of War, Hon. W. L. Marcy, we clearly see why it was that General Kearny felt called upon to make the remarks made at Las Vegas and at other points between that place and the Capital.[15] The War Department did not furnish General Kearny with a proclamation, printed in the Spanish language, such as was given to General Zachary Taylor, but a few copies of the one sent to General Taylor were sent to General Kearny, and he was requested not to use them.[16] The Republic of Mexico, at that time, was in a most deplorable condition in its administration of civil and military affairs. This condition had existed and continued, more or less, ever since the defeat of Santa Ana at San Jacinto. In December, 1845, General Herrera resigned the Presidency and yielded up the government to General Paredes without a struggle. Thus a revolution was accom-

---

[15]Ex. Doc. No. 60, page 155.

[16]Ex. Doc. No. 60, W. L. Marcy to Col. S. W. Kearny, page 168.

plished solely by the army commanded by Paredes, and the supreme power in Mexico passed into the hands of a military dictator and usurper who was bitterly hostile to the United States.

In the month of August, just at the time when Kearny arrived in New Mexico, the government of Paredes was overthrown and General Santa Ana, who had been in Havana since 1844, an exile from his country, returned. Revolution followed revolution. The country was divided into races, classes and parties, and with so many local divisions among departments and personal divisions among individuals, it is no wonder that, in many portions of Mexico, the people were not in harmony with the powers that attempted to rule the country. The men of Spanish blood monopolized the wealth and power of the country and the mixed Indian races bore its burdens.

Some of the military chieftains desired a monarchical form of government, notably Paredes, and desired to place a European prince upon a throne in Mexico. Naturally there was jealousy and animosity between them. It was the policy of General Kearny, and of every other American general commanding an army in the war with Mexico, to reach the interests, passions or principles of some one of the parties, thereby conciliating their good will and securing active cooperation in bringing about a speedy and honorable peace. Policy and force were combined and the fruits of the former were prized as highly as those of the latter. The inhabitants were encouraged to remain in their towns and villages. They were continued in office. Kind and liberal treatment was accorded them and they were made to believe that the American army had come as a deliverer from oppressive dictatorship of military governors. Rights of person and property were carefully guarded, respected and sustained, and the troops were restrained from every act of license or outrage.

GENERAL KEARNY'S FIRST PROCLAMATION.

On the 31st day of July, prior to his departure from the Arkansas river, General Kearny issued a proclamation, which soon reached the hands of General Armijo. In this he declared that his entry into New Mexico with a large military force was for the purpose of seeking union with and ameliorating the condition of the inhabitants of New Mexico. That his coming was by order of the American government and that he would be amply sustained in his efforts. The people were enjoined to remain quietly at home in the pursuit of their peaceful occupations and that in this they would not be interfered with, but would be respected and protected in their civil and religious rights, but admonishing all that those who took up arms or encouraged resistance against his government would be regarded as enemies and treated accordingly.[17]

The fact that during the entire march from the Arkansas to Las Vegas, not one act of oppression had been committed by Kearny's command doubtless had found its way into the hearts of the people who had been ruled with the sword of tyranny. But General Armijo is not to be too severely criticised for his official acts. These speak for themselves. With his personal character it is unnecessary to deal. His authority came from the City of Mexico, a capital so remote that presi-

---

[17]Ex. Doc. No. 60, No. 12, page 168.

Raising American Flag Over Old Palace.
Santa Fé, N. M., August 18, 1846.

dent might succeed president, the government itself might be overturned, and the news not reach Santa Fé for several months. He was governor of the province furthermost north in the Republic. In his official conduct, he probably knew his people better than some of his critics. His acts as governor and commanding general were no different than those of other military chieftains and governors in his nation.

When he assembled his army at the Apache Pass and the dissensions arose between his officers and men, no doubt already the diplomatic leaven used by General Kearny in his several addresses, together with his acts and deeds of kindness, as well as the well known strength of the American army, had produced the effect desired, and Armijo, too well appreciating the final outcome, used this situation as an excuse and fled southward, accompanied by a personal body-guard of one hundred dragoons, not knowing that at the very moment of his flight, a substantial force under Colonel Ugarte was on its way up the valley of the Rio Bravo to assist him in the defense of his country and its citizens.

GENERAL ARMIJO AND THE TEXAS-SANTA FÉ EXPEDITION.

In judging General Armijo's policies and official acts, small attention should be given to the treatment received by the Texans at his hands at the time of the Texas-Santa Fé Expedition, which had traveled across the plains of Texas under the pretense of establishing commercial relations with New Mexico. Theirs was something beside a commercial invasion. [18]Under the circumstances, Governor Armijo is not to be severely

[18]Kendall's Texas-Santa Fé Expedition, Vol. 1, pages 14-15.

Old Palace, 1909.

blamed for his official conduct. When this expedition was organized it was given out officially, by General Mirabeau B. Lamar, then president of the Republic of Texas, that the expedition was commercial in its intentions, the object being to open a direct trade with Santa Fé by a route known to be much shorter than the old Santa Fé Trail from the Missouri River. The diversion of this trade, at that time very considerable, was undoubtedly the primary and ostensible object, but General Lamar's ulterior motive, the bringing of so much of the province of New Mexico as lies upon the eastern side of the Rio Grande under the protection of his government, was not generally known until after the expedition had left Austin and was far on its way to Santa Fé. General Lamar had been led to believe that nine-tenths of the inhabitants of New Mexico were discontented under the Mexican yoke and anxious to come under the protection of the Lone Star Republic. In fact he had received assurances from Texans, living in Santa Fé, that such was the popular feeling, and that the people would hail the coming of the expedition with joy. Governor Armijo may have been regarded as extremely cruel toward these invaders, carrying arms into a country from which only a short time before it had achieved its independence, but it was but natural that Armijo should so regard them, particularly when it was well known that Texas was claiming as its western boundary, the Rio Grande, a contention which Mexico was resisting with all its power and diplomacy. A parallel case in more recent times is that of Dr. Jameson and his raiders in South Africa.

Fac-simile of First Page of Proclamation of General Kearny, August 19, 1846.

Last Page of Proclamation of General Kearny, August 19, 1846.

IN SIGHT OF SANTA FÉ.

The advance of the American column arrived in sight of the City of Santa Fé at three o'clock in the afternoon of the 18th of August, 1846; by six o'clock the entire army was in the capital. The general and his staff, and other officers of the army, were received at the old palace by Lieutenant Governor Vigil, assisted by about thirty representative citizens of the city. Refreshments were ordered served by Governor Vigil and as the sun sank behind the far distant Jemez and Valles Mountains, painting the clouds which overhung the lofty ranges with a glorious combination of saffron, opal, purple and golden color, the flag of our country was hoisted over the ancient palace and a salute of thirteen guns from cannon planted on the eminence, afterwards known as Ft. Marcy, declared the conquest of New Mexico complete.

There, in the Old Palace, sat the American general and his principal officers, the guests, enforced it is true. but still welcome, of all that was left of the men who had derived authority from the Mexican Republic; seated in a building, which, in historic interest, surpasses any other within the confines of the United States; built in the first years of the 17th century, and, down through all the succeeding years, until 1886, whether the country was under Spanish, Pueblo, Mexican or American control, it remained the seat of authority; whether the ruler was called viceroy, captain-general, political chief, department commander or governor and whether he presided over a kingdom, a province or a territory, the Old Palace has been his official residence.[19] Thoughts of the most pleasant

---

[19] Prince's History of New Mexico.

character filled the minds of both officers and men; the former being entertained in various places in the city, at the houses of the most prominent people, the men mixing with the populace in the various resorts and bailles of the city.

On the following morning General Kearny addressed nearly all of the people of Santa Fé, assembled in the plaza for the purpose of hearing him, saying:

"New Mexicans:—We have come amongst you to take possession of New Mexico, which we do in the name of the government of the United States. We have come with peaceable intentions and kind feelings toward you all. We come as friends, to better your condition and make you a part of the Republic of the United States. We mean not to murder you or rob you of your property. Your families shall be free from molestation; your women secure from violence. My soldiers shall take nothing from you but what they pay for. In taking possession of New Mexico, we do not mean to take away from you your religion. Religion and government have no connection in our country. There, all religions are equal; one has no preference over the other; the Catholic and the Protestant are esteemed alike. Every man has a right to serve God according to his heart. When a man dies he must render to God an account of his acts here on earth, whether they be good or bad. In our government, all men are equal. We esteem the most peaceable man, the best man. I advise you to attend to your domestic pursuits, cultivate industry, be peaceable and obedient to the laws. Do not resort to violent means to correct abuses. I do hereby proclaim that, being in possession of Santa Fé, I am therefore virtually in possession of all New Mexico. Armijo is no longer your governor. His power is departed; but he will return and be as one of you. When he shall return you are not to molest him. You are no longer Mexican subjects; you are now become American citizens, subject only to the laws of the United States. A change of government has taken place in New Mexico and you no longer owe allegiance to the Mexican government. I do hereby proclaim my intention to establish in this Department a civil government, on a republican basis, similar to those of our own states. It is my intention, also, to continue in office those by whom you have been governed, except the governor, and such other persons as I shall appoint to office by virtue of the authority vested in me. I am your governor—henceforth look to me for protection."[20]

Immediately upon the delivery of the proclamation by General Kearny a response was made by Juan Bautista Vigil y Alarid, which is fairly expressive of the opinions entertained by a large number of the representative and influential citizens of the territory. Vigil was the official left in charge by Governor Armijo and his address is given here for the first time:[21]

"General:—The address which you have just delivered, in which you announce that you have taken possession of this great country in the name of the United States of America, gives us some idea of the wonderful future that awaits us. It is not for us to determine the boundaries of nations. The cabinets of Mexico and Washington will arrange these differences. It is for us to obey and respect the established authorities, no matter what may be our private opinions.

---

[20]Lt. Emory's Account, page 6.
[21]Vigil Papers, N. M. Historical Society.

The inhabitants of this Department humbly and honorably present their loyalty and allegiance to the government of North America. No one in this world can successfully resist the power of him who is stronger.

Do not find it strange if there has been no manifestation of joy and enthusiasm in seeing this city occupied by your military forces. To us the power of the Mexican Republic is dead. No matter what her condition, she was our mother. What child will not shed abundant tears at the tomb of his parents? I might indicate some of the causes for her misfortunes, but domestic troubles should not be made public. It is sufficient to say that civil war is the cursed source of that deadly poison which has spread over one of the grandest and greatest countries that has ever been created. To-day we belong to a great and powerful nation. Its flag, with its stars and stripes, covers the horizon of New Mexico, and its brilliant light shall grow like good seed well cultivated. We are cognizant of your kindness, of your courtesy and that of your accommodating officers and of the strict discipline of your troops; we know that we belong to the Republic that owes it origin to the immortal Washington, whom all civilized nations admire and respect. How different would be our situation had we been invaded by European nations! We are aware of the unfortunate condition of the Poles.

In the name, then, of the entire Department, I swear obedience to the Northern Republic and I tender my respect to its laws and authority.

JUAN BAUTISTA VIGIL y ALARID (Rubric)
    Governor."
Santa Fé, August 19, 1846.

Fac-simile of Acceptance of Allegiance by Juan Bauptista Vigil y Alarid, Acting Governor, August 19, 1846.

Last Page of Acceptance of Allegiance of Juan Bauptista Vigil y Alarid, Acting Governor, August 19, 1846.

The following day the principal chiefs of several tribes of Pueblo Indians presented themselves at the palace and gave in their submission and expressed great satisfaction over the arrival of the American forces. Their interview was long and very interesting and, as stated by Lieutenant Emory,[22] they narrated what is a tradition with them, that the white man would come from the far east and release them from the bonds and shackles which the Spaniards had imposed, not in the name of, but in a worse form than slavery.

The same night a message was received from General Armijo, asking on what terms he would be received; but this proved to be only a ruse on his part to gain time in his flight to the south. From trustworthy accounts, Armijo's force, at the Canyon, was about four thousand men, tolerably well armed, and six pieces of artillery. Had he been possessed of the slightest qualifications as a general, it was possible for him to have given the American forces a great deal of trouble. During the week various deputations came to the capital to see General Kearny, some of them from Taos, all giving in their allegiance and asking protection from the Indians.[22]

KEARNY'S SANTA FÉ PROCLAMATION.

On the 22nd day of August, 1846, General Kearny issued a proclamation which produced a most salutary effect upon the people. In this document he says:[23]

"As, by the act of the Republic of Mexico, a state of war exists between that government and the United

---
[22]Lt. Emory's Account, page 6.
[23]Ex. Doc. No. 60, pages 170-171.

States; and as the undersigned, at the head of his troops, on the 18th instant, took possession of Santa Fé, the capital of the department of New Mexico, he now announces his intention to hold the department, with its original boundaries (on both sides of the Del Norte) as a part of the United States, under the name of the Territory of New Mexico."

"The undersigned has come to New Mexico with a strong military force, and an equally strong one is following him in his rear. He has more troops than is necessary to put down any opposition that can possibly be brought against him, and therefore it would be but folly or madness for any dissatisfied or discontented persons to think of resisting him."

"The undersigned has instructions from his government to respect the religious institutions of New Mexico, to protect the property of the church, to cause the worship of those belonging to it to be undisturbed, and their religious rights in the amplest manner preserved to them; also to protect the persons and property of all quiet and peaceable inhabitants within its boundaries against their enemies the Eutaws, the Navajos and others; and when he assures all that it will be his pleasure, as well as his duty, to comply with those instructions, he calls upon them to exert themselves in preserving order, in promoting concord, and in maintaining the authority and efficacy of the laws. And he requires of those who have left their homes and taken up arms against the troops of the United States, to return forthwith to them, or else they will be considered as enemies and traitors, subjecting their persons to punishment and their property to seizure and confiscation for the benefit of the public treasury."

"It is the wish and intention of the United States to provide for New Mexico a free government, with the least possible delay, similar to those in the United States; and the people of New Mexico will then be called on to exercise the rights of freemen in electing their own representatives to the territorial legislature. But, until this can be done, the laws hitherto in force will be continued until changed or modified by competent authority; and those persons holding office will continue in the same for the present, provided they will consider themselves good citizens and are willing to take the oath of allegiance to the United States."

"The United States hereby absolves all persons residing within the boundaries of New Mexico from any further allegiance to the Republic of Mexico, and hereby claims them as citizens of the United States. Those who remain quiet and peaceable will be considered good citizens and receive protection—those who are found in arms, or instigating others against the United States, will be considered traitors and treated accordingly."

"Don Manuel Armijo, the late governor of this department, has fled from it; the undersigned has taken possession of it without firing a gun, or spilling a single drop of blood, in which he most truly rejoices, and for the present will be considered as governor of the territory."

"Given at Santa Fé, the capital of the Territory of New Mexico, this 22nd day of August, 1846, and in the 71st year of the independence of the United States." S. W. KEARNY,
Brigadier General, U. S. Army."
"By the Governor:
Juan Bautista Vigil y Alarid."

PLAN OF SANTA FE AND ITS ENVIRONS.

On the same day General Kearny wrote to Brigadier General Wool, at Chihuahua, Mexico, saying that "everything is quiet and peaceable. The people now understand the advantages they are to derive from a change of government and are much gratified with it."

On the 2nd day of September, General Kearny and a portion of his command, consisting of a battery of eight pieces and one hundred artillerymen, a battalion of one hundred dragoons, under Captain Burgwin, and five hundred mounted volunteers, marched south to the valley of the Rio Grande, moving by way of Agua Fria, five miles from Santa Fé, thence to the Galisteo river, and, following this stream to its junction with the Rio Grande where the Pueblo of Santo Domingo now stands. His command numbered seven hundred and twenty-five. The general and his officers were hospitably entertained by the *principales* of the pueblo and were entertained at the residence of the priest.[24] The general was shown into the priest's parlor which was tapestried with curtains stamped with likenesses of all the presidents of the United States up to the time of President Polk. The cushions were of spotless damask and the couch was covered with a white Navajo blanket worked in richly colored flowers.

The air was redolent with the perfumes of grapes and melons and every crack of door and window glistening with the bright eyes and arms of the women of the capilla. The old priest was busily talking in the corner, and little did he know of the game of sighs and signs carried on between the young fellows and the fair inmates of his house. The gayest array of young men in the command were out and the women seemed

---

[24]Lt. Emory's Account, page 7.

to those present to drop their usual subdued look and timid wave of the eyelash for good hearty twinkles and signs of unaffected and cordial welcome, signs supplying the place of conversation, as neither party could speak the language of the other.[25]

A fine repast was served by the priest, and afterwards, standing in front of the portal, General Kearny delivered a speech to the assembled Indians which was first interpreted into Spanish and then into Pueblo. The command then proceeded down the valley, stopping at the principal Indian villages and Mexican towns and arriving at Tomé, in the county of Valencia, on the 7th of September, and thereafter returning to Santa Fé, arriving on the eleventh of the month.

General Kearny, having occasion to transfer some public property into the hands of a public functionary, took up a bit of blank paper and commenced writing, when the Alcalde, who happened to be present, remarked to the general that an instrument of writing was not legal, unless it was drawn upon paper stamped with the government seal or coat-of-arms, for the State of New Mexico. He then stepped out and brought a few sheets of the government paper to General Kearny, politely observing "that the government sold it at only eight dollars per sheet, a very moderate sum to pay for having an important document strictly legal." With out ceremony, General Kearny changed his purpose for the moment, and wrote, in substance, as follows: "The use of the 'stamp paper' by the government of New Mexico, is hereby abolished. Done by the Governor,

S. W. KEARNY, Brig. Gen."

---

[25]Lt. Emory's Account, page 7.

"I will now," continued he, "take it at its real value, just as other paper." The Alcalde was astonished, for his prospects of further extortion were blasted. The common people who had been compelled to pay the exorbitant sum of eight dollars for a sheet of paper, when an instrument of writing was wanted which required a seal, rejoiced that they were now relieved of so burdensome a tax.

On the 22d of September, General Kearny, claiming to have authority to do so, made appointments of territorial officials as follows: Charles Bent, governor; Donaciano Vigil, secretary; Richard Dallam, marshal; Francis P. Blair, Jr., United States Attorney; Charles Blumner, treasurer; Eugene Leitensdorfer, auditor, and Joab Houghton, Antonio Jose Otero and Charles Beaubien, judges of the superior court.[26]

KEARNY CODE PROMULGATED.

On the same day General Kearny promulgated the laws which he had prepared for the government of the territory. In his letter to the Adjutant General of the Army, transmitting a copy of these laws, General Kearny says:

"I take great pleasure in stating that I am entirely indebted for these laws to Colonel A. W. Doniphan, of the 1st Regiment of Missouri Mounted Volunteers, who received much assistance from private Willard P. Hall, of his regiment. These laws are taken, part from the laws of Mexico, retained as in the original—a part with such modifications as our laws and constitution made necessary; a part are from the laws of Missouri Territory; a part from the laws of Texas and Coahuila, a part from the statutes of

---

[26]Ex. Doc. No. 60, page 22, page 176.

Charles Bent, First Governor of New Mexico.

Missouri; and the remainder from the Livingston Code; the organic law is taken from the organic law of Missouri Territory."

This letter, together with the copy of the laws and the list of General Kearny's appointees, was received at Washington, November 23d, following.

GENERAL KEARNY LEAVES FOR CALIFORNIA.

On the 24th of September, 1846, general orders were issued designating the force to accompany Kearny on his march to California. It consisted of three hundred United States 1st Dragoons, under Major Sumner, who were to be followed by the battalion of Mormons, five hundred in number, commanded by Captain Cooke.

Colonel Doniphan's regiment was to remain in New Mexico until relieved by Colonel Price's regiment, which was daily expected to reach Santa Fé from the United States, when the 1st Missouri Mounted Cavalry, under Doniphan, was directed to join General Wool, at Chihuahua. The two batteries of artillery were divided; one company, Captain Fisher's, to be left in New Mexico; the other, Captain Weightman's, to accompany Colonel Doniphan. The battalion of infantry, under Captain Angney, was directed to remain in Santa Fé. Thus was the Army of the West divided into three columns, to operate in regions remote from each other and never again to be united in one body.[29]

On the morning of the 25th, the column was ready for its long march to the Coast, and, at two in the afternoon, left Santa Fé and reached Albuquerque on the 29th, at which place the Rio Grande was crossed; thence the valley was followed to the Jornado del

---

[29]Lt. Emory's Account.

Muerto and thereafter, across the plains into the valley of the Rio Mimbres, from which locality Kearny proceeded westward to the Pacific Coast, reaching San Diego in December.

The conquest of New Mexico was complete; achieved without the loss of a man or the firing of a gun, the work was finished. Kearny and Doniphan, going out from the then western border of civilization, marching upwards of a thousand miles through lands overrun with hostile Indians, making a circuit equal to a fourth of the circumference of the globe, providing for the army as they went, returned with trophies taken from fields the names of which were unknown to themselves[30] and their country. History has but few such expeditions to record. "New Mexico, itself so distant and so lately the Ultima Thule, the outside boundary of speculation and enterprise, so lately a distant point to be obtained, became itself a point of departure for new and far more extended expeditions."

The fruits of this great expedition, coupled with the great successes of the naval and military forces of the United States operating simultaneously on the coast of California, time has shown to have been inestimable in value to our country. New Mexico and California, conquered but afterwards ceded by Mexico to the United States, an area of territory embracing nearly ten degrees of latitude, lying adjacent to Oregon and extending from the Pacific Coast to the Rio Bravo, gave an empire to the United States and its acquisition was second only in importance to the purchase from Napoleon, of Louisiana, in 1803. Gold had not been discovered in California; the great copper mines of the

---

[30]Hon. Thomas H. Benton—address, July 2d, 1847.

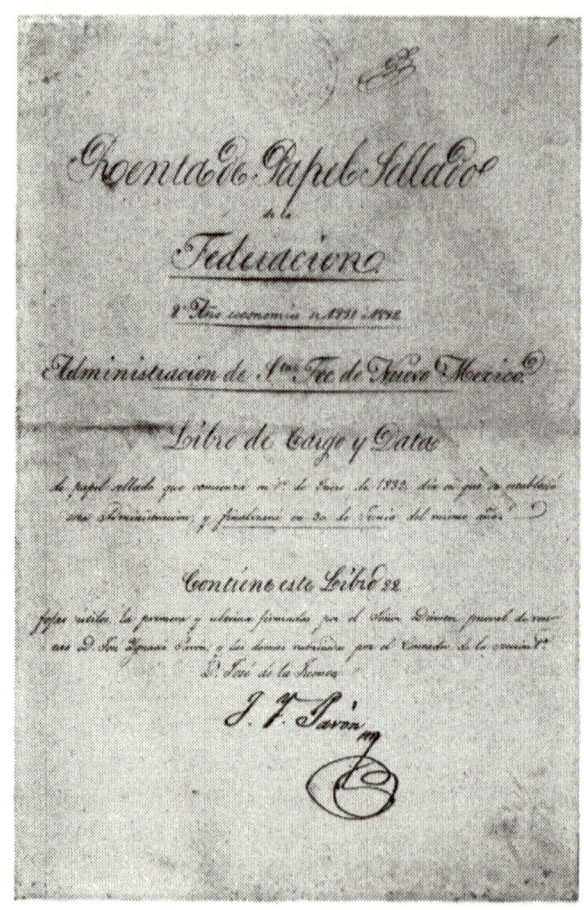

Fac-simile of Page of Stamped Paper, the Use of Which Was Abolished by General Kearny.

present territory of Arizona had not been dreamed of by men of Anglo-Saxon blood, and the immense agricultural and horticultural resources of the golden state, not to mention those of the territories of New Mexico and Arizona, had not been given the slightest thought by the statesmen of that day. The possession of the ports of San Diego, Monterey and San Francisco immediately enabled the United States to command the commerce of the Pacific Coast, and at that time, in the whaling business alone, the capital invested exceeded forty millions of dollars. To-day the assessed valuation of property in some of the cities of California exceeds by many millions of dollars the entire cost of the war with Mexico; a single copper mine in the Territory of Arizona has produced copper bullion of greater value, in dollars, than the total amount of the national debt of our country after the war with Mexico was over, and the value of the coal and coke already produced in the coal regions of New Mexico and Southern Colorado, at the time of the occupation, a part of New Mexico, exceeds the cost of all that portion of the United States embraced within the Louisiana Purchase and the territory acquired by the annexation of the Republic of Texas, as well as that secured under the terms of the Treaty of Guadalupe Hidalgo.

KEARNY'S ACTIONS PARTLY DISAPPROVED AT WASHINGTON.

Exactly four months after General Kearny had established a civil form of government in New Mexico and named the officials of the Territory, President Polk, in answer to a resolution of the House of Representatives asking for all documents containing any orders or instructions to any military, naval or other officer of the government in relation to the establish-

General Kearny and Command on the Gila En Route to California.

ment or organization of civil government in any portion of the Territory of New Mexico, which has or might be taken possession of by the Army or Navy of the United States, said:—"Among the documents accompanying the report of the Secretary of War will be found a "form of government" "established and organized" by the military commander who conquered and occupied with his forces the Territory of New Mexico. This document was received at the War Department in the latter part of last month, and, as will be perceived by the report of the Secretary of War, was not, for the reasons stated by that officer, brought to my notice until after my annual message of the 8th instant was communicated to congress."

"It is declared on its face to be a temporary government of the said territory," but there are portions of it which purport to "establish and organize" a permanent Territorial government of the United States over the Territory and to impart to its inhabitants political rights, which, under the Constitution of the United States, can be enjoyed permanently only by citizens of the United States. These have not been "approved and recognized" by me. Such organized regulations as have been established in any of the conquered territories for the security of our conquest, for the preservation of order, for the protection of the rights of the inhabitants, and for depriving the enemy of the advantages of these territories while the military possession of them by the forces of the United States continues, will be recognized and approved.[31]

"It will be apparent from the reports of the officers who have been required by the success which has

---

[31]Message of President Polk, Dec. 22d, 1846.

Indians of Santo Domingo Dancing for General Kearny and Staff.

crowned their arms to exercise the powers of temporary government over the conquered territories, that, if any excess of power has been exercised, the departure has been the offspring of a patriotic desire to give to the inhabitants the privileges and immunities so cherished by the people of our own country, and which they believed calculated to improve their condition and promote their prosperity. Any such excess has resulted in practically no injury, but can and will be early corrected in a manner to alienate as little as possible the good feelings of the inhabitants of the conquered territory."

LEYES

para

El Gobierno del Territorio de

NUEVO MEJICO

LAWS

for

THE GOVERNMENT OF THE TERRITORY OF

NEW MEXICO.

TESTAMENTARIAS.

Seccion 1 Las leyes hasta ahora vigentes relativas á herencias, repartimientos, ultimas voluntades y testamentos segun estan contenidas en el tratado sobre estas materias escrito por Pedro Murillo de Lara, quedarán vigentes en todo lo que son conformes con la constitucion de los Estados Unidos y estatutos tambien vigentes

2 Los Prefectos concederan letras credenciales para testamenterias y para Abintestatos.

3. Las latras para testamentarias y Abintestatos serán concedidas en el condado en que el hogar ó lugar de residencia del difunto estubiere ubicado. Si no tenia hogar ó lugar de residencia al tiempo de su muerte y poseyera tierras las letras credenciales se concederán en el condado en que estubieren las tierras ó parte de ellas. Si el difunto no tenia hogar ó lugar de residencia y no poseía tierras, las letras podrán concederse en el condado en que murió ó donde entuvieren la mayor parte de sus bienes. Si

ADMINISTRATIONS.

Section 1 The laws heretofore in force concerning descents, distributions, wills and testaments, as contained in the treatise on these subjects written by Pedro Murillo De Lorde, shall remain in force so far as they are in conformity with the Constitution of the United States and the State laws in force for the time being.

2 The prefects shall grant letters testamentary and of administration

3 Letters testamentary and of administration shall be granted in the county in which the mansion house or place of abode of the deceased is situated. If he had no mansion house or place of abode at the time of his death, and be possessed of lands, letters shall be granted in the county in which the lands or a part thereof lies. If the deceased had no mansion house or place of abode, and was not possessed of lands, letters may be granted in the county in which he died or where the greater part of his

CHAPTER III.

1. The March to Chihuahua. 2. Doniphan Ordered Against the Navajos. 3. Treaty with the Navajos. 4. Doniphan Proceeds Down Valley of Rio Grande. 5. Battle of Brazito. 6. Doniphan Occupies El Paso. 7. Marches on Chihuahua. 8. Battle of Sacramento. 9. Occupation of Chihuahua. 10. Departure of Army for Saltillo. 11. Return to the United States.

When General Kearny left Santa Fé for California the command of the forces remaining in New Mexico was turned over to Colonel Doniphan. Two days after the departure of Kearny, Colonel Sterling Price, accompanied by his staff, arrived in the city in advance of his command. Colonel Price's troops arrived a few days later and consisted of 1,200 mounted volunteers from Missouri and a Mormon battalion of 500 infantry, which had been organized at Council Bluffs. These troops marched across the plains in fifty-three days. Santa Fé was now a great military camp, the aggregate effective force of the army at the time being in the neighborhood of three thousand five hundred men.

Great preparations were made for the campaign to be commenced by Colonel Doniphan, his objective point being Chihuahua, where it was supposed he would be able to join with General Wool, who had been ordered there by the President, operating under orders from General Zachary Taylor, at that time commanding the army of occupation in Mexico, and under whose leadership the battles of Palo Alto and Resaca de la Palma had been fought on the 8th and 9th days of May previous.

When Colonel Doniphan had completed all his arrangements for the campaign to the south, advices were received by him, in the nature of a special order from General Kearny, who had reached La Joya, a point in the valley of the Rio Grande, a short distance above the present city of Socorro, directing him, prior to his march against Chihuahua, to undertake a campaign against the Navajo Indians, who had been raiding the valley in the neighborhood of Polvodera. Without a moment's delay, everything being in readiness, Colonel Doniphan began the work.

CAMPAIGN AGAINST THE NAVAJO INDIANS.

Colonel Price was left in command at Santa Fé, and on the 26th day of October, having divided his force into two parts, at the head of one Doniphan proceeded to Albuquerque, thence to the Rio Puerco, following that stream to its headwaters. Major Gilpin was placed in command of a force of two hundred men, marched up the valley of the Chama from Abiquiu, crossed the Continental Divide and proceeded down the San Juan river to the valley of the Little Colorado. Captain John W. Reid, with thirty men, led an expedition into the heart of the Navajo country, which was of a most daring and brilliant kind. The whole country was traversed and the Navajos finally assembled at Ojo del Oso (Bear Spring), where a treaty was signed, after a campaign lasting only six weeks, and at the conclusion of which the command returned to the valley of the Rio Grande, reaching Socorro on the 12th day of December, 1846.

Thus early in the history of American rule of New Mexico, the army of the United States, traversing the Great Plains, the heroes of a bloodless conquest of

General A. W. Doniphan at Seventy.

New Mexico, became the champions and protectors of a people not yet citizens of the United States. In negotiating with the Navajos, Colonel Doniphan outlined the purposes of the American government in taking possession of New Mexico. He was answered by Sarcilla Largo, a young chief, an Indian of prominence and ability in his tribe, who said that he was gratified to learn the views of the American general. It was explained to the Indians that the United States had taken military possession of the country; that the laws of the United States were now in force and that all citizens would be protected against violence, invasion and depredation; that the government was also anxious to enter into a treaty of peace with the Navajos; that the same protection would be given to them; that the United States claimed everything by right of conquest and that the Mexicans and Indians were now equally citizens of his country.

Sarcilla Largo replied: "Americans! You have a strange case of war against the Navajos. We have waged war against the New Mexicans for many years. We have plundered their villages, killed many of their people and have taken many prisoners. Our cause was just. You have lately commenced a war against the same people. You are powerful. You have great guns and many brave soldiers. You have therefore conquered them, the very thing we have been attempting to do for many years. You now turn upon us for attempting to do what you have done yourselves. We cannot see why you have cause to quarrel with us for fighting the New Mexicans on the West, while you do the same thing on the East. Look how matters stand! This is our war. We have more right to complain of

Reprint from Hughes' Doniphan Expedition.

you for interfering in our war, than you have to quarrel with us for continuing a war we had begun long before you got here. If you will act justly you will allow us to settle our own differences."

It was then explained that the New Mexicans had surrendered and were no longer bearing arms against the American forces. The Indians were informed that according to the usages of civilized warfare, when a man surrendered he was treated thereafter in a friendly manner. That, by right of conquest, all of New Mexico and all the inhabitants had become a part of the United States; that, if the Navajos continued to steal from the New Mexicans, they were stealing from citizens of the United States and that, when they killed them, they were killing our own people. That the American government had guaranteed protection to the New Mexicans from whatever source they should be threatened, and that no further warfare against them on the part of the Navajos would be tolerated.

It was finally agreed to execute the treaty, the Navajo chief declaring that New Mexico, being in the possession of the American army, and it being the intention to hold it, all depredations by his tribe would cease and that thereafter they would refrain from making war upon our people. "We have no quarrel with you," said Sarcilla, "and want no war with so great a nation. Let there be peace between us."

The entire column commanded by Doniphan was concentrated near Socorro, in the valley of the Rio Grande, and on December 14th began its march down the Rio Bravo, a wonderful undertaking, an expedition which made the name of Doniphan a household word

Colonel Doniphan Treating With the Navajo Indians.
Sarcilla Largo: "We can not see why you have cause to quarrel with us for fighting the New Mexicans on the west, while you do the same thing on the east."

in the Great West and raised him to that pinnacle of glory which gave a great American poet an inspiration, a comparison with the deeds and march of Xenophon and the Retreat of the Ten Thousand.[32]

After crossing the Jornado del Muerto (journey of death), Colonel Doniphan and command entered the Mesilla Valley of the Rio Grande, and, a few miles south of the present town of Las Cruces, camped at what is known as the Brazito, on the east bank of the river, in a level, bottom prairie, partially covered with mesquite and cottonwood undergrowth.

BATTLE OF BRAZITO, DECEMBER 25, 1846.

While the men were scattered in quest of wood and water for cooking purposes, for fresh grass for the animals, and while the wagon trains and teamsters were scattered along the road for miles in the rear, a great cloud of dust was observed to the southward, and shortly it was announced by men scouting in the advance that the enemy was approaching. Every man flew to his post; assembly was sounded; the men, dashing down their loads of wood and buckets of water, came running from all directions, seized their arms and fell into line under whatever flag was most convenient; those in the rear fell into line, under the nearest standards, as fast as they came up.

By this time the Mexican General had drawn up his forces in front and on the right and left flanks of Doniphan's lines. His force was about one thousand three hundred men, regulars and volunteers, cavalry and infantry and four pieces of artillery. They exhibited a most gallant and imposing appearance, for

---

[32]William Cullen Bryant.

Colonel Doniphan's Army marching through the Jornada del Muerto, the "Journey of Death." Reproduced from the work of William H. Richardson.

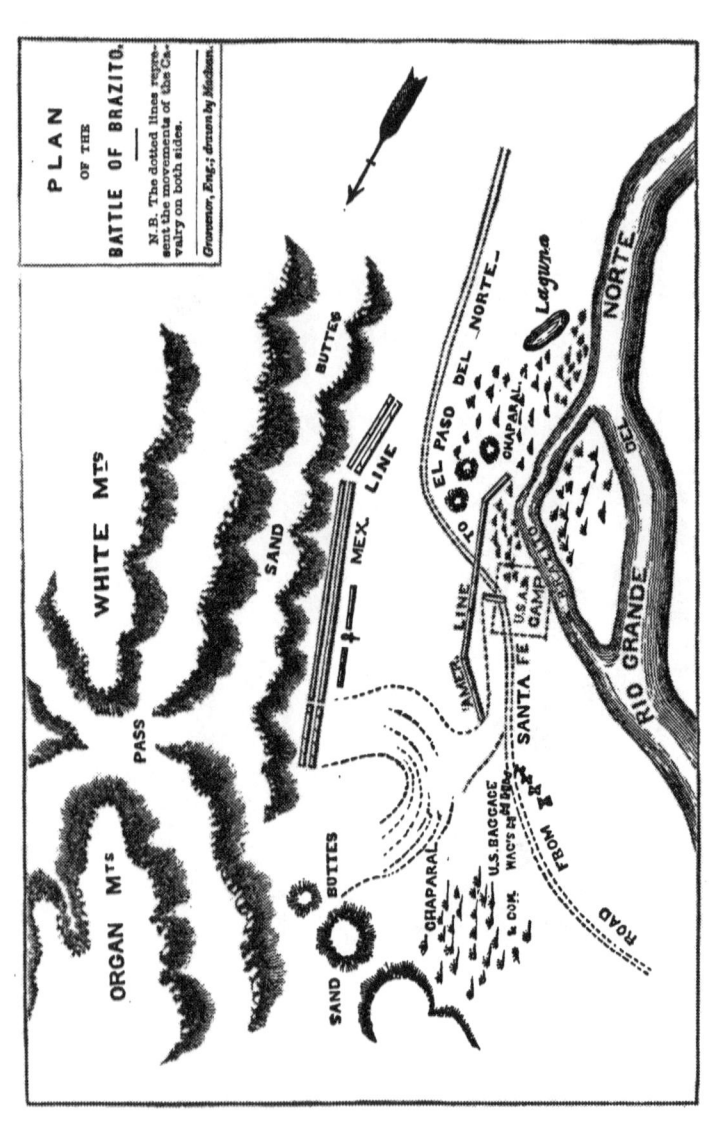

the dragoons were dressed in a uniform of blue pantaloons, green coats, trimmed with scarlet and wearing tall caps, plated in front with brass, on the tops of which waved plumes of horsehair.

Before the battle commenced and while the two armies stood marshaled front to front, the Mexican commander, General Ponce De Leon, despatched a lieutenant to Colonel Doniphan, bearing a black flag. The messenger, coming with the speed of lightning, halted when within sixty yards of the American line and waved his ensign gracefully in salutation. Colonel Doniphan advanced toward him a short distance, accompanied by an interpreter, and asked his demands. The response was a demand from the Mexican General that the American commander appear before him. Doniphan replied: "If your General desires peace, let him come here," when the messenger cried out: "Then we will break your ranks and take him there." "Come then and take him," cried Doniphan, and immediately the battle began.[33]

"Dios y Libertad," shouted the Mexican commander, and in a whirlwind of sand and dust the cavalry came thundering on. Through the rising clouds of dust the bright lances and sabres glittered in the sheen of the sun; the Vera Cruz dragoons were leading and charged on Doniphan's left. Not until within a few yards did the Americans open fire. The shrill voice of Doniphan could be heard above the cries of the Mexicans and the fire of the yagermen. The execution was deadly; his line was broken. At this moment Captain Reid, with only sixteen mounted men, the balance on foot, charged the enemy, broke through his

---

[33]Hughes' Doniphan's Expedition, pages 264 and 265.

Black Flag Carried by Mexicans at Battle of Brazito.
In Museum of Battery "A," St. Louis, Mo.

ranks, hewed them to pieces with their sabres and
threw them into complete confusion. Hand to hand
conflicts were everywhere in evidence. The Mexican
General had his horse killed under him and was
wounded in a sabre duel with one of Reid's troopers.
The Chihuahua infantry and cavalry charged Doniphan's right. They were met with a galling fire at
sixty paces and, wheeling, fled in great confusion. The
consternation became general in the ranks of the enemy
and they commenced a retreat. The Mexican loss
was seventy-one killed, five prisoners and not less than
one hundred and fifty wounded, among whom was the
commanding general, Ponce De Leon. The American
loss was none killed and eight wounded.

By this defeat the Mexican army was completely
disorganized and dispersed. Their volunteers returned
with the utmost expedition to their respective homes,
while the regulars, under Ponce De Leon, continued
their flight to Chihuahua. This was the only battle
fought by Doniphan's command on what is now American soil.

On the following morning Doniphan moved southward, and, on the 28th, occupied El Paso, which surrendered without a struggle. Here he remained for
about six weeks awaiting the arrival from Santa Fé
of the artillery under Major Clark and Captain
Weightman. These re-enforcements arrived on the 1st
of February, 1847, and consisted of one hundred and
seventeen men and six pieces of cannon. On the 8th
the entire army began its advance upon the City of
Chihuahua. The men were buoyant with hope, expecting a harvest of undying fame and looking for
victory or death on the field of battle. This little

The Battle of Brazito, December 25, 1846.

army, only a handful of volunteers, essayed to conquer the greatest city in Northern Mexico, defended by regulars and volunteers from the entire state of Chihuahua and the neighboring state of Durango. The march led through sandy plains; the water was bad and scarce and everything physically was a menace to the success of the enterprise. The capture of Chihuahua had been deemed of the greatest importance by the American government, so much so that General Wool, with 3,500 men and a heavy park of artillery had been directed thither for its subjugation. Colonel Doniphan was only too well aware of the dangers that confronted him, but he had been ordered to report to General Wool and, brave frontiersman that he was, had no idea of remaining at El Paso waiting for reenforcements; no doubt was in his mind as to his ability to defeat the enemy and capture the city, notwithstanding the fact that both the great states of Chihuahua and Durango were in arms to oppose his advance.

On the 28th, near the City of Chihuahua, the American army came in sight of the enemy encamped at a place called Sacramento. All day long an immense eagle, sometimes soaring aloft and sometimes swooping down amongst the fluttering banners, followed the lines of march and seemed to herald the news of victory. Like the Romans of old, the men regarded the omen as good.

The enemy had occupied the brow of a rocky eminence rising upon a mesa between the Sacramento river and the Arroyo Seco. The approaches were fortified by a line of field works consisting of twenty-eight strong redoubts and intrenchments. This pass

Cannon Captured by Colonel Doniphan at Battle of Sacramento, Now in State House Grounds, Jefferson City, Missouri.

MILITARY OCCUPATION OF NEW MEXICO. 111

was the key to the capital—the far-famed City of Chihuahua, the Mecca of the merchants of the Santa Fé Trail. Thus fortified and intrenched, the Mexican army, consisting, according to a consolidated report of the adjutant general, which fell into the hands of Doniphan after the battle, of four thousand two hundred and twenty men, commanded by Major General Heredia, aided by General Conde, formerly Minister of War of Mexico, as commander of cavalry; General Ugarte, in command of the infantry, and General Trias, commanding the artillery, awaited the approach of the American army.[34]

As the American volunteers advanced nothing could exceed in point of solemnity and grandeur the rumbling of the artillery, the firm moving of the caravan, the dashing to and fro of horsemen, the fluttering banners and guidons waving defiance to the enemy. The Mexicans began the engagement with a cavalry charge, led by General Conde. Down the fortified heights he charged, with sabres flying, leading twelve hundred men, a magnificent sight, the glistening brass upon their accoutrement shining with the flash of a thousand sabres. This force was greater than Doniphan's entire command, and quickly he ordered the artillery to begin its work; at less than a thousand yards the six-pounders and howitzers did deadly work. The charge was broken; Conde fell back in some confusion, unmasking, however, a battery which immediately commenced a fire upon the American army. The artillery battle continued for upwards of an hour, resulting in great loss to the Mexicans. General Conde

---

[34]Hughes' Doniphan's Expedition. Campaigning with Doniphan-Edwards.

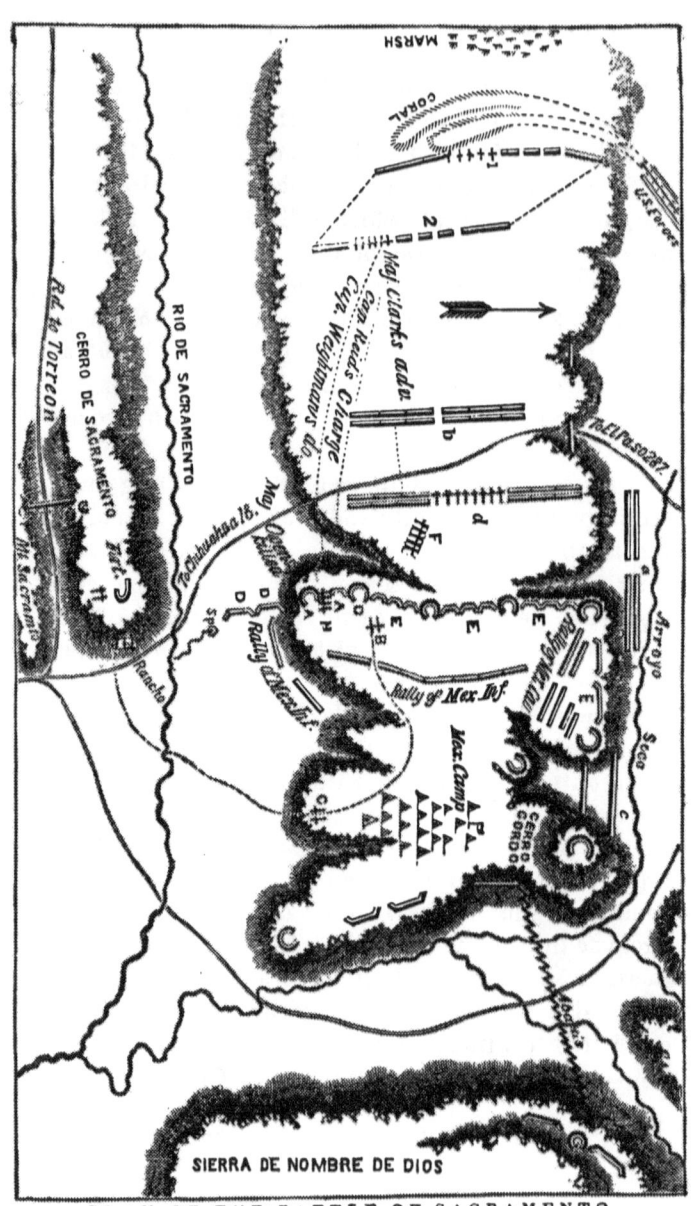

PLAN OF THE BATTLE OF SACRAMENTO

fell back and attempted to reorganize his command behind the retrenchments. Meanwhile the Americans advanced to storm the redoubts. Sixteen pieces of cannon from the redoubts opened a heavy fire upon our army as it moved up the hill, but, owing to the fact that the enemy was compelled to direct his fire plungingly down hill, the army sustained but little damage. When within four hundred yards of the redoubts a charge was ordered. Here it was that Captain Reid again distinguished himself, for with twenty-five troopers he charged the redoubt in his front and carried the battery, silencing the guns. He was too weak to hold it, however, and overwhelmed by the enemy he was beaten back. His horse was killed under him. Within a few moments the remainder of Reid's troop was with him and a section of Weightman's howitzers. Together they swept the intrenchments with grape and canister and the battery was retaken and held.

Meanwhile the American left, under Major Gilpin, boldly scaled the heights, passed the intrenchments, cleared the redoubts and, with great slaughter, forced the enemy to retreat. The Mexican artillerymen were brave fighters; some of them were made prisoners while in the act of touching off their cannon. Great efforts were made by the Mexican generals to rally their forces, but they were unavailing. The rout of the Mexican army became general and the slaughter continued till night put an end to the conflict.

The Mexican loss on the field was three hundred and four men, and a large number wounded, not less than five hundred and seventy were taken prisoners.

Thus was the army of Northern Mexico totally defeated and completely disorganized by a column of

Charge of Captain Reid, at Sacramento.
Reprint from Hughes' Doniphan Expedition.

MILITARY OCCUPATION OF NEW MEXICO. 115

Missouri volunteers. The American loss was one killed, Major Owens of Independence, Mo., and eleven wounded.

Colonel Doniphan, immediately following up this sweeping victory, took possession of the City of Chihuahua, together with a vast quantity of provisions, six thousand dollars in silver, fifty thousand head of sheep, one thousand five hundred head of cattle, one hundred mules, twenty wagons, twenty-five thousand pounds of ammunition, ten pieces of cannon, one hundred stands of small arms, one hundred stands of colors, several fine carriages and other things of lesser note, belonging to the departed commander, Heredia.

On the same day, in the center of the Plaza, amid the thunder of twenty-eight guns, a national salute, Old Glory was hoisted over the stronghold of northern Mexico.

On the 18th of March, Doniphan learned of the great conflict at Buena Vista, and, on the 20th, despatched a messenger to General Wool protesting against remaining at Chihuahua as a mere wagon-guard for the garrisoning of a city with troops never intended for such duty. On the 9th of April following, despatches were received from General Taylor, by way of General Wool at Saltillo, and were sent to Colonel Doniphan by the hands of Captain Pike, with an escort of twenty-six cavalry-men, reaching Doniphan on the 23d, and on the 25th Colonel Doniphan ordered the evacuation of the city and began his march to Saltillo.

Isolated from every other branch of the army, barred by intervening deserts from all communication with his government, thrown entirely upon his own resources, compelled to draw supplies from a hostile country and in the absence of instructions from any superior authority, Doniphan and his command had been practically abandoned by the United States government and left to cut its way through the country of a subtle enemy. Destitute of clothing and the means of procuring it, the army not having received a dollar in pay since the day of enlistment, the soldiers indeed were become rough and uncouth samples of frontier existence.

Their long beards flowed in the wind like the hair of the Cossack on the Russian Steppes. Their buckskin apparel, their unusually stern appearance, their determined and resolute mien attracted the gaze and won the admiration of the people everywhere.

When General Wool, with three thousand five hundred men, with heavy artillery, set out from San Antonio on his intended expedition against Chihuahua, many predicted his complete annihilation, and yet, Doniphan, with a force of less than a thousand effective men, captured the city, although desperately defended at Sacramento, a feat at that time unrivalled in the history of American armies.

In compliance with the orders of General Taylor, the services of the Missouri Volunteers being no longer required in the war with Mexico, General Doniphan and command were sent to the United States by way of Matamoras and the Gulf of Mexico. They were discharged at New Orleans and returned to their native state, graced with the trophies of the vanquished foe, the cannon captured at Sacramento afterwards presented to the state of Missouri, having in twelve months travelled more than three thousand five hundred miles by land, over two thousand five hundred miles by sea,

The Missouri Mounted Volunteer.
Sketch from Life, on Arrival of Doniphan's Command at Chihuahua, 1847.
Reprint from Hughes' Doniphan Expedition.

conquered the state of New Mexico, concluded a great campaign against the Navajo Indians, in which a treaty of peace was secured, fought the battles of Brazito and Sacramento, conquered the state of Chihuahua, marched over six hundred miles through sandy, desert wastes to Saltillo, joining General Wool, all accomplished with a loss of less than one hundred of their original number.

The expedition of Cyrus against his brother, Artaxerxes, and the retreat of the Ten Thousand Greeks under Xenophon form the only parallel to Doniphan's expedition recorded in the history of the world.[35]

The returning soldiers were welcomed on every hand by the patriotic citizens of their native state. Great public meetings were held, one at St. Louis on the 2d day of July, 1847, being addressed by Hon. Thomas H. Benton, then a United States senator from Missouri, who in a most thrilling and eloquent manner recounted with astonishing accuracy and extraordinary minuteness the events of the great campaign.[36]

In the latter part of the month, at a meeting held in Independence, Colonel Doniphan was crowned with the hero's laurel wreath, and a Mrs. Buchanan, on behalf of the ladies of the state, delivered from the stand, in the presence of the assembled thousands, a most eloquent address, saying:—[37]

"Volunteers of Missouri:—In the history of your country no fairer page can be found than that which records your heroic achievements. Many of you had

---
[35]Hughes' Doniphan's Expedition.
[36]Missouri Republican—July 3d, 1847.
[37]Hughes' Doniphan's Expedition, page 383.

never welcomed the morning light without the sunshine of a mother's smile to make it brighter. Many of you had known the cares and hardships of life only in name, still you left the home of your childhood and encountered perils and sufferings that would make the cheek of a Roman soldier turn pale, and encountered them so gallantly that time in his vast calendar of centuries can show none more bravely, more freely borne."

"We welcome you back to your homes. The triumph which hailed the return of the Caesars to whose war chariot was chained the known world is not ours to give, nor do you need it. A prouder triumph than Rome could bestow is yours, in the undying fame of your proud achievements. But if the welcome of hearts filled with warm love and well merited admiration, hearts best known and longest tried, be a triumph, it is yours in the fullest extent."

"Colonel Doniphan:—In the name of the ladies who surround me, I bestow on you this laurel wreath—in every age and every clime, the gift of beauty to valor. In placing it on the brow of him who kneels to receive it, I place it on the brow of all who followed where so brave, so dauntless a commander, led. It is true that around the laurel wreath is twined every association of genius, glory and valor, but I feel assured that it never was placed on a brow more worthy to receive it than his on which it now rests—THE HERO OF SACRAMENTO."

Alexander William Doniphan was born on the 9th day of July, 1808, in Mason county, Kentucky. There his tender years were spent and his youthful mind received its first impressions. Amidst Kentucky's wild, romantic mountain scenery, his young faculties developed, unfolded and expanded. Here he learned sentiments of honor, honesty and patriotism. He was a great admirer of the patriots of the American Revolution. He was educated at a college located at Augusta, Kentucky, conducted by the Methodist Episcopal Church and graduated in his 19th year with high honors. He read law under Martin Marshall and finally moved to the state of Missouri and located at Lexington, removing later to Liberty, in Clay county, about twelve miles from Kansas City. His success at the bar was almost unexampled.

Colonel Doniphan, in 1838, held the office of Brigadier General of militia, and in that year was in command of a brigade belonging to the division of Major General Lucas, operating against the Mormons, who were creating disturbances in the Far West, led by their great Prophet, Joseph Smith. Military preparations were being actively pushed forward by the Prophet to meet the emergency and General Doniphan rendered important service in overawing the insurgent forces and quelling the disturbances without bloodshed. This was his first campaign. His biographers say that[38] in all the relations of his social life, and his public career as well, his conduct was most exemplary. In all his dealings he was just and honorable. He was most interesting and fluent in conversation; his manner and deportment were most prepossessing, and, as an orator, he had wonderful and shining powers. His air was commanding, his language full and flowing, his gestures graceful, his enunciation distinct, his voice sonorous, his arguments convincing and his mind clear

---

[38]Hughes and Allen.

and comprehensive. His was a great imagination. It was not only brilliant but dazzlingly brilliant, vivid and strong, and when excited the tide of his eloquence was almost irresistible. In stature he was six feet and four inches, well proportioned, dignified and gentlemanly in his manners. His features were bold, his eye keen and expressive and his forehead massive. No fitter man could have been chosen by the volunteers for the command of the regiment. It was his sagacity that planned, his judgment that conducted and his energy and bravery, together with that of his officers and men, that accomplished the most wonderful campaign of any age or country. It was done without an outfit, without money, almost without ammunition, by a citizen-commander of citizen soldiers. The history of this expedition is his monument. His deeds will ever live to praise him. He died at Richmond, Missouri, August 8, 1887, beloved by all who knew him.

CHAPTER IV.

1. General Price in Command at Santa Fé. 2. The Archuleta Conspiracy. 3. The Taos Revolution. 4. The Killing of Governor Bent. 5. The Battles of Cañada, Embudo, Taos and Mora. 6. The Leaders Are Tried by Court-martial and Hanged. 7. Fight with Indians at Red River Canyon. 8. Fight at Las Vegas; the Town Is Burned. 9. Indian Fight at Arroyo Hondo. 10. Fr. Antonio Jose Martinez. 1. Legislature Under Military Rule; Governor Vigil. 12. Differences Between Military and Civil Authorities. 13. Formation of Territory of New Mexico.

Upon the departure of Colonel Doniphan and his command for the Chihuahua campaign, Colonel Sterling Price, afterwards commissioned a Brigadier General, and later Governor of Missouri and a Major General in the Confederate army, in the war between the States, assumed command at Santa Fé. About the 1st of December following the departure of Doniphan some very distinguished native citizens of New Mexico began to hold secret cabals, plotting the overthrow of the existing government. These revolutionists had been prominent in the affairs of New Mexico during the rule of Armijo and longed for return to power and authority. The leaders of this revolution were Don Tomas Ortiz, who aspired to become governor, and Don Diego Archuleta, who had been nominated as commanding general. Many other prominent men, of great and restless ambition, joined in the plot, among whom, it has been declared, was the priest, Fr. Antonio Jose Martinez, of Taos.

The 19th of December, at midnight, was the time first fixed for the revolt, which was to be simultaneous throughout the department. Owing to a want of complete organization, the conspiracy not yet having fully matured, the commencement of the revolution was suspended until the evening of the 24th of December, when it was believed the chances for the successful capture of the city of Santa Fé and its garrison would be better. It was believed that Christmas evening was a most favorable time, for the reason that the soldiers would be indulging in wine in the resorts of the city and would be taken unarmed. Every American, without distinction, throughout the entire department, and such natives as had favored the American government and accepted office under General Kearny, were to be massacred and the reins of government seized. This revolution, however, failed, owing to the vigilance of Colonel Price, his officers and men. The leaders fled, some south to Chihuahua and others to the mountains of Rio Arriba. The rebellion was immediately suppressed.

But the leaders of this revolution were men of restless and unsatisfied ambition. They remained inactive only a brief period. A second and still more dangerous revolution was plotted. Some of the most powerful and dangerous men in the department are known to have favored the design. The experience derived from the failure of the first brought about the most profound secrecy in the formation of the plans for the second. Upon the surface everything throughout the department was quiet and yet the machinations of the revolutionists were daily gaining strength. Even the priests gave counsel. The people everywhere, in the towns, villages and settlements began to arm and equip themselves unknown to the military authorities, and on the 19th of January, 1847, the rebellion broke out in several parts of New Mexico.

THE TAOS REVOLUTION—KILLING OF GOVERNOR BENT.

On the 14th of January, Governor Charles Bent had left Santa Fé to visit Taos and five days later he was foully assassinated in his own residence in that village.

Governor Bent, it seems, was aware of the discontent which prevailed among certain leaders and classes of the people, for, subsequent to the first conspiracy, he issued, as governor, a proclamation, among other things declaring:

"You are now governed by new statutory laws and you also have the free government promised to you. Do not abuse the great liberty which is vouchsafed you by it, so you may gather the abundant fruits which await you in the future. Those who are blindly opposed, as well as those whose vices have made them notorious, and the ambitious persons who aspire to the best offices, also those persons who dream that mankind should bow to their whims, having become satisfied that they cannot find employment in the offices which are usually given to men of probity and honesty, exasperated (Thomas Ortiz and the old revolutionist, Diego Archuleta) have come forth as leaders of a revolution against the present government. They held a meeting in this Capital about the middle of last month, which was also attended by some foolish and imprudent men who were urged to follow the standard of rebellion. Their treason was discovered in time and smothered at its birth. Now they are wandering about and hiding from the people, but their doctrines are scattered broadcast among the people, thereby causing uneasiness, and they still hold to their ruinous plans. * * * There is still another pretext with which they want to alarm you and that is the falsehood that troops are coming from the interior in order to re-conquer the country. What help could the department of Chihuahua, which is torn by factions and reduced to insignificance afford you? Certainly none. * * * I urge you to turn a deaf ear to such false doctrines and to remain quiet, attending to your domestic affairs, so that you may enjoy under the law, all the blessings of peace, and by rallying around the government, call attention to the improvements which you deem material to the advancement of the country and that by so doing you may enjoy all the prosperity which your best friend wishes you."

While he knew of the discontent prevailing, Governor Bent was in no wise alarmed for his personal safety. The native people had always professed the warmest admiration and friendship for him, and his treatment of them was of the most cordial and generous kind.

Governor Bent misjudged the people and underestimated the influence of the treacherous men who professed to be his friends. Early on the morning of the 19th of January, the insurrectionists, under the leadership of Pablo Montoya and a Taos Indian, known as Tomasito, entered the city, joined the resident members of the revolutionary movement and began the attack. They destroyed the houses of the resident Americans. The Indians, under the leadership of Tomasito, visited the home of Governor Bent, and, firing through the door, while engaged in conversation with him, wounded him in the chin and stomach. The

Old Church at Taos, N. M.

MILITARY OCCUPATION OF NEW MEXICO. 127

door was broken down and the Indians filled his body with arrows, three of which the prostrate governor pulled from his face before he was killed. His wrists and hands were slashed with knives and axes. Amidst the fiendish yells of the Indians, he was scalped, while yet alive, and afterwards his head was hacked from his body. Immediately after the killing of Governor Bent, the remaining Americans hid themselves as best they could. Pablo Jaramillo, the brother of Mrs. Bent, and Narcisco Beaubien, a son of Charles Beaubien, buried themselves in the straw of a stable near by, but were discovered and their bodies pierced through with lances. Among others who were massacred were Louis Lee, the acting sheriff of the county, Cornelio Vigil, prefect and probate judge, and J. W. Leal, circuit attorney. Leaving Taos, the insurrectionists proceeded to the Arroyo Hondo, where they destroyed a distillery and killed Jesse Turley and six other Americans.[39]

While these bloody scenes were being enacted in Taos and at the Arroyo Hondo, similar attacks were made upon Americans in other parts of the Territory. Seven were killed at Mora.[40] These were Santa Fé traders, the most prominent of whom was Lawrence L. Waldo, of Westport, Missouri, father of Henry L. Waldo, of Las Vegas. Mr. Waldo had been engaged in trade for several years and had made several trips over the Santa Fé Trail. Like Governor Bent, he was respected and liked by the masses of the Mexican people and by the Indians. He was just entering Mora with his companions, in charge of a caravan, ignorant

[39]Hughes' Doniphan's Expedition, page 393.
[40]Hughes' Doniphan's Expedition — Culver, Noyes and others.

of the fact that a revolution had been started, when all were shot from ambush and killed. When the news reached Las Vegas, a detachment of troops was sent to Mora, which returned with the bodies of the murdered men, and later they were buried in the cemetery on the hill west of the present old town of Las Vegas.

GENERAL PRICE STARTS FOR TAOS. BATTLES OF CAÑADA, EMBUDO AND TAOS.

As soon as Colonel Price learned of the massacre of Governor Bent and his retinue, word having been brought to him by a brother of the sheriff, who had lost his life with Bent, he left for Taos with a strong force.

The insurgents were assembled in force near the present village of Santa Cruz, twenty-five miles north of Santa Fé, under Generals Ortiz and Montoya, with a view of making an assault upon the Capital. Colonel Price met them at Cañada, the enemy numbering about two thousand men. The American force consisted of four hundred and eighty men and four pieces of artillery, mountain howitzers. The insurgents were posted on both sides of the main road to Taos, occupying the hills. A sharp fire from the howitzers was directed against the enemy, but with little effect, where upon Colonel Price ordered Captain Angney to charge the hill, which was gallantly done, being supported by Captain St. Vrain with a company of citizen soldiers. The conflict continued until sundown. The American loss was two killed and seven wounded. The insurgent loss was thirty-six killed and forty-five taken prisoners. The insurgents retreated toward Taos. The enemy was hotly pursued by Price and was again encountered at Embudo, where he was discovered in the thick piñon and cedar thickets which lined the road side. A charge was ordered and was made by three companies under Captain Burgwin and Captain St. Vrain and Lieutenant White, resulting in the total route of the insurgents.

The march was resumed the following day and no opposition was had until the third day of February, at which time Price arrived at the Pueblo of Taos, where he found the insurgents strongly fortified. A few rounds were fired by the artillery that evening, but was soon discontinued on account of its ineffectiveness.

General Price gives a very vivid description of the battle of Taos; it is as follows:—"Posting the dragoons under Captain Burgwin about two hundred and sixty yards from the western flank of the church, I ordered the mounted men under Captains St. Vrain and Slack to a position on the opposite side of the town, whence they could discover and intercept any fugitives who might attempt to escape toward the mountains or in the direction of San Fernando. The residue of the troops took ground about three hundred yards from the north wall. Here, too, Lieutenant Dyer established himself with the six-pounder and two howitzers, while Lieutenant Hassendaubel, of Major Clark's battalion, light artillery, remained with Captain Burgwin, in command of two howitzers. By this arrangement a crossfire was obtained, sweeping the front and eastern flank of the church. All these arrangements being made, the batteries opened upon the town at nine o'clock a. m. At eleven o'clock, finding it impossible to breach the walls of the church with the six-pounders and the howitzers, I determined to storm the building. At a signal Captain Burgwin, at the head of his own company and that of Captain McMillin, charged the western flank of the church, while Captain Angney, in-

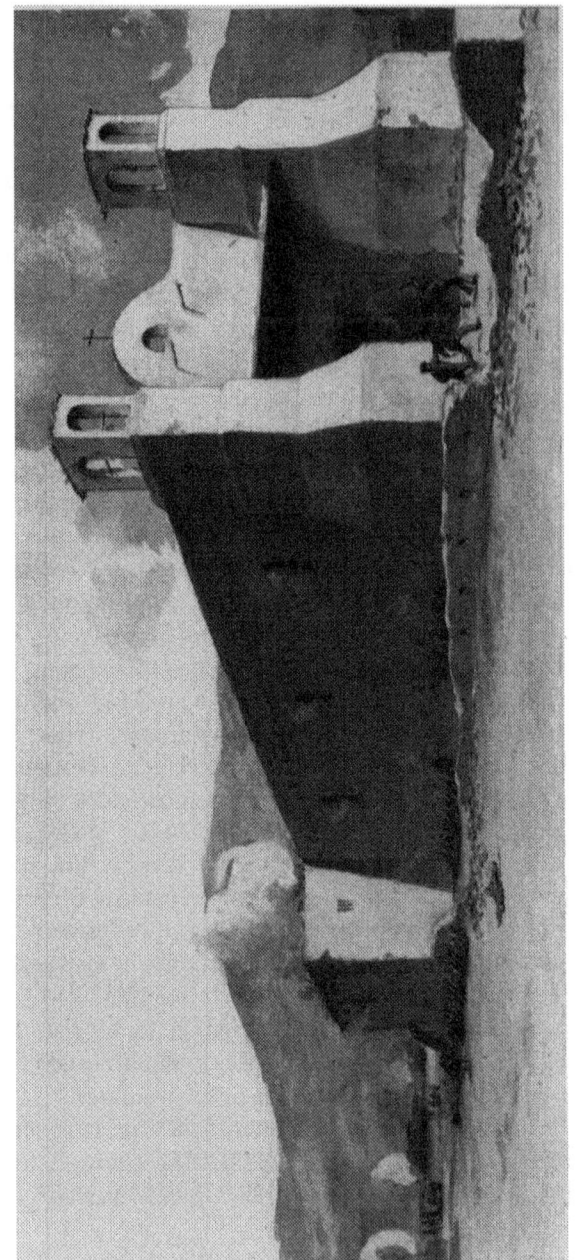

The Battle of Taos, N. M., February 4, 1847—Death of Captain Burgwin, U. S. A.

fantry battalion, and Captain Barber and Lieutenant Boon, Second Missouri Mounted Volunteers, charged the northern wall. As soon as the troops above mentioned had established themselves under the western wall of the church, axes were used in the attempt to breach it, and a temporary ladder having been made, the roof was fired. About this time Captain Burgwin, at the head of a small party, left the cover afforded by the flank of the church, and, penetrating into the corral in front of that building, endeavored to force the door. In this exposed situation Captain Burgwin received a severe wound, which deprived me of his valuable services, and of which he died on the 7th instant. Lieutenants McIlvane, First United States Dragoons, and Royall and Lachland, Second Regiment Volunteers, accompanied Captain Burgwin into the corral, but the attempt on the church door proved fruitless, and they were compelled to retire behind the wall. In the meantime small holes had been cut in the western wall, and shells were thrown in by hand, doing good execution. The six-pounder was now brought around by Lieutenant Wilson, who, at a distance of two hundred yards poured a heavy fire of grape into the town. The enemy, during all this time, kept up a destructive fire upon our troops. About half-past three o'clock the six-pounder was run up within sixty yards of the church, and after ten rounds, one of the holes which had been cut with the axes was widened into a practicable breach. The storming party, among whom were Lieutenant Dyer, of the ordnance, and Lieutenants Wilson and Taylor, First Dragoons, entered and took possession of the church without opposition. The interior was filled with dense smoke, but for which circumstance our storming party would have suffered great loss. A few of the enemy were seen in the gallery, where an open door admitted the air, but they retired without firing a gun. The troops left to support the battery on the north side were now ordered to charge on that side."

"The enemy then abandoned the western part of the town. Many took refuge in the large houses on the east, while others endeavored to escape to the mountains. These latter were pursued by the mounted men under Captains Slack and St. Vrain, who killed fifty-one of them, only two or three men escaping. It was now night, and our troops were quietly quartered in the house which the enemy had abandoned. On the next morning the enemy sued for peace, and, thinking the severe loss they had sustained would prove a salutary lesson, I granted their supplication on the condition that they should deliver up to me Tomas, one of their principal men, who had instigated and been actively engaged in the murder of Governor Bent and others. The number of the enemy at the battle of Pueblo de Taos was between six and seven hundred, and of these one hundred and fifty were killed, wounded not known. Our own loss was seven killed and forty-five wounded; many of the wounded have since died."

In this battle fell Captain Burgwin, than whom a braver soldier or better man never poured out his blood in the cause of his country. The total loss of the insurgents in the three engagements was two hundred and eighty-two. The American loss was fifteen killed and forty-seven wounded.[41]

---

[41]Hughes' Doniphan's Expedition and official report of Col. Price. The killed were Captain Burgwin, Lieutenant Van Valkenburg; sergeants Caldwell, Rose and Heart; privates Graham, Smith, Papin, Bower, Brooks, Levicy, Hansuker, Truax, Austin and Beebe.

After the battle the leading spirits in the insurrection were captured and placed in prison awaiting trial, but a dragoon, named Fitzgerald, shot Tomasito, killing him instantly. On the 6th, Montoya, who had styled himself the "Santa Ana of the North," was tried by court-martial and sentenced to be hung, which was done in the presence of the army, along with fourteen others.[42]

The home of Fr. Antonio Jose Martinez was generally regarded as the headquarters for the insurrectionists prior to the uprising and until after the assassination of Governor Bent. His power over his parishioners was absolute and his hatred of Americans and American institutions was recognized by all. This fact was regarded by such men as Governor Bent, Colonel St. Vrain and Col. Kit Carson[43] as ample proof of his complicity in the revolution. His brother, Captain Pascual Martinez, had been in command of a company of soldiers under Governor Armijo, prior to the coming of General Kearny, and there are persons still living who are authority for the statement that he actively participated in the uprising at the instigation of his brother, the priest.

Governor Bent was a native of Virginia, having been born in Charleston, in 1797. His father was of English ancestry; his mother was part French. He was a very highly educated man and graduated from

---

[42]The court-martial consisted of six officers — Captains Angney, Barbee and Slack; Lieutenants Ingalls, White and Eastin, the last named being Judge-Advocate of the Court.

[43]Col. Carson was not in this battle, although his home was in Taos; at the time he was in California with Kearny, having been a scout under him in his march from the Gila river to San Diego, California.

134 MILITARY OCCUPATION OF NEW MEXICO.

the United States Military Academy at West Point. He resigned from the army and engaged in mercantile pursuits at St. Louis, Missouri. In 1829 he left for the Far West over the Santa Fé Trail, looking for a location for the establishment of business. For some time he was with his brother at Bent's Fort, on the Arkansas, and, in 1832, came to Santa Fé, where, with his brothers, William and George, he established a general merchandising business. He was afterwards a business partner with Colonel Ceran St. Vrain, which continued until the death of Governor Bent.

Governor Bent married Maria Ignacia Jaramillo, a daughter of Don Francisco and Apolonia (Vigil) Jaramillo, who died in Taos, April 13, 1883. Mrs. Bent's sister, Josefa Jaramillo, was the wife of Christopher—Kit—Carson. His headless remains are buried in the National cemetery at Santa Fé.

Fr. Antonio Jose Martinez, who was regarded by many as one of the chief authors of the revolution, was one of the most remarkable men ever identified with the history of New Mexico. He was born in the county of Rio Arriba, in 1793, and was a grandson of General Martinez, who came from Chihuahua in the early part of the seventeenth century. His opposition to Americans and their institutions was made manifest in many ways. He realized that the coming of the American was a death blow to his power and prestige in the country and he is said to have used all his power to incite a sentiment of suspicion and distrust of the American people. He was acknowledged to be one of the most brilliant men of his time in New Mexico. No one, except those who were actually engaged as principals in the insurrection, knew positively just

Father Antonio Jose Martinez.

what part Fr. Martinez took in the uprising. He was a very crafty man and the American authorities never could affirmatively fix upon him any active participation, although in later years there were many native citizens, who had been identified with the movement, who did not hesitate to declare that they had been guided by his counsel and advice. He died at Taos, July 27, 1867, and is buried in the cemetery at that place.

BATTLE AT MORA.

Immediately after the killing of Governor Bent, news of the fact was brought to Captain Hendley, who was in command of a grazing detachment of the army on the Pecos river. He learned that the insurgent forces were gathering near Las Vegas. In a short time he was joined by various detachments of the army and marched on the City of the Meadows, which he at once occupied.

Leaving the greater part of his force at Las Vegas, with eighty men, Captain Hendley started for Mora, where he learned that the insurgents had gathered a force of two hundred men. He arrived at Mora on the 24th. A general engagement ensued, the insurgents retreating and firing from windows in the houses of the village. A large body of insurgents had taken possession of an old fort and commenced to fire upon the Americans. Hendley charged the fort and was in possession of a small apartment, and was making ready to fire it, when he was struck by a ball from an adjoining room and died immediately. The Americans, having no artillery, retired with a loss of one killed and three wounded. The insurgent loss was twenty-five killed and seventeen taken prisoners.

The Battle of Mora, N. M., February 1, 1847.

On the first of February, the death of Hendley as well as that of Messrs. Waldo, Noyes, Culver and others was avenged by Captain Morin and his men by the complete demolition of the village of Mora. The insurgents fled to the mountains.

The battles of Cañada, Embudo, Taos and Mora, in all of which the insurgents were defeated with heavy loss, suppressed the insurrection and once more quiet, law and order were restored. A military force was left at Taos by Colonel Price under command of Captain Angney. Price returned to Santa Fé, where he continued to discharge the civil and military functions of the territory. The energy and ability displayed by Colonel Price in the suppression of this rebellion were most commendable; in two weeks all was over; the leaders were executed after trial on a charge of treason; the insurgent armies dispersed; the people returned from the hills to their homes, their daily avocations were resumed and peace and harmony were at once restored, to the great satisfaction of the masses of the people. The plans that had been laid for the uprising were far more extensive than anyone had believed possible. They covered the entire territory from Taos to El Paso, and were known even to the City of Mexico, for, in a letter to General Santa Ana, from that city, dated nearly three months after the killing of Governor Bent, the General is advised that "Intelligence has been received from New Mexico of certain Sicilian vespers which the inhabitants have enacted upon the Yankees there. Being no longer disposed to submit to the extortions exacted, they fell upon them simultaneously, and had killed even to the general, who was there with the Yankees.[44]

At a term of court held by Judge Houghton at Santa Fé immediately following the return of Colonel Price from Taos, several indictments for treason were presented. The accused men were mostly residents of Taos county. Prior to the conflict which resulted in the killing of Governor Bent, a circular letter had been sent out, dated January 20, 1847, by Jesus Tafolla, and countersigned by Antonio Maria Trujillo, addressed to the several native military commanders, which urged them to rebellion in the following words:

"To the Defenders of Their Country: With the end to shake off the yoke bound on us by a foreign government, and as you are Military Inspector General appointed by the Legitimate Commander for the Supreme Government of Mexico, which we proclaim in favor of: The moment you receive this communication, you will place in readiness all the companies under your command, keeping them ready for the 22d day of this month, so that the forces may be, on the day mentioned, at that point. Take the precaution to observe if the forces of the enemy advance any toward these points, and if it should so happen, appoint a courier and despatch him immediately, so that exertions may be doubled, understanding that there must not be resistance or delay in giving the answer to the bearer of this official document."

These dispatches were accompanied by orders reading as follows: "By the order of the Inspector of Arms, Don Antonio Maria Trujillo, I herewith send

---

[44]Letters of J. P. De Mora to Gen. Santa Ana—Ex. Doc. No. 60, page 1088.

you this dispatch (or order) that the moment this comes to hand you will raise all the forces, together with all the inhabitants that are able to bear arms, connecting them also with persons in San Juan de Los Caballeros, by to-morrow, counting from the 22d day of the present month, and not later than eight o'clock in the morning.

"We have declared war with the American and it is now time that we shall all take our arms in our hands in defense of our abandoned country.

"You are held responsible for the execution of the above order.

"JUAN ANTONIO GARCIA,
"Sor. So. Dn. Pedro Vigil."

The indictment against Trujillo, drawn by Hon. Frank P. Blair, Jr., United States Attorney, appointed by General Kearny, reads as follows:[45]

"UNITED STATES OF AMERICA, } ss.
TERRITORY OF NEW MEXICO,

"In the United States District Court, at the March Term, 1847.

"The Grand Jurors for the district of New Mexico, on the part of the United States of America, on their oaths, present that Antonio Maria Trujillo, of the County of Taos, in the Territory of New Mexico, being a citizen of the United States of America, but disregarding the duty of his allegiance to the government of the United States aforesaid, and wholly withdrawing the allegiance, duty and obedience which every true and faithful citizen of the said government and of right ought to bear toward the said government of the

---

[45]Records in office District Court, Santa Fé, N. M.

United States, on the 20th day of January, in the year 1847, and on divers other days, as well before as after, with force and arms, at the county aforesaid and territory aforesaid, together with divers other false traitors, to the jurors, aforesaid, unknown, did, then and there, maliciously, wickedly and traitorously levy war against the government of the United States of America, and did then and there maliciously and traitorously endeavor and attempt to subvert the laws and constitution of the government, to the evil example of all others in like cases offending, and against the peace and dignity of the government of the United States * * *."

Trujillo was tried before Judge Houghton and promptly found guilty. The sentence imposed by the court is worthy of a place in this connection, as it is the only sentence of the kind passed by any court in the history of New Mexico. The record at Santa Fé shows the sentence to have been in the following words:[46]

"Antonio Maria Trujillo:—A jury of twelve citizens, after a patient and careful investigation, pending which all the safeguards of the law, managed by able and indefatigable counsel, have been afforded you, have found you guilty of the high crime of treason. What have you to say why the sentence of death should not be pronounced against you?

"Your age and gray hairs have excited the sympathy of both the court and the jury. Yet, while each and all were not only willing but anxious that you should have every advantage placed at your disposal that their highly responsible duty under the laws to

---

[46]Court records, Santa Fé District Court, date March 16, 1847.

their country would permit, you have been found guilty of the crime alleged to your charge. It would appear that old age has not brought you wisdom, nor purity, nor honesty of heart. While holding out the hand of friendship to those whom circumstances have brought to rule over you, you have nourished bitterness and hatred in your heart. You have been found seconding the acts of a band of the most traitorous murderers that ever blackened with the recital of their deeds the annals of history. Not content with the peace and security in which you have lived under the present government, secure in all your personal rights as a citizen, in property, in person, and in your religion, you gave your name and influence to measures intended to effect universal murder and pillage, the overthrow of the government and one widespread scene of bloodshed in the land. For such foul crimes an enlightened and liberal jury have been compelled, from the evidence brought before them, and by a sense of their stern but unmistakable duty, to find you guilty of treason against the government under which you are a citizen. And there only now remains to the court the painful duty of passing upon you the sentence of the law, which is that you be taken from hence to prison, there to remain until Friday, the 16th day of April next, and that, at two o'clock in the afternoon of that day, you be taken thence to the place of execution, and there be hanged by the neck till you are dead! dead! dead! And may the Almighty God have mercy on your soul!"

This trial and its outcome were made the subject-matter of a resolution passed by the congress of the United States calling upon President Polk to advise

Fight at Las Vegas, N. M., June 6, 1847.

congress whether any persons had been tried and condemned for "treason against the United States in that part of New Mexico lying east of the Rio Grande since the same has been in the occupancy of our army" and, if so, before "what tribunal," and "by what authority of law such tribunal was established."

In response to this request, President Polk said: [47]"It appears that after the territory in question was 'in the occupancy of our Army' some of the conquered Mexican inhabitants, who had at first submitted to our authority, broke out in open insurrection, murdering our soldiers and citizens and committing other atrocious crimes. Some of the principal offenders who were apprehended were tried and condemned by a tribunal invested with civil and criminal jurisdiction, which had been established in the conquered country by the military officer in command. That the offenders deserved the punishment inflicted upon them there is no reason to doubt, and the error in the proceedings against them consisted in designating and describing their crimes as 'treason against the United States.' This error was pointed out, and its recurrence thereby prevented, by the Secretary of War, in a dispatch to the officer in command in New Mexico, dated on the 26th day of June, 1847."

There is doubt as to the authority to try and condemn Trujillo for "treasonable" acts. The error consisted in the manner in which it was done. In the prosecution of the war with Mexico, the United States had the right, by conquest and military occupation, to exercise rights of sovereignty over it. The sovereignty of Mexico was suspended and the laws of

---

[47]Message of President Polk, July 24, 1848.

OF THE TERRITORY OF NEW MEXICO. 145

Mexico could not be rightfully enforced over the conquered territory or be obligatory over its inhabitants, who remained and submitted to the authority of our government. By the surrender the inhabitants at least passed under a temporary allegiance and were bound by such laws and such laws only as the United States saw fit to recognize and impose. From the nature of the case no other laws could be obligatory upon them, for where there is no allegiance or protection or sovereignty there can be no claim to obedience.[48]

The only affairs occurring during the year 1847, in which the military took an important part, were those at Red River Canon, about 180 miles from Santa Fé, where Major Edmonson, with a detachment of two hundred men, was vigorously attacked by a large force of Indians, estimated to have been about five hundred in number. In the engagement the American loss was one killed and several wounded.

In the month of June, Lieutenant Brown and two private soldiers were killed near Las Vegas and the bodies of the enlisted men burned. Major Edmonson determined to punish the men who committed these murders and marched upon the town with a small force of cavalry, leaving the infantry and artillery to follow. On reaching the Gallinas, he divided his force into two parties, under command of Captains Holloway and Horine, and charged the place on the right and left of the plaza. In less than fifteen minutes many Mexicans were slain, the fugitives captured and the town with fifty prisoners taken. The dead body of Lieutenant Brown, having the cross suspended from

---

[48]Debates in Congress, 1848.

his neck, was found secreted in the rocks west of the plaza. The clothes, guns, sabres, pistols and bowie knives of the murdered soldiers were discovered secreted in various houses. The greater portion of the town was reduced to ashes, only a sufficient number of houses being left to shelter the women and children. The mills, a few miles from the town, which belonged to the alcalde, Juan de Dios Maes, were also destroyed. The prisoners, by order of Colonel Price, were conveyed to Santa Fé, where they were tried before a court martial and six of them sentenced to death. This sentence was carried out on the 3rd day of August in the presence of the army.

On July 9th a detachment of thirty-one men, belonging to Captain Morin's company, stationed about 18 miles from Taos, was furiously attacked two hours before daylight by two hundred Mexicans and Pueblo Indians. Five Americans were killed and nine wounded.[49]. The loss of the enemy was never ascertained.

As before stated, the government established by General Kearny, had the instructions given to him by the Secretary of War been carried out, should have been of a character purely military, with the right to perform only such civil duties as were necessary to the full enjoyment of the advantages resulting from the conquest and to the due protection of the rights of all persons and the property of the people.[50]

In the latter part of 1847 it became very patent to all that the jurisdiction of the courts established by

---

[49]The killed were Lieut. Larkin, W. Owens, J. A. Wright, W. S. Mason and Wilkinson.

[50]Letter to General Kearny from W. L. Marcy, Sec. of War—Ex. Doc. No. 60, page 179.

Kearny was very limited, particularly when any conflict arose between the civil and military authorities. The citizens of the territory were not aware of the position of the administration at Washington relative to the rights of the United States over the territory and its people.

As late as October 20, 1847, nearly a year after the message of President Polk to the congress of the United States, in which he approved only a part of the official acts of General Kearny, as declared in his proclamation, in the giving of the code of laws and the making of civil appointments, a periodical published at Santa Fé at that time, in a long editorial upon the existing state of affairs, says:[51] "Recently the American citizens here have seen the powers properly falling under the jurisdiction of the civil tribunals arrogated by the military, bringing the former into contempt and disrepute, and that there is in effect only the form of a civil government in the territory, and that for all practical purposes it is paralyzed and ineffectual. This being the state of things, the will of the commanding officer is the law. The citizens here are not aware that the laws framed and established by General Kearny and confirmed by the president have been revoked. They wish to know whether the organic laws of General Kearny are still in full force, or whether they have been revoked. They wish to know whether this has been done by the order of the President or not. Why call together a legislative body, if its acts may be annulled and made void by the will or caprice of a commanding officer? Why frame laws, if the order of a commanding officer is para-

---

[51]Editorial, Santa Fé Republican, Oct. 20, 1847.

mount? Why have judges and courts if they can only act at the pleasure of the military authorities?"

A grand jury,[52] duly sworn and empaneled by Judge Houghton, the presiding judge of the court sitting at Santa Fé, in its report of matters before it during the October Term, 1847, very pertinently says: "They have found the honorable court which they now address has virtually acknowledged the existence of a superior authority by refusing to issue a writ of habeas corpus in behalf of a citizen. They have also found that the settlement of civil contracts has been arrogated by another authority than the regularly appointed civil courts; that the military commander has been the self-constituted judge and jury of a case which concerned his own private interests. They recommend that the civil authorities request from the military that, when a citizen is arrested for any offense against the existing statutes of the territory, he be handed over for trial to them."

This grand jury report is significant. No copy of it is found in the court records, but the newspaper, in which it was published, is on file in the records of the Historical Society of New Mexico. The conclusion is inevitable that in the disposition of matters involving violations of the criminal code, Judge Houghton had very little to say, particularly if the commanding officer thought best to exercise his authority. The learned judge was not a member of the legal profession when Kearny clothed him with the judicial ermine, neither was Otero or Beaubien, but it does not require a lawyer to ascertain that Judge Houghton's stock of good

---

[52]Report of Grand Jury—Santa Fé Republican, Oct. 20, 1847.

common sense was great enough to cause a denial of a writ of habeas corpus rather than have a clash with the commanding officer, who, at that time, happened to be General Sterling Price. The judge, not learned in the law, evidently desired to continue dealing out justice, even though his jurisdiction was somewhat warped and hazy. The covert sarcasm of the word "request," as used by the grand jury in its report, shows beyond all question that, even with the so-called courts and other officials created by Kearny endeavoring to exercise their official functions, the real and supreme authority was the commanding general of the department. Judge Houghton evidently had some of the characteristics of a Solomon in declining to have a serious clash with an American General, who, when occasion required, saw fit to constitute himself a "judge and jury of a case which concerned his own private interests."

LEGISLATURE AT THE TIME OF MILITARY OCCUPATION.

On the 6th day of December, 1847, a so-called Legislative Assembly, under the military government, convened at Santa Fé. Donaciano Vigil had been named governor, after the death of Bent. Governor Vigil was a native New Mexican and was born September 6, 1802. He had occupied a number of public positions, both civil and military, and enjoyed the confidence of the people. He had been active in expeditions against the Navajos in 1823, 1833, 1836 and in 1838. For more than four years he was the military secretary of the governor and was twice a member of the Departmental Assembly, and was an official of great experience.

The address of Governor Vigil to the first legislative assembly forcibly demonstrates him to have been a man of marked ability. He had been accustomed to methods and a system of government radically different from those of the great republic whose protection he was then enjoying and to which, when Kearny came, he had been among the first to render allegiance. He must have been well informed as to our institutions, or else in one short year he absorbed more than many of his people have succeeded in attaining in the many years that have elapsed since that memorable occasion. His ideas of public education and the mental emancipation of his people are well worth considering even to-day. On this subject Governor Vigil said: "If your government here is to be republican, if it is to be based upon democratic-republican principles, and if the will of the majority is to be one day the law of the land and the government of the people, it is evident, for this will to be properly exercised, the people must be enlightened and instructed. And it is particularly important in a country, where the right of suffrage is accorded and secured to all, that all should be instructed and that every man should be able to read to inform himself of the passing events of the day and of the matters interesting to his country and government. This is the age of improvement, both in government and society, and it more particularly becomes us, when commencing, as it were, a new order of things, to profit by and promote such improvements, and they can only be encouraged and promoted by diffusing knowledge and instruction among the people. The diffusion of knowledge breaks down antiquated prejudices and distinctions, introduces the people of all countries to a more intimate and attached acquaint-

OF THE TERRITORY OF NEW MEXICO. 151

ance, and is calculated to cultivate these sympathies among the masses in all nations which induce comparison and insure improvement. The world at large is advancing, and how can we profit by the advance unless the people are educated? It is true that the available means which could be applied at present to the cause of education are small, but for the promotion of so desirable an object they might be both increased and economized. All that the legislature can do in the cause of education for the people is most earnestly pressed upon them and will meet with my hearty approval and co-operation."

This first session of a legislative assembly ever held in New Mexico under American control was organized by the election of Don Antonio Sandoval as Speaker of the Legislative Council and Captain W. Z. Angney as Speaker of the House of Representatives. Ten acts were passed, among which were acts establishing a University and raising funds for its support; an act in relation to replevin; one regulating ejectments, and one calling for a convention of delegates to meet in the City of Santa Fé, in the month of February, 1848. These laws all bear the approval of Governor Vigil, and were also approved by the Military Commander, General Price, by special orders, as follows:[53]

"Headquarters, 9th Military Department,
"Santa Fé, N. M., February 5, 1848.

"The foregoing Legislative enactments of the Territory of New Mexico, having been duly reviewed by

---

[53]Pamphlet of Laws, Sess. 1847, in library of Frank Springer, Esq., Las Vegas, N. M.

the Commanding General of the Territory, they are hereby approved, and will be duly observed.

"By order of the Brigadier General,

"STERLING PRICE."
"W. E. PRINCE,
"A. D. C. & A. A. A. Gen."

On the same day, the Commanding General, having become convinced that a Territorial Secretary, a United States District Attorney and a United States Marshal were unnecessary in the carrying on of the government, and without requesting the resignation of either of the officials named by General Kearny, abolished the offices by Special Order. By the same order he also decreed that an import duty of six per centum, ad valorem, should be levied upon all merchandise introduced into the Territory, and named the Territorial Treasurer as Collector of Customs on such imports, establishing sub-collectorships at the town of Taos, the town of San Miguel and the town of Valencia.

Licensed gambling houses were established by General Price, by the same general order, the license being fixed at two thousand dollars per annum.[54]

Thus it will be seen that the government of New Mexico was essentially military in character and that everything in the way of law and order was strictly within the control of the commanding officer of the Military Department. This condition continued for two years after the signing of the treaty of Guadalupe Hidalgo. The commanders of the department succeeding General Price, who left New Mexico in the summer

---

[54]Orders No. 10, Gen. Price, commanding 9th Military Department. War Rec. Washington, D. C. Reports of General Sterling Price.

of 1848, were Colonel Newby, Major Beall, Major Washington and Colonel John Munroe.

In the month of February, 1848, General Price published an address to the members of the convention which was to be held in Santa Fé in the following October, and which was provided for by the second Act passed by the general assembly of 1847. In that address General Price said: "You can now secure the protection of a government which imposes no bonds upon the conscience, which will protect you in the unmolested enjoyment of your personal, political and religious rights, under the regulation of equal laws. In short, you have it in your power to secure for New Mexico all the rights and privileges of citizens under the freest government in the world. * * * And I express the hope that, in view of your serious and important duties, the deliberations of the convention will be conducted with the strictest propriety and decorum; and though the right freely and properly to express opinions should not be restricted, yet I desire all clearly to understand that seditious and indecorous language against the constituted military or civil authorities, calculated to inflame or excite the people against the government, my desire for the peace and welfare of the Territory will induce me immediately to notice. The utterers of such language will be held responsible and called to a strict account."

The time for the holding of this convention had been set by the legislative assembly for the month of February, 1848, but it did not convene until the following October, nearly four months after the signing of the Treaty of Guadalupe Hidalgo. When this treaty was executed many claimed that the military authority in New Mexico ceased to exist, but those in authority at Washington thought differently and claimed that the civil government established during the war must remain as a *de facto* government until the congress should provide a territorial organization. Meanwhile the military authorities continued to govern, although many efforts were made on the part of the new comers from the states to form a civil government, and secure recognition at the capital of the nation. These new settlers belonged to that class of restless Americans who opposed military rule in times of peace, and immediately they began striving for recognition as a territory.

On the 10th of October the convention met and continued in session for four days. Fr. Antonio Jose Martinez, of Taos, was chosen president, and James M. Giddings was made clerk. The convention accomplished little more than the drawing up of a memorial to Congress. The memorial throws considerable light upon the thought and opinion of the day and it is therefore reproduced in full. It follows:

"Petition to Congress of the people of New Mexico by representatives in convention assembled:

"We, the people of New Mexico, respectfully petition Congress for the speedy organization of a territorial civil government.

"We respectfully petition Congress to establish a government purely civil in its character.

"We respectfully represent that the organic and statute law promulgated under military orders of September 22, 1846, with some alterations would be acceptable.

"We desire that the following offices be filled by appointment of the President, by and with the advice and consent of the Senate, the Governor, Secretary of State, Judges, United States Attorney and United States Marshal.

"We desire to have all the usual rights of appeal from the courts of the territory to the Supreme Court of the United States.

"We respectfully but firmly protest against the dismemberment of our territory in favor of Texas or from any cause.

"We do not desire to have domestic slavery within our borders; and, until the time shall arrive for admission into the union of states, we desire to be protected by Congress against the introduction of slaves into the territory.

"We desire a local legislature, such as is prescribed by the laws of New Mexico, September 22, 1846, subject to the usual veto of Congress.

"We desire that our interests be represented by a delegate admitted to a seat in Congress.

"Considering that New Mexico has a population of from 75,000 to 100,000, we believe our request to be reasonable, and we confidently rely upon Congress to provide New Mexico with laws as liberal as those enjoyed by any of the territories.

(Signed)   Santiago Archuleta,
Antonio J Martinez,   James Quinn,
Elias P. West,   Manuel A. Otero,
Donaciano Vigil,   Gregorio Vigil,
Francisco Sarracino,   Ramon Luna,
Juan Perea,   Charles Beaubien,
Antonio Sais,   Jose Pley.
Santa Fé, October 14, 1848."

The records of the debates in congress, the messages of the president of the United States, all show that there was at this time, at Washington, an almost endless discussion of the true status of New Mexico. The petition from the people of the Territory accomplished nothing, and, in the course of another year, a second convention was·called, which met in Santa Fé in September, 1849. This convention adopted a plan of territorial government and urged its adoption by congress, and elected Hugh N. Smith as delegate to congress, but that body refused to admit him to a seat.

To quote a contemporary writer, "About this time two opposite parties sprang up, one in favor of a state, and the other of a territorial form of government, which engendered a great deal of excitement and ill feeling. Several large public meetings were held by the respective parties at Santa Fé. The agitation of a state government originated with the national administration. In the spring of 1849 James S. Calhoun went to New Mexico as Indian agent, but, upon his arrival, he declared that he had secret instructions from the government at Washington to induce the people to form a state government. The matter continued to be discussed without much effect in favor of the state until the spring of 1850, when Col. George A. McCall arrived from the states upon a mission like Calhoun's. He informed the people that no territorial government would be granted by Congress, and that President Taylor was determined that New Mexico should be erected into a state government, in order to settle the question of slavery and also that of the boundary of Texas. The delegate in Congress, Mr. Smith, wrote home to the same effect."[55]

The President of the United States, Zachary Taylor, was in favor of the immediate admission of California and New Mexico as states. He advised the people of New Mexico to make application, being actuated by an earnest desire to give to Congress an opportunity of avoiding occasions of bitter and angry dissensions among the people of the entire country. In a message to Congress he asserted that "under the constitution every state has the right of establishing and, from time to time, altering, its municipal laws and domestic institutions, independently of every other state and of the general government, subject only to the prohibitions and guaranties expressly set forth in the Constitution." He maintained that these subjects were left exclusively to the respective states, and were not designed to become subjects of national agitation, meaning the slavery question. That this question had arisen after the acquisition of all new territory, and that the excitement throughout the land, at former periods, upon this question, would again obtain, so far as California and New Mexico were concerned, until they were admitted as states or organized into territories, and that, under all the circumstances, he believed it his duty to put the matter before the congress, so that the admission of New Mexico and California as states would remove all occasion for the unnecessary agitation of the public mind.[56]

On the subject of the claims made by Texas to a very large portion of what is now New Mexico, Presi-

---
[55]W. H. H. Davis.
[56]Message of President Taylor, January 4, 1850.

dent Taylor was of the opinion that if the people of New Mexico had formed a plan of a state government, as ceded under the treaty of Guadalupe Hidalgo, and had been admitted as a state, the courts of the United States would have had jurisdiction in the matter of determining the boundaries, but inasmuch as New Mexico had not been admitted, it was the duty of Congress to devise some method for the adjustment of the boundary question. He did not express an opinion upon, but submitted to congress, the question whether it would be most expedient before such adjustment to establish a territorial form of government for New Mexico, which, by including the district claimed by Texas, would practically decide the claims of that state adversely to her, or, by excluding the district, would decide in her favor. President Taylor believed that such a course would not be expedient, for the reason that New Mexico was at the time enjoying the benefit and protection of the laws and had a large military force stationed at various points which were a protection against the Indians. He could not see that any material difference would result to New Mexico for the want of a government established by congress for only a brief period, his reason being based upon the opinion that New Mexico would shortly apply for admission into the Union as a state. During all the period of American occupation, up to the time when the question of the west boundary of the state of Texas was determined, the military authorities at Santa Fé paid no attention whatever to the claims of Texas and would not recognize the attempt on the part of that state to extend the jurisdiction of the courts of Texas over the disputed territory. The State of Texas, in 1850, sent a special commissioner to Santa Fé, with full power and instructions to extend the civil jurisdiction of the State over what the Texas legislature had seen fit to designate as the "unorganized counties of El Paso, Worth, Presidio and Santa Fé." Upon arrival at Santa Fé, the Texan commissioner met with opposition to his purpose by the military authorities. The four counties named covered all of the territory east of the Rio Grande, which prior to the treaty of Guadalupe Hidalgo, had been regarded by Mexico, and by the people living within the limits indicated, as an essential and integral part of the department of New Mexico, and actually governed and possessed by her people, until conquered by General Kearny and severed from the Mexican republic by force of American arms.

President Millard Fillmore declared that these claims and acts, on the part of the authorities of the state of Texas, were such as to demand immediate attention on the part of all branches of the general government and feared that a crisis might ensue, which would necessitate the summoning of the two houses of congress, and compel, also, immediate action on the part of the executive branch of the government.

The governor of the state of Texas was notified by the president that New Mexico was a Territory of the United States, with the same extent and the same boundaries which belonged to it while in the actual possession of the Republic of Mexico, before the treaty of Guadalupe Hidalgo. The president defined his position in the following language:[57] "The executive government of the United States has no power or authority to determine what was the true line of boundary be-

---

[57]Message of President Taylor.

tween Mexico and the United States before the Treaty of Guadalupe Hidalgo, nor has it any such power now, since the question has become a question between the State of Texas and the United States. So far as this boundary is doubtful, that doubt can only be removed by some act of congress, to which the assent of the State of Texas may be necessary, or by some appropriate mode of legal adjudication; but, in the meantime, if disturbances or collisions arise or should be threatened, it is absolutely incumbent on the executive government, however painful the duty, to take care that the laws be faithfully maintained; and he can regard only the actual state of things as it existed at the date of the treaty, and is bound to protect all the inhabitants, who were then established and who now remain, north and east of the line of demarcation, in the full enjoyment of their liberty and property, according to the provisions of the ninth article of the treaty. In other words, all must be now regarded as New Mexico which was possessed and occupied as New Mexico, by citizens of Mexico, at the date of the treaty, until a definite line of boundary shall be established by competent authority."

The importance of immediate action by the congress of the United States, in the settlement of this boundary question, was most apparent. All considerations of justice, general expediency and domestic tranquility demanded it. It was seen that no government could be established for New Mexico, either state or territorial, until it was ascertained just what New Mexico was, and what were her rightful limits and boundaries, and the president recommended to congress that the general government "would be justified in allowing an indemnity to Texas not unreasonable or extravagant, but fair and liberal, and awarded in a just spirit of accommodation."

On the 9th day of September, 1850, the congress of the United States passed an act entitled "An Act proposing to the State of Texas the establishment of her northern and western boundaries, the relinquishment by the said state of all territory claimed by her exterior to said boundaries, and of all her claims upon the United States, and to establish a Territorial Government for New Mexico."

On the 25th day of November following, the State of Texas agreed to and accepted the propositions contained in this act, and, from common sources of public information, a very remarkable degree of unanimity prevailed, not only in the legislature, but among the people of Texas, in respect to the happy solution of the difficulties which had confronted the nation.

The difficulties felt and the dangers apprehended from the vast acquisition of territory under the treaty with Mexico were overcome by the wisdom of congress in the passage of the act of September 9, 1850.

There were many rival politicians in New Mexico during this period, some of them of more than ordinary ability, the more prominent being Hugh N. Smith, William Z. Angney, Richard Hanson Weightman, Ceran St. Vrain, W. S. Messervy, Joab Houghton, Henry Connelly, Manuel Alvarez and James H. Quinn. These politicians were in constant warfare. Senator Thomas H. Benton was an ardent supporter of the civil government for New Mexico, as against the military regime, and he counseled the New Mexicans "to meet in convention, provide cheap and simple government and take care of yourselves until Congress can provide for you." The people who had come from the states of the Union did not take kindly to the rule of a military commander in time of peace. To them a government of this sort was intolerable, and the only question for determination for them was the securing of a strictly civil form of government at the earliest possible moment. The situation was aggravated by the apparent subserviency of the so-called judicial branch of the government to the orders, will, whims and caprices of the military commander and his subordinates.

The state movement was set on foot by sixteen civilians, citizens of the United States, some Democrats and some Whigs, some natives of southern and some of northern states. The address prepared by them appeared in the columns of a Santa Fe newspaper[58] and was replied to by a counter address in the columns of the same paper, signed by sixty-two other civilians, among whom were included all the judges of the circuit courts, the prefects, the sheriffs, the alcaldes and, in fact, the great body of the officers of the civil government of the military commander, all of whom held their offices at his absolute will and pleasure.[59]

The state movement was by them denounced as a factious movement and the movers as the "Alvarez faction." As the movement progressed it was discovered that the military commander had a decided leaning toward the territorial party; indeed his acts were decidedly partizan and against the state party.

The state party triumphed in the election, and this was accomplished despite the partisan acts of the mili-

[58]New Mexican, December 8, 1849.
[59]Letter of R. H. Weightman, October 7, 1850—Cong. Globe, 32d Cong., 1st Sess., page 324.

tary commander, despite the almost unanimous opposition of the judges, prefects, alcaldes and others, who held their offices at the will and pleasure of the military commander and despite the vote of the employes of the quartermaster's department.

The Legislative Assembly, which convened after this election was held, memorialized the congress of the United States, giving expression to sentiments of no uncertain kind, and are reproduced as showing the feeling of the majority of the people of New Mexico at that time. This memorial is as follows:

"The inhabitants of New Mexico, since February 2, 1848, have groaned under a harsh law, forced upon them in time of war, when they were thought undeserving of confidence.

"The military is independent of and superior to the civil power.

"The inhabitants have no voice or influence in making the laws by which they are governed.

"Some power, other than the Congress of the United States, has made judges dependent on its will alone for the tenure of their offices, and the amount and payment of their salaries.

"Some power, other than the Congress of the United States, has subjected us to a jurisdiction foreign to the constitution and unacknowledged by our laws.

"We are taxed without our consent, and taxes, when collected, are not applied to the public benefit, but embezzled by officers irresponsible to the people.

"No public officer in New Mexico is responsible to the people. Judges, unlearned in the law, decide upon life, liberty and property. Prefects and alcaldes impose fines and incarcerate without the intervention of a jury.

"Alcaldes assail the rights of the people freely who exercise their religion without restriction, and dictate to congregations what priest shall administer the sacraments of the church.

"The full extent of the power to control and injure, which this unrestrained and organized band of office holders wielded can only be entirely understood when it is known that the military commander held to no accountability civil officers charged with assaults upon the religion of the country and embezzlement of the public funds.

"The influence of the quartermaster's department in the elections was by no means an inconsiderable one. With its army of employes, with its contracts to let, with its agencies to purchase the entire surplus of the corn and forage of the country, and with its easy means of communication by express at government expense, it proved itself very formidable; and this influence, with some honorable exceptions, was thrown against the state party.

"This web of influence, extending to the frontiers of New Mexico, was, like the other, organized, and, like it, also easily managed from the center; and the managers of both webs were acting in concert, and, as has already been told, against the state party.

"At this time there was available only one printing press in the entire country, and it belonged to the government. This press was sold and fell into the hands of the territorial party. It was used solely for the advancement of the interests of that faction, and, being owned by an army sutler and contractor, and edited by Judge Houghton and the chief clerk of the quartermaster, all communications of the State party were excluded from the columns of the paper. That party could not secure the printing of its ballots, and upwards of twenty thousand tickets, issued by the State party, were written out by hand.

"With the press against the state party, the office holders against it and the moneyed interests of the government against it, it cannot be said that the state movement was born of or grew to manhood by Executive influence. It appears clearly that the voice of the people, as expressed by their ballots, made itself heard under very difficult circumstances.[60]

Many charges were preferred, by men of consequence, against the so-called civil government. These charges were filed with the commanding general, Munroe, but he paid small attention to them; in fact, ignored them. The controversies between individuals were of the most dangerous sort; the language used in the trial of cases, directed to the court, was of a most vituperative character. Chief Justice Houghton seems to have been the unfortunate individual against whom was hurled charges, which, if they were true, ought to have subjected him to trial for almost every crime known to the law.

In December, 1849, Richard Hanson Weightman, an attorney practicing in Judge Houghton's court, and the successful candidate for delegate to congress in the election of 1851, filed with the commanding officer the following statement, which is a most interesting document:

---

[60]Letter of R. H. Weightman—32d Cong., 1st Sess., page 325.

"Influenced, sir, by duty and inclination, I lay before you charges of a most serious nature against the highest judicial officer in this Territory—Judge Joab Houghton; charges so serious that, if true, it is an act of mere justice to the community that he should be removed from office.

"In consequence of peculiar, agitating and dangerous questions which now exist in the United States, it has been thought proper, and even patriotic, in Congress, to withhold from us a territorial organization, which, except for the agitating questions there existing, we would doubtless long since have obtained.

"As it is, a *de facto* government obtains here of a most anomalous character, having no parallel in our history, opposed to the spirit and genius of our institutions and laws, and unrecognized by any competent authority.

"This government *de facto* was established under the laws and usages of war; and, upon the conclusion of the peace, February 2, 1848, having been found in existence here, to prevent anarchy, continues by the acquiescence of the authority, whatever it may be, which is competent to change it.

"Under this government, as it actually exists, the Governor exercises military, executive and legislative functions.

"To show that he has exercised legislative functions, I make reference to Order No. 10, dated February 5, 1848, laying duties and taxes, providing for their collection and for the payment of salaries, creating offices, etc."[61]

---

[61] Order No. 10 was made by General Sterling Price.

I presume, however, that no argument is necessary to prove that the Governor has the power, under this government, as it actually exists, whether legally or not, to relieve the community of a corrupt, ignorant or objectionable judge.

In making charges, it is necessary to be precise, and to enter into particulars; otherwise, the accused will have just cause to complain that he is tried on charges which are undefined, and to which, therefore, it is not possible to make a defense.

Though by entering into unpleasant, though necessary, details, I may, in the eyes of the undiscerning, appear to want good taste, I shall not refrain from so doing; preferring rather to deserve this censure than to subject myself to the charge of concealing from the accused that which is brought against him.

In the form, then, of charges and specifications, I accuse Judge Joab Houghton as follows:

Charge 1st. His conduct has been characterized by breaches of faith of such a nature that the continuation of him, in so elevated and responsible a station, can but have the effect of lowering, in the eyes of the public, the standard of American character.

Specification 1st. It has been substantiated in a court, to the satisfaction of a jury, that he has received, as the agent of Colcord and Hall, a sum of money exceeding three thousand dollars, and not paid the same to his principals.

Specification 2nd. He has received money, as the agent of East and Anderson, for the specific purpose of paying duties under order No. 10, of date February 5, 1848, and, instead of paying the money into the hands of the collector, placed therein, in lieu of money, his audited accounts for his salary as judge, which accounts were received as cash, and, subsequently, when that part of Order No. 10, paying and collecting of duties, was annulled, he withdrew said audited accounts from the hands of the collector, and replaced the bonds of East and Anderson, which said bonds are now in the hands of the collector and the money of East and Anderson in the hands of Judge Houghton.

Specification 3rd. That on or about the 19th day of June, 1848, he was engaged in business as a merchant, being a partner in the firm of E. Leitensdorfer & Company; that about that date the firm of Leitensdorfer & Company introduced into Santa Fé goods, the original cost of which, including the outfit, was not less than $100,000; that subsequently, on or about the 21st day of September, E. Leitensdorfer and Joab Houghton dissolved partnership; that, on or about that date E. Leitensdorfer left Santa Fé, appointing Joab Houghton his agent and attorney for the transaction of business; that, on or about the 11th day of December, 1848, E. Leitensdorfer made an assignment of all his effects, for the benefit of his creditors; that the effects assigned amounted to about $40,000 and the ascertained debts of the firm to more than $116,- 000; that between the dates, June 19th and December 11th, E. Leitensdorfer was, for the greater or a great part of the time, absent from Santa Fé, the place of the house of business of the firm, and that the deficit is not accounted for; but nearly all, if not all, of the goods taken south for sale by the said Leitensdorfer are accounted for, while the part left in Santa Fé, generally under the charge of said Houghton, is the part not accounted for; and that this failure is fraudulent and Judge Houghton guilty of the fraud.

Specification 4th. So much of the specifications under charge 2nd and 3rd as may be applicable to this charge.

Charge 2nd. His occupying his position on the bench amounts to a denial of justice in a large class of cases.

Specification 1st. The case of Campbell vs. Leitensdorfer & Co., involving about $8,000, was brought by attachment, based upon an affidavit of fraud, on the 26th day of May, 1849, and was in due course for trial at the June term of that year, but could not be tried because the Judge was interested; it could not be tried at the October term for the same reason, and cannot be tried for the same reasons, under existing circumstances, so long as Judge Houghton occupies his present position.

Specification 2nd. The case of Kelly vs. Leitensdorfer & Co., involving about $8,000, based on affidavit of fraud, was filed June 30th, 1849, and was for trial in due course at the last October term, but could not be tried, and cannot be tried, for the same reason as above.

Specification 3rd. The case of Welsh vs. Leitensdorfer & Co., involving about $8,000, based on affidavit of fraud, was filed June 3, 1849, and was for trial in due course, at the last October term, but could not, and cannot be tried for the reasons set forth in Specification 1st, of this charge.

"Specification 4th. There are now, in the hands of the undersigned, liabilities of the firm of Leitensdorfer & Company and bills against it for the gross sum of $3,659.70, to recover which six suits will be necessary; but have not filed suits because he has not been able to discover property of that firm, the court having declared that it will adjudicate no point about which there is a contest.

"Specification 5th. There is now in the hands of Mr. Biggs, by the agreement of all the parties to the suits, a large sum of money biding their issue, and must there remain until they are decided, to the great damage of the owners thereof.

"Specification 6th. There are a number of other creditors of E. Leitensdorfer & Company who would bring suits, if they believed justice could be obtained.

"Specification 7th. By the death or going away of important witnesses the ends of justice, which are now delayed, may be entirely defeated.

"Specification 8th. So much of the specifications under charges 1st and 2nd as may be applicable to this charge.

"Charge 3rd. Ignorance of law and disregard to his obligations as a judge.

"Specification 1st. Before trial, out of court, he has expressed the opinion that a man about to be tried for his life was a murderer.

"Specification 2nd. He has admitted to bail the man whom he said was a murderer.

"Specification 3rd. He has written articles in the Santa Fé Republican concerning a point of law, about, in due course, to come before him for decision, on which depended a large class of cases involving a sum of money, exceeding $80,000.

"Specification 4th. Had he adjudicated on the bench as he adjudicated in the newspapers he would have been benefited by the adjudication.

"Specification 5th. At a meeting of the bar, held in the city of Santa Fé, on or about the 26th of July, 1849, at which meeting were present Messrs. Smith, Tully, Angney, Wheaton, West, Pillans, Ashurst, Beach, Hall and Weightman, the question was discussed as to the propriety of inviting Judge Houghton to resign; at this meeting, it was the opinion of all the members present, that he was incompetent to fill the office, and eight of their number signed a letter, requesting him to resign, two of them declining to sign the letter on personal grounds; the two who declined being Messrs. Smith and Hall.

"Specification 6th. So much of the specifications of charges 1st and 2nd as may be applicable to charge 3rd.

"The witnesses to prove the above charges and specifications are at present in New Mexico; how long they will remain there it is impossible to say.

I have to request, therefore, as early notice as possible may be afforded me that an investigation may be had; the commission, or whatever other body to whom these charges, etc., may be referred, should have power to send for persons and papers.

"With much regret that I have to trouble you with so disagreeable a matter, I am, sir, very respectfully, your obedient servant,

"R. H. WEIGHTMAN.
"Brevet Colonel John Munroe.

"Civil and Military Governor of New Mexico."

Judge Houghton was notified by Major Weightman of the fact that these charges had been preferred against him and was advised that if he did not substantiate the charges as made, he would freely and cheerfully retract them. The distinguished gentleman, however, declined an investigation, but immediately sent a challenge to Major Weightman. Colonel Munroe declined to entertain the charges and nothing officially was done by him in relation thereto.

The challenge, in its wording, ignores the charges as filed with Colonel Munroe, but accuses Weightman of having slandered Judge Houghton. The fact that there is no record in New Mexico of the wording of a formal challenge to meet upon the "field of honor," and as this course adopted by Judge Houghton was in a sense an appeal to the old English "wager of battle," the exact language of the challenge is worth recording, and follows:

"Santa Fé, September 9, 1849.

"Sir: In consequence of slanderous words used by you in conversation with Lieutenant Taylor, at the Sutler's store in Albuquerque, with J. L. Hubbell, Esq., at Socorro, at Santa Fé, and generally throughout the Territory, within the last few ——, I demand of you an unequivocal retraction of such slanders, or the satisfaction due from one gentleman to another.

"J. HOUGHTON.

"R. H. Weightman, Esq."

This letter brought forth a characteristic reply from Weightman, in which he seems determined to have the record appear without a flaw, in giving publicity to his opinion of the learned "fountain of justice," as he was described by Weightman in a number of public addresses. This reply was directed to James H. Quinn, Esq., a practicing attorney of Judge Houghton's court, who acted as his second in the duel which followed. The letter to Quinn is interesting, and, while of some length, should be read in connection with the charges against Judge Houghton. In this letter Weightman says:

"Santa Fé, September 19, 1849.

"Sir: I received at your hands a note from Judge Houghton, of this date, in which he is pleased to say that, in consequence of words, which he characterizes as slanderous, used by me to Lieutenant Taylor, in Albuquerque, to J. L. Hubbell, Esq., in Socorro, at Santa Fé, and generally throughout the Territory, within the last few 'days' (I suppose was intended, a word being left out), he demands of me an unequivocal retraction of such slanders, or the satisfaction due from one gentleman to another.

"Besides the application of the word slanderous to my words, I have an objection to make to the general tenor of his note, which is this: it leaves open the inference that I made the remarks alluded to not in Judge Houghton's presence. To rebut which inference, I have to say, that three or four months ago, it became my duty, as counsel in the case of Colcord & Hall vs. Smith D. Town, to comment upon the conduct of Judge Houghton, in receiving, as agent of Colcord & Hall, a large sum of money, in the neighborhood of $3,400.00, and not paying the same over to his principal, as it was intended he should, and as he was trusted to do. In my remarks to the jury, the judge was spoken of as a faithless agent, and it may, perhaps, not be inappropriate to mention that the jury found a verdict in accordance with the theory laid down by myself and the other gentlemen with whom I was associated on that occasion. Judge Houghton was not present on this occasion, but my remarks and the finding of the jury are matters of public notoriety.

"Again, in Socorro, at which place he refers to a conversation with Mr. Hubbell, I made the same, or similar, remarks in a public speech to the people, Judge Houghton being present, and distant perhaps six feet from me at the time.

"I deem this statement due to myself, in order to make it apparent that I have in no wise secretly assailed the character of Judge Houghton.

"In conclusion I have to say that in consideration of the fact that Mr. Houghton occupies at this time the important position of chief judge of this Territory, and is recognized as a gentleman by persons of high standing, yourself among the number, I feel myself at liberty to accept the latter of the alternatives he has been pleased to offer me. I accept his challenge, and will meet him this day at as early an hour as can conveniently be agreed upon between yourself and the gentleman who will hand you this.

"Very respectfully, etc.,

"R. H. WEIGHTMAN.

"James H. Quinn, Esq."

This duel was fought on the same day, no blood was shed, and while no apology was offered by Weightman, the outcome of the meeting was to a degree laughable. The parties met in an arroyo, near the city of Santa Fé, and when the command "fire" was given, only one shot was heard—that from Weightman's pistol, the ball from which passed close to Houghton's ear. Houghton, who was slightly deaf, insisted that he had not heard the word of command; Weightman then lifted both his hands in the air and told Houghton to shoot; the seconds interposed, however, and the party left the grounds, Weightman still insisting that what he had said concerning Judge Houghton was the truth.

There was a great deal of dissatisfaction in many parts of the Territory, at this time, growing out of the actions of the so-called civil authorities concerning the property and priests of the Catholic church. Ever since the revolution of 1847, the military commander, owing to the belief which was entertained by many that prominent representatives of the church had been cognizant of the plans of the revolutionists, and were active sympathizers in the movement which resulted in the death of Governor Bent, regarded the chief representative of the church, the Vicario, Juan Felipe Ortiz, as an enemy to the American institutions which were being gradually established by his authority. It was insisted that the rights of that church freely to exercise its functions were being infringed. Major Weightman seems to have been the friend of the Church, and its attorney as well, and on several occasions complaints of a very serious character were lodged with the military commander, but no notice was taken by him in relation to the same. The military commander was advised officially that the Vicario fully understood the responsibility resting upon him to the United States government, but contended that the Church should not be deprived of the "right freely to exercise its religion," that right being guaranteed by the Constitution of the United States. The commander was informed that the Catholic Church, as well in New Mexico as in other parts of the United States, confided the care and control of all the property of the church to the Bishop of the Diocese. The Bishop of Durango had placed this custody, care and control in the hands of the Vicario, who was held responsible for the judicious exercise of the power conferred upon him. This law, custom and usage of the Church was being set aside by the actions of the civil authorities in many ways; the limits of parishes, as arranged under the authority of the Church, were being altered by the civil officials with a view to their ideas as to propriety and convenience. This was done, certainly so far as the parishes of Socorro, Albuquerque, Belen and Tomé were concerned, and it was claimed that the interference came from the influence of Judge Antonio Jose Otero.

Don Donaciano Vigil, the secretary and acting governor of the Territory, after the death of Governor Bent, issued an order suspending the Vicario, Juan Felipe Ortiz, from exercising his ecclesiastical functions; the acting governor also threatened to banish a priest, who had the temerity to declare that the acting governor had no power to do so, and, in the end, advised the priest to take the first advantage of leaving the country.

One of the alcaldes, while the parish priest was absent, demanded the keys of the church from the sacristan at Tomé and took from it the sacred vestments and consecrated vases and delivered them to Nicolas Valencia, a non-conformist and suspended priest, for the purpose of celebrating a marriage and mass.

Another alcalde directed Fr. Benigno Cardenas, a non-conformist, suspended priest, a refugee from justice, to go to the parish of Tomé, and receive without excuse or protest, from Jose de Jesus Baca, the regularly appointed priest, the delivery of the church property, taking an inventory of the same. The alcalde, who thus undertook to control the affairs of his precinct as well as those of the church, was Don Vicente Armijo; the word and order of Don Vicente was most effectual, for the Fr. Cardenas took possession and the Fr. Baca was excluded from the performance of his priestly functions. All of these ousters were confirmed by the appointing authorities—the so-called civil governor, Vigil, and his superior, the military commander, endeavoring to correct the action of the alcalde, sent an official order to the prefect of the county, Don Manuel Otero, directing him to restore Padre Baca to his rights and the property of the church, which order was not obeyed.

Every one of these infringements upon the rights of the priests was presented to Colonel Munroe, in the way of charges and memorials signed by hundreds of citizens, but all were deemed unworthy of notice by that arbitrary satrap.

The true state of affairs is most graphically painted in a letter to Colonel Munroe[62] from Major Weightman. Word had been received from Don Jose Chaves, one of the most influential men of the country, that he feared, unless the people were pacified, violence might be committed, for the reason that the civil authorities were attempting to force upon the people, against their will, the Padre Cardenas. This Padre was the same one who was attempted to be forced upon the people of Tomé. Major Weightman, who was the recipient of the letter from Don Jose Chaves, immediately proceeded to Los Lunas, where he was advised that Judges

---

[62]Letter of R. H. Weightman of June 18, 1850, to Col. Munroe—Cong. Globe, 32d Cong., 1st Session, page 326.

Houghton and Otero had arrived and that for the present all was quiet. The following day the judges and the prefect left for Sabinal, where it was claimed the people were in a state of revolution and that Colonel May of the army was present with troops to quiet the disturbance. Major Weightman proceeded to Sabinal, where he found everything quiet, the people working in the fields and neither Colonel May nor any troops were present. Later on Colonel May appeared and declined to interfere. Immediately the alcalde cited, through an order issued to his constable, armed men to be present, for the purpose of assisting the constable in keeping order. It was asserted that the entire proceeding was little less than an electioneering trick to intimidate the people into voting for a continuance in office of those then exercising civil authority. Judges Houghton and Otero were on the ground and there were persistent rumors of revolution, assassination and other disturbances, but nothing occurred, other than a conclusive demonstration that the people, so lately come into the rights of American citizens, were beginning to appreciate their full importance.

The alcalde at Sabinal was one Jesus Silva, whose ideas of his authority were most unique. On Sunday, the 16th of June, 1850, this alcalde attempted to compel the people to receive the Fr. Cardenas as the priest of the parish. The alcalde maintained that inasmuch as the regular priest, Otero, had not performed mass for some time, that it was necessary for the spiritual welfare of the people that mass be said. The reasons for the absence of the cura, Otero, were that the same alcalde had placed him in jail a short time prior and he had left, fearing a repetition of the incarceration and a continued disregard for the rights of the church, as long as Alcalde Silva continued in the administration of his office. The actions of the alcalde were approved by the Prefect, Ramon Luna, as well as by Judges Houghton and Otero, who were all present and undertook to reprove the people for their alleged insubordination to the lawfully constituted authority of the alcalde.

More than one hundred citizens, the owners of the church property, made vigorous protest to the military commander, at Santa Fé, against the actions of the alcalde and the judges and prefect, but no action was ever taken, although an investigation was asked for at his hands.

On the 18th of June an order was issued and placed in the hands of the constable, commanding him to arrest one, Jose Armijo, and about one hundred others, who had protested against the action of the alcalde, Silva, and take them before the Prefect, Ramon Luna, at sunrise the following morning, where their offenses would be examined into. The following morning was the day of election, and, even to the uninitiated, this order of arrest and proceeding may be readily understood, when it is known that every man thus arrested was opposed to the re-election of the existing officials, everyone of whom was a candidate for office. All of these people were taken to the northern limits of the county, a distance of thirty miles, passing by the doors of neighboring alcaldes, and, but for the timely assistance of Don Jose Chaves, who gave bail for them, in the sum of fifteen thousand dollars, all would have been incarcerated until the next term of the court. When court was held, notwithstanding the statement of the public prosecutor that no offense had been committed, they were indicted, and those who could not give bail a second time were thrown into prison, where they remained until the appointment of James S. Calhoun as governor of the Territory. And what was their offense? Don Jose Armijo, an elderly gentleman of good repute, acting as spokesman for the citizens who objected to Fr. Cardenas, had said to the Alcalde that it was against the will of the people that he say mass. To which the alcalde replied, "I have the power, and do not recognize the people." Whereupon Mr. Armijo said: "If you do not recognize the people or their sovereignty, the people will not recognize you as alcalde." This was held to be rebellion by the learned judges, the alcalde and the prefect.

This, then, was the sort of government to which the authorities of the United States introduced its newly acquired citizens. Not that government which Kearny had promised them, but another and different sort, a government upheld and maintained by the bayonets, under command of Colonel Munroe, who was supposed to be protecting the new citizens in their rights rather than in oppressing them, as the facts clearly show was the case.

The War Department at the nation's capitol was laboring under the belief that the military in New Mexico was only taking a partial participation in the civil affairs of the Territory, and it was only after the election of June 20, 1850, that matters were brought to a full determination as to who was the real authority in New Mexico and what was his power.

Pursuant to a meeting held at Santa Fé, April 20, 1850, Colonel Munroe, the military governor, issued a proclamation calling for an election of delegates to meet in convention on May 15th. At this convention, whose presiding officer was James H. Quinn, a constitution for the state of New Mexico was framed. Three days afterwards Colonel Munroe issued another proclamation calling for a popular election on the adoption of the constitution, and also to choose state and federal officers, whose authority should become valid as soon as the state government was recognized at Washington by the congress.

The election was held on June 20th. Henry Connelly and Manuel Alvarez were elected governor and lieutenant-governor over Baca and St. Vrain, and William S. Messervy was chosen representative in congress. The vote on the constitution was overwhelmingly in favor of its adoption, only thirty-nine votes being recorded against it.

The officials elected at this time were thoroughly at variance with the military officers in respect to the powers and prerogatives of each.

The commanding officer, Colonel Munroe, insisted upon exercising all the authority which had been his and which had been used wherever deemed necessary since the beginning of the war with Mexico and the taking possession of the country by General Kearny in August, 1846. The position taken by both Colonel Munroe and by Lieutenant Governor Alvarez, who was acting in the absence of Governor Connelly, who was ill and visiting in the states, is well outlined in an official communication from Governor Alvarez to Colonel Munroe, of date July 13, 1850, and which is given in full:

"Governor's Office,
"July 13, 1850.

"Sir:—In my notes of yesterday, I intimated that I would take an early occasion to answer your communication of the 11th instant, in which you are pleased to allude to a conversation, solicited by yourself through your adjutant, which we held on the 10th, in which, among other matters, you intimated a disposition to disregard any acts of the Legislature overstepping the bounds of your proclamation of date May 28, 1850, a determination to sustain the authorities hitherto administering the functions of government, and alluded to the course of the new government in organizing its departments and proceeding to exercise legislative power, as unwarranted and revolutionary.

"From the terms of your conversation, I learned that you entertain the idea that the people, in organizing a government, were bound to follow your proclamation literally, strictly, and that they can exercise no power beyond its license. In this construction of the people's right, our opinions are entirely different, since I hold the true ground to be:

"1st. That the people had an undoubted right to hold a convention, form a constitution, and organize a civil government, without either your first or second proclamation, or without even consulting with you.

"2d. That any private citizen, as well as the commandant of the ninth military department, could have issued the proclamation, or could, by common consent, have been designated for that purpose; and, if obeyed, it would have been just as effectual and obligatory on the people and yourself.

OF THE TERRITORY OF NEW MEXICO. 183

"3d. That in the absence of any congressional legislation over us, we have as free and undoubted a right to reform and remodel our old system, or to establish a new and different one, not violating the constitution of the United States, as the people of New York or Virginia.

"4th. That the civil power exercised by you, under a military order from General Scott, can be no greater nor more restrictive of the rights of the people than that exercised by the President of the United States.

"5th. That the President of the United States can not delegate a greater power than he could himself exercise, and nothing is clearer than that he, without the sanction of congress, has no power either to dictate a government to us or to prevent us from making such a one as we may prefer.

"6th. That it has never been pretended, even by the President of the United States, that he had any authority to make a government for us or to insist that we should observe the one left to us on the termination of the war. President Polk, in his message of December 5, 1848, holds this emphatic language in speaking of New Mexico and California: 'Since that time (13th May) the limited power possessed by the executive has been exercised to preserve and protect them from the inevitable consequences of a state of anarchy. The only government which remained was that established by the military authority during the war. Regarding this to be a *de facto* government, and that, by the presumed consent of the inhabitants, it might be continued temporarily, they were advised to conform and submit to it for a short intervening period before congress would again assemble and legislate on the subject.' And, again, in his previous message of 8th July, President Polk declares that 'the war with Mexico having terminated, the power of the executive to establish or to continue temporary civil government over these territories, which existed under the laws of nations while they were regarded as conquered provinces in our military occupation, has ceased.' Secretary Crawford, in his late report (November 30, 1849), advances a similar view: 'The peculiar condition of the territories of California and New Mexico, in respect to their internal governments, and the absence of any clearly defined authority by congress for this object, has imposed delicate and difficult duties on the army. One of its assigned duties is to aid civil functionaries, when required, in the preservation of public tranquility; but it is believed that the civil authority, so far as it has its origin in political power, in a great measure disappeared by the transfer of the sovereignty and jurisdiction from Mexico to the United States. The military regulations established for their government during the war were superseded by the return of peace.' I refer you also to the instructions given to Lieutenant-Colonel McCall. Not having these instructions, I can only refer you to them.

"All of these opinions, emanating from distinguished statesmen, are indorsed by the great politicians of the country. There is hardly any question of state rights better settled than that the people have an inalienable right peaceably to assemble to take steps to reorganize or remodel the government, and to establish such laws as are by them deemed more just and salutary. These extracts show—

"1st. That the government, hitherto existing in New Mexico, is one simply of consent—a consent presumed; and the people are advised to submit temporarily to it.

"2nd. They show that the president disclaims any power to establish or continue temporary civil governments.

"3rd. That the military regulations established for (our) government were superseded by the return of peace.

"If the positions above stated are true—and I am not aware that statesmen differ about them—it has always been competent for the people to take the step they have recently taken; and that the commanding officer of the 9th military department has exercised the functions of a civil governor, has arisen solely from the consent of the people. That consent is now withdrawn. The people have amicably, and through the recommendation of yourself, proceeded to the full organization of a civil polity. Until the national congress shall undo it, or refuse to sanction it, by the law of nations and the rights of states, it will remain our only legitimate government.

"Had the President power to make us a government, long ago he would have so ordered. This power is reserved to congress; and, until it acts, the people must adopt such a government as to them may seem best.

"The people of California have pursued a similar course. The government went into immediate operation; the officer commanding the troops of the United States retired from the discharge of his civil functions, and his conduct, and the course of the people, have met with general approbation in the United States.

"If a state government is likely to be beneficial to the people of New Mexico, why should they be delayed in its enjoyment? Are they less able to sustain it now than they would be in six months or a year? And what right has the military commandant of the 9th military department, when the President himself has no such power, to say that such a government should be indefinitely withheld from the people?

"If I understand the second proclamation issued by you, it contemplates the organization of the government, so far as may be necessary to elect United States senators—that is, it contemplates that at least the executive and legislature should qualify and proceed in this election. The governor and legislature, by the very law that constituted them—the popular voice—were, before entering upon the discharge of their duties, required to take an oath to support the constitution of New Mexico. Before an election could take place it was necessary to pass a law on this subject, and to provide the mode of authenticating the credentials of the senators. This the proclamation did not contemplate; yet it was necessary, and the signature of the vice-governor, acting in the absence of the governor, became necessary, to perfect the law. The signature of the commanding officer of the 9th military department to the credentials of the senators would, to say the least of it, have been novel, and expose them to the commentary of asking for seats with an unusual and unconstitutional evidence of an election. Why were the formation of the constitution and the election of an executive and a legislature necessary to choose United States senators? Simply because by the constitution of the United States such officers must be chosen by the legislatures of the states, and they are necessary to authenticate the credentials. If, then, it was competent for the legislature to make one law, is it not competent for them to make two or as many as they may deem proper? Was the vice-governor an officer constituted with full power yesterday to perfect the law 'to regulate the election of United States senators,' and is he less an officer to-day, or his signature to another law, adopted by the same legislature, less efficacious, or absolutely null and void? He cannot be an officer with full authority one day, the next without such authority, and on the third again vested with his official dignity and power; and if he has been governor for one hour he is so until his term expires, and, being so, there is no other; for the co-existence of two governors coeval in the same State is impossible, and contrary to all law and experience.

"I have failed to discover in the extract you were pleased to send me any principle contradictory of the positions here laid down. The propositions are stated generally, and are the law as commonly received. The questions discussed are not the ones that at this time vitally affect New Mexico.

"It is certainly true that, so long as we are not constituted a State, the congress has power to make all needful rules and regulations respecting us. But we are not a Territory until these needful rules are made. Congress has done nothing—has not declared us a Territory, nor extended over us the laws of the United States. The doctrines asserted (although inartificially stated) in the extract are sufficiently true, and, as general propositions, will not be discussed;

yet, applied to our present attitude, they lose all applicability.

"I have deemed it proper to say this much in reply to your communication of the 11th, and, while I assert an earnest desire to see the early prosperity of my adopted country, subscribe myself your most obedient servant,

"MANUEL ALVAREZ."

In reply to this communication, stating the position taken by the Governor, Alvarez, and his advisers, for the wording of the letter shows that it was written by a lawyer, and not by the governor personally, the commander of the military department, Colonel Munroe, declared that "having in my proclamation of the 28th of May last, calling an election for an executive and legislature to consummate the proper arrangements for the presentation of the state constitution to the congress of the United States," etc., stated "that all action by the governor, lieutenant-governor, and of the legislature, shall remain inoperative until New Mexico be admitted as a state under said constitution, except such acts as may be necessary for the primary steps of organization, and the presentation of said constitution properly before the congress of the United States;

"The present government shall remain in full force until, by the action of congress, another shall be constituted.

"Applying principles clearly in accordance with the constitution of the United States, with the decisions of the supreme court and the laws of congress, I had no right to suppose that the officers elected under its provisions would assume to themselves authority

Monument to General Doniphan, Liberty, Mo.

beyond the conditions on which they were elected by the people, or that they would engage in any acts to supersede the present government. But, soon after the meeting of the legislature, I became convinced, from expressed opinions of members, of other gentlemen occupying important positions, and from the acts of both houses, in addition to its legitimate business, there was an obvious intention of subverting the government by legislative action. In a sincere hope that a purpose so repugnant to law and injurious to the wellbeing of New Mexico might, by conciliation on my part, be averted, I have done whatever laid in my power to avoid the possibility of opposition, either in feeling or in action by the legislature, or the party by which its majority was elected, against the constituted authorities and established government.

"Reluctantly as I approach the subject, I now declare that the nomination of officers, and their confirmation, to assume the exercise of functions which (by superseding the officers now in commission) will affect the laws of this Territory, as at present constituted, will be deemed and considered as an act on the part of all concerned in direct violation of their duties as citizens of the United States.

"My official obligations imperatively require that the present government be sustained until superseded by another legally constituted; and this duty I will fulfill with all the means at my disposal."

Immediately upon the receipt of this letter by Governor Alvarez, its contents were communicated to the legislature then in session, whereupon that body, undoubtedly voicing the sentiments of the people of New Mexico, adopted a joint resolution, the tenor of which is expressive and vigorous.

This resolution is as follows:

"Whereas, a letter signed by John Munroe, styling himself civil and military governor of New Mexico, and directed to Lieutenant-Governor Manuel Alvarez, has just been communicated to the legislature, in which said Munroe expresses a determination to maintain the civil authorities hitherto administering the government in New Mexico, and also threatens to use all the forces at his disposal to resist the effective operation of the state government now in complete organization, with an evident intention to overawe the people, legislature and the different departments of the government, and to annul, by means of military power, the peaceable desires of the people; and,

"Whereas, seven-eighths of the entire population of New Mexico are clearly in favor of putting in immediate operation the civil state government lately adopted by them by an unheard of unanimity, and to be relieved from the sinking, ineffective and abhorrent system which they have peacefully respected for nearly four years;

"Resolved:

"1. That it is the indisputable right of the people, in the absence of congressional legislation on the subject, to organize a civil government and put it in immediate operation.

"2. That the right of exercising any civil function by the commander of the 9th military department (if it ever existed) was superseded by the organization of the state government.

"3. That we heartily approve the communication despatched by Vice-Governor Alvarez to Colonel Munroe, dated July, 1850.

"4. That we heartily approve the intention of Governor Alvarez to establish and maintain in operation the government just organized.

"5. That the people have a clear and sacred right to take any step to put in operation the state government, and that this right was superior to, and entirely independent of, the military government hitherto existing in this Territory.

"6. That Colonel J. Munroe has no legal or other right to restrict the peaceful action of the people in organizing a government; nor had he authority, either in law, or from the general government, to subject the action of the late convention to any conditions or limitations whatever.

"7. That the commander has assumed a power not delegated to the President of the United States and directly in opposition to the expressed principles of President Taylor in his reply to the investigations made by the congress of the United States.

"8. That the Secretary of State be required to furnish copies of the above preamble and resolutions to Colonel J. Munroe, Governor Alvarez and to the Senators and Representatives to congress."

When these resolutions had been presented to Colonel Munroe, and, realizing the earnestness of the spirit which prompted their passage, he made formal report to the Adjutant General of the Army at Washington, Major General R. Jones, in the following language:

"Headquarters 9th Military Department,
"Santa Fé, New Mexico, July 16, 1850.

"Sir: The political affairs of New Mexico have assumed so grave a character that it has become my imperative duty to make the executive of the United States acquainted through you with the material fact that the new state government, organized so far only as to take the preliminary steps towards admission into the Union, has assumed to supersede the actual government, and go at once into operation.

"The ratification of the constitution and the election of an executive and legislature by the people was held under the proclamation I issued on the 28th day of May last, and there has been no official expression of their dissent from that instrument, nor any authority given by them to the governor and legislature to act beyond its provisions.

"Merely adverting to the unadjusted claim of Texas and the probability of a territorial organization as causes of delay, I have, independent of these questions of expediency, decided that my obligations are not to acknowledge the authority above assumed, but to await the determination of the congress of the United States as to the legality of that authority, or the orders of the Executive in relation to the course I am to pursue.

"The purpose of the new state government being, by the appointment of its officers and other acts, to supplant the present establishment with as little delay as possible, you will perceive how important it is that instructions for my guidance be sent me without loss of time.

"A reasonable delay on the part of the legislature, at a time when there is every prospect that the people of New Mexico will soon have a government in accordance with their wishes, is a policy which I have no doubt the New Mexicans in that body would have adopted as best suited to their interests, and as respectful to the government of the United States; but opinions have been prepared for them here by those having no ties binding them to the Territory, except the possession and expectation of office, and, if any serious consequences arise from the adoption of their advice, will be found safely beyond its limits.

"Those persons well understand the unstable elements of the Mexican character, the general ignorance of the people, their manifest dislike (although latent) to Americans, and the strong sympathies a large number entertain for Mexican institutions and its government, as opposed to that of the United States, yet, with this knowledge, they have pursued a course, understandingly, from which sooner or later disagreeable consequences will undoubtedly arise.

"As charges, both general and specific, have been made, and will be urged at Washington against those who have administered the affairs of this Territory, an investigation into their conduct is due both to the people and themselves. If such an investigation should be ordered, I am satisfied it will be shown that the persons and property of the inhabitants of New Mexico have been protected to the full extent of the guaranty provided by the treaty with Mexico.

"A separate paper will enumerate the documents which accompany this communication."

With all the information concerning the contest for power between the people and the military, as presented by Colonel Munroe himself, the President directed the Secretary of War to instruct Colonel Munroe to abstain from all further interference in the civil and political affairs of New Mexico, which instructions are found in the following order:

"War Department, Washington,
"September 10, 1850.

"Sir: Your letter addressed to the Adjutant General, dated Santa Fé, New Mexico, July 16, 1850, having reached this department, and, together with the documents accompanying the same, been submitted to the President, I am directed to make the following reply: The President has learned with regret that any misunderstanding should exist between a portion of the people of New Mexico and yourself in relation to the government of that country, and hastens to relieve you from the embarrassment in which that misunderstanding has placed you.

"I have now the pleasure to inform you that congress has at length passed a law providing for the es tablishment of a Territorial government in New Mexico. The President will proceed with the least possible delay to organize the government; and, as soon as it goes into operation, all controversy as to what is the proper government of New Mexico must be at an end, and the anomalous state of things which now exists there will be determined. You will perceive, however, that the same act (a duly authenticated copy of which accompanies this communication) also fixes the boundary between New Mexico and Texas, and that its operation is suspended until the assent of Texas shall have been given to the boundary established by the act.

"Although there is little doubt that such assent will be given, yet, as some time must elapse before it can be obtained, it is proper that some instructions should be given for your guidance in the interval.

"It is at all times desirable that the civil and military departments of the government should be kept entirely distinct. Although circumstances may occasionally arise which require a temporary departure from this principle, that departure should cease with the necessity which occasioned it. No necessity seems to exist at present for departing from it in regard to New Mexico. The country is represented to be tranquil; and, although the inhabitants have undertaken to establish a government for themselves without the authority of a previous act of congress, nevertheless there is no reason to believe that in so doing they intended to throw off their allegiance to the United States; and, as the government they seek to establish is entirely consistent with the lawful authority and dominion of the United States in and over the Territory and its inhabitants, the President does not consider himself called upon to suppress it by military force. Unless, therefore, it should become necessary to suppress rebellion, or resist actual hostilities against the United States (an event hardly to be apprehended), or unless the inhabitants, or a portion of them, should demand from you that protection which is guaranteed to them by the ninth article of the Treaty of Guadalupe Hidalgo, you are directed to abstain from all further interference in civil or political affairs of that country.

"In case you should have any further communications to make to this department in relation to the civil and political affairs of New Mexico, you will address them directly to the head of this department.

"C. M. CONRAD,
"Secretary of War."

Matters in New Mexico were believed by the President and his cabinet to be in so strained a condition, owing to the position taken by the commander of the ninth military department and his unwarranted mixing in the civil and political affairs of the Territory, that the President ordered the letter from his Secretary of War, Mr. Conrad, sent to Santa Fé by special messenger. At that time, it required only about six weeks for a letter to be transmitted from Washington to New Mexico, and the orders to Colonel Munroe did not reach him until the 22d day of October. The special messenger, entrusted with the carriage of this letter, was Henry Hardy.

Colonel Munroe, however, did not perform the orders of his chief, and kept the people in ignorance of the tenor of his instructions and kept on in the performance of the functions of civil and military governor of the Territory until the organization of the territorial government and the installation of Governor Calhoun, which took place in March, 1851. He thus kept in power those officials who were unsatisfactory to the people; maintained a government which was civil only in name and purely military in all matters deemed by the commandant demanding it; a government which harassed and oppressed the people, interfered with their religious worship, disturbing parishes in the administration of their own churches and religious affairs; a government which fined and imprisoned the people without the intervention of juries, which taxed them without their consent, which embezzled the taxes when collected, and which, in one or two flagrant cases, scourged them without trial.[63]

---

[63]R. H. Weightman — speech in Congress, 1st Sess. 32d Congress.

Colonel Munroe had unwittingly allied himself with a few persons who had impressed him with the firm belief that the Mexican people were degraded and vicious and always looking for an opportunity to create trouble with those in authority. His ideas of government were purely of the sort entertained by almost all military officers, and he was jealous of any interference with the authority with which he deemed himself vested.

The passage of the act of September 9, 1850, did not dispose of the complaints and dissatisfaction which existed in the Territory, and it was not until the inauguration of Governor Calhoun, the following spring, that the people had any confidence in the government which had been promised them at the time of the proclamation of General Kearny.

The first legislative assembly of the Territory of New Mexico, pursuant to the provisions of the act of September 9, 1850, met at Santa Fé on the 2d day of June, 1851, and among its enactments was one providing "that all laws that have previously been in force in this Territory that are not repugnant to or inconsistent with the constitution of the United States, the organic law of this Territory, or an act passed at the present session of the Legislative Assembly, shall be and continue in force, excepting in Kearny's Code, the law concerning registers of land."

There had been no substantial reason for the denial to the people of New Mexico of a territorial form of government for so long a period as had intervened since the treaty with Mexico. In the first petition for admission, the people of New Mexico had declared that her people were opposed to slavery. The fact that the domestic institutions of some of the states were distasteful to New Mexicans was not a sufficient reason for withholding some sort of government other than the strange mixture of civil and military which continued after the Treaty of Guadalupe Hidalgo. Had New Mexico been admitted to the Union in 1850, her constitution would have prohibited slavery. There were not a thousand residents in the Territory at that time, who had been born in the United States, and the Mexican population was over sixty-five thousand, all of the latter being opposed to slavery, but the factious temper of the times was such that the slightest pretext for argument gave rise to angry conflict and in the light of events transpiring during that period and until the actual breaking out of hostilities in the war between the States, there was no chance for the admission of New Mexico into the Union.

The true sentiment of the people of New Mexico was reflected ten years later by her contribution in men for the Federal armies, in the great conflict for the preservation of the Union and the suppression and eradication of an institution which, at the first opportunity, in convention assembled, her people had declared to be obnoxious to all liberty loving citizens.

BIOGRAPHICAL SKETCHES.

It was intended, at the time of the commencement of the writing of this volume, to incorporate, as far as possible, many incidents occurring during the Occupation Period, all of which were a part of the story of the acts and deeds of the men who were prominent in the affairs of New Mexico at that time. This plan was found to be impracticable. In order that nothing of interest should be omitted, it was deemed wise to bring out all these events in the form of biographical sketches. This has been done with a plainness and a simplicity which may recommend it to the general reader and certainly to the descendants of those individuals whose biographies are presented. The limits within which it has been necessary to confine this portion of the volume have rendered unavoidable some omissions and occasional compression; but, on the whole, there has been included that which is memorable and interesting. It was an essential object to bring in all these events within a moderate compass and in a manner available for those who have little time for special study or reading, and yet may reasonably desire to know something of the history of the conquest of New Mexico not to be gathered from ordinary histories.

Interesting studies of other men, taking a prominent part in the affairs of New Mexico at that time, might have been included; but their deeds and participation in the events of the period were practically the same as those narrated in the sketches which follow. It has been believed that this modest effort to place within the reach of the public a comprehensive relation, carefully based upon the best authority available, written entirely without bias or prejudice, will serve to rectify, to a great extent, the mistaken opinions which have found lodgment in the minds of the American people relative to the Territory of New Mexico and its citizens.

General Stephen Watts Kearny.
From a Picture belonging to his son, Henry S. Kearny, of New York City.

STEPHEN WATTS KEARNY.

Stephen Watts Kearny was a student of Columbia college, in the City of New York, in 1812, and would have graduated in the summer of that year. As soon, however, as it became a certainty that war must ensue between the United States and Great Britain he applied for and obtained a commission in the United States army. On the 12th of March, 1812, while still in his eighteenth year, he was appointed, from New York. First Lieutenant in the Thirteenth United States Infantry. He distinguished himself particularly in storming a British battery, and throughout the assault on Queenstown Heights, 13th October, 1812. Lieutenant-Colonel Christie, commanding his regiment, himself wounded in this action, presented young Kearny with his sword on the field of battle for the cool and determined manner with which he executed the command which devolved upon him. A companion in arms states that, as 'First Lieutenant of Captain Ogilvie's company, he (S. W. K.) enjoyed at an early age the character of high promise his after years developed. He was made prisoner on this occasion and sent to Quebec, and was long detained in captivity. He became Captain in April, 1813; Brevet Major in April, 1823, and Major in May, 1829. Upon the organization of the First United States Dragoons he was appointed their Lieutenant-Colonel, 4th March, 1833, and Colonel, 4th July, 1836. On the 30th of June, 1846, he was commissioned Brigadier-General, was placed in command of the Army of the West, and made the conquest of the Territory of New Mexico. He received the Brevet of Major-General. United States Army, for gallant and meritorious conduct in New Mexico and California, to date from the battle of San Pascual, 6th December, 1846, in which he was twice wounded. He commanded the combined force, consisting of detachments of sailors, marines and of dragoons, in the battles of San Gabriel and Plains of Mesa, 8th and 9th January, 1847, and was Governor of California from the date of his proclamation, 1st March, 1847, down to June of the same year. On the 31st of October, 1848, he fell a victim, at Vera Cruz, to illness contracted in the course of his arduous service during the Mexican War. Like his nephew, Major General Philip Kearny, he died for his country.

One who knew him well, being competent to judge, said: "If ever there was a man whom I considered really chivalrous, in fact, a man in all that noble term conveys, that natural soldier and gentleman was Stephen Watts Kearny."

He was descended from chivalric ancestors. He was the son of Philip Kearny and Lady Barney Dexter (Ravaud) Kearny, his wife. The founder of the family in America was Michael Kearny, who came from Ireland and settled in Monmouth, N. J., prior to 1716. Among his ancestors were the DeLanceys, glorious soldiers for ages. John Watts, Senior, married Anne, the second daughter of Stephen De Lancey, who immigrated to New York in 1686. They were his grandparents and the great-grand-parents of Major General Philip Kearny. Their youngest son, Stephen, commanded the First Battalion, New York Volunteers, during the War of the Revolution.

In the unfortunate controversy which arose in California between General Kearny and Commodore Stockton, Colonel Fremont was involved. General Kearny deemed it his duty to arrest Colonel Fremont and prefer charges against him, which he did, the result of which was the court-martial which tried and convicted Colonel Fremont. Colonel Fremont was the son-in-law of Senator Thomas H. Benton. Senator Benton developed an enmity towards General Kearny such as he only could hold. No more uncompromising man than Benton ever lived. No man ever in public life was more intolerant, and often he was, despite his greatness, rash and unreasonable. The conviction of Fremont was the cause of Benton's hatred of Kearny. No one can read the correspondence between General Kearny, Commodore Stockton and Fremont without a feeling that General Kearny maintained his position well. The controversy was very distasteful to General Kearny, but he believed the instructions given him had placed upon him a great responsibility, and he believed that he was acting as the personal representative of the President of the United States. He would not surrender any part of the prerogatives entrusted to his care. He acted solely from a sense of duty. He was a faithful officer, devoted to his duty, and was always trusted by his government.

Donaciano Vigil, Second Governor of New Mexico.

DONACIANO VIGIL.

The ancestors of Donaciano Vigil came from Spain, were of limited means, and without the power and influence which accompanied wealth, even in the eighteenth century. His parents were Don Juan Cristobal Vigil and Dona Maria Antonia Marin. His father, while of liberal education, was a soldier, and fought in many Indian campaigns in New Mexico. From 1815 to 1821 he was an Alcalde of the first instance, an official having about the same jurisdiction and authority as a judge of our district courts.

Donaciano Vigil was born in Santa Fé, the capital of the province of New Mexico, on the 6th day of September, 1802. He had an older brother, Juan, and two sisters.

Education under the Spanish regime was under a strict censorship, and very much restricted in curriculum. A reverend Father, who was master of ancient languages, but ignorant of the first principles of mathematics and other sciences, explained this enigma to Captain Zebulon Pike, U. S. A., when that officer was in Santa Fé in 1807, by informing him of the care "the Spanish government took to prevent any branch of science from being made a pursuit, which would have a tendency to extend the views of the subjects in the provinces to the geography of their country, or any other subject which would bring to view a comparison of their local advantages and situations with other countries."

In addition to this mistaken policy of the Spanish government, there were no schools worthy of the name in the province of New Mexico provided with teachers capable even in the branches permitted to be taught.

About this time—1811—the magnificent sum of eight hundred dollars had been expended by the government of New Mexico in the conduct of two so-called public schools, one at Santa Fé and the other at San Miguel.[64] Opportunities for education proper in those times were limited to home instruction. Fortunately the father of Donaciano Vigil was educated, and fully appreciated the advantages of an education to his children. He gave them instruction and reviewed their studies as they advanced. Donaciano and his brother Juan, as also a cousin, Juan Bautista Vigil y Alarid, had a natural liking for books and study, and naturally were men of brilliant minds. Accelerating the instruction received at home by availing themselves of the limited supply of books in those times among their friends and neighbors, they soon became well grounded in the history of their country and time. Their superior attainments soon brought their services into demand in positions of responsibility and trust. It was a current remark among those most familiar with men and times under the Republic of Mexico that Donaciano Vigil and his brother, Juan, were among the best educated men in public life in the department. Juan had served in the provincial assembly, and had frequently been called to other positions of trust and responsibility in local affairs.

Donaciano Vigil was married at Santa Fé, the marriage ceremony having been performed by the Very Reverend Vicar, Juan Felipe Ortiz. The union was blessed with ten children, of whom five, all boys, grew to manhood. Antonio B. was appointed a cadet to the Military Academy in the City of Mexico in 1841, was

[64]Manuscript copy of report of Pedro Bautista Pino to King of Spain, Nov. 12, 1811; in possession of author.

commissioned a lieutenant and served in the Mexican army during the Mexican War; was engaged in the battle of Palo Alto, and returned to New Mexico in 1848. Jose Epifanio was at one time auditor of public accounts of the Territory of New Mexico, and held many other positions of trust and profit under the Territorial government, and died at Santa Fé, beloved and respected by all who knew him. Antonio B, with the other sons, Desiderio, Hermenijildo and Epitacio, resided at Pecos, in San Miguel county, and during their lives were engaged in stockraising and agricultural pursuits. Don Heremenijildo Vigil served in the Legislative council from San Miguel county in 1890. Desiderio and Epitacio served during the war of the rebellion of 1861-65, respectively, three years in the First New Mexico Infantry and six months in the Second New Mexico Infantry.

The Vigil homestead in Santa Fé, where the old governor, and the judge, his father before him, resided, is near the old Guadalupe church, on the banks of the Rio de Santa Fé. It was a retired, quiet retreat, once abounding in magnificent trees, planted by the hands of Judge Vigil. It was here that Governor Vigil lived with his amiable consort during the heyday of his distinguished career, and until he removed in 1855 to his ranch on the Pecos river, some twenty-five miles to the southeast of Santa Fé. In the year 1823 he made his reputation as an intrepid Indian fighter, having been engaged during that year and taking a leading part in a campaign against the Navajos, whose warriors had been raiding the valley of the Rio Grande. In the years 1833 and 1836, respectively, he again participated in the chastisement of this powerful tribe.

The insurrection of 1837 found Vigil a military prisoner in the *cuarto de los venderas*, at the Palace, where, it may be remarked, many distinguished people had been held in duress, including a former Territorial governor of New Mexico, Merriweather, in 1821.

The circumstances under which he thus became a prisoner, briefly stated, may serve to indicate a sturdy characteristic. The military forces in the department at that date, in consequence of there being no money to pay them, had been temporarily discharged, so as to allow them to return to their homes or to engage in such pursuits as they might be able to find, and thus gain that subsistence which the government had acknowledged itself unable to furnish.

Vigil had found employment in the store of one, Tomas Valencia, a merchant of Santa Fé, as a clerk, receiving imperative instructions that he was to credit no person whatever. While thus employed, and a short time previous to the insurrection against Perez, Captain Cavallero, commandant of the forces in New Mexico, called at the store and demanded credit. Vigil explained the nature of his instructions, but the Captain persisted, even to abuse and personal violence. In the latter, however, the belligerent captain found himself second best, in that the future governor of New Mexico gathered him in his arms and put him outside the store room. Taking a cowardly advantage of the relations then existing, Vigil still being a sergeant in the army, the captain, as "Commandante," issued an order placing Vigil under arrest for assaulting his superior officer. And thus, as before indicated, Governor Perez found Sergeant Vigil, while the insurrectionary hordes were descending upon him from the

North. He was released, and, with the few others who still stood by the ill-fated governor, accompanied him in a forlorn hope to the Cañada, where, meeting the insurrectionists, Governor Perez was defeated by overpowering numbers, Perez, with a few followers, barely escaping, while Vigil, with many others, was taken prisoner, confined at Santa Cruz and placed in manacles of rawhide. The revolutionary forces were largely composed of Pueblo Indians, who were highly excited and turbulent under the vicious and designing misrepresentations which had incited the uprising. Thus situated, the prisoners were in constant expectation of being summarily put to death.

In a few days, however, and immediately following the assassination of Governor Perez, and the issuing of a pronunciamento by the insurgent commander, declaring himself provisional governor, an order came from the latter for the removal of Vigil from Santa Cruz to Santa Fé, where he was set at liberty. It was believed by Vigil that this clemency was owing largely to the fact of his unjust incarceration by Cavallero. Sergeant Vigil, after visiting his family, reported to Captain Ronquillo, of his company, for duty. Ronquillo, however, said to him that he was alone and powerless; that the insurgents were in full possession of the capital, and that he was at liberty to pursue such a course as, in his judgment, was best, in view of the situation.

In the meantime, the Provisional Governor had called a meeting of the citizens generally to meet in the portal of the Palace, to consider the exigencies of the situation. Among those present and participating were the Fr. Antonio Jose Martinez, Manuel Armijo and Juan Jose Esquibel, who were appointed a committee to draft a statement of the grievances of the people and their loyalty, by them to be presented to the Supreme Government of Mexico. The proceedings of the meeting also show that the following named officers were authorized to sign and authenticate the statement, who were: "His Excellency, the Acting Governor, Jose Gonzales; the Commanding General, the Inspector, Jose Ma. Ronquillo; and the Acting Secretary, Sergeant Donaciano Vigil." This meeting was held on the 27th and 28th days of August, 1837, being eighteen days after the assassination of Governor Perez. It is proper to state that in the month of January following, on the 28th, Manuel Armijo, who was present at this meeting, having enlisted a force of some six hundred men in the Rio Abajo (Valley of the Rio Grande), executed a *coup de main* on the government of Gonzales, shot him, caused others to be executed, and then, in turn, issued his pronunciamento, proclaiming himself governor. A few months later, Armijo having gone to the City of Mexico and presented his own case, returned with an appointment as governor of the Territory.

In 1838, Vigil led another expedition against the Navajos. In the meantime he had been elected a member of the Departmental Assembly. It was about this time, also, that Captain Cavallero emerged from his hiding place and again demonstrated his soldierly qualities by ordering the arrest of Vigil on the old charges, and he was again placed in the Palace.

On the 19th of September, 1839, however, Governor Armijo ordered his release and gave him a detail as Military Secretary, the Governor remarking to the

Secretary: "Let Cavallero and all your enemies do their best; I will stand by you." Thus ended this cowardly persecution.

It is a peculiar factor in the career of Governor Armijo, that while Vigil was frequently found standing as a bulwark between Armijo and the people, with all the courage of conviction, risking even his life against his autocratic policy and oppressions, Armijo soon came to acknowledge his strength among the people, by yielding to his advice at times, and to appreciate the value of maintaining friendly relations, by his respectful bearing toward Vigil, and in having him detailed for service in his immediate office. As a rule, he was overbearing and despotic in the extreme to those around him or whom he suspected of being opposed to him. Except at brief intervals, Vigil remained as private and Military Secretary at the office of the executive until the 8th day of December, 1843, at which date he retired with a change of administration.

In the meantime, however, he had been promoted, in 1841, to Ensign in the company of Taos; in the year following, to First Lieutenant of his old company of El Bado; for gallant services in the capture of the Texas invaders, the same year, brevetted captain and, under date of April 18, 1842, was commissioned Captain of his company by President Santa Ana. In 1843 he was a second time elected to the Departmental Assembly. In 1845 he was sent to Chihuahua to purchase military supplies. His mission, by reason of the pressing local demand to meet the advance of General Taylor, with the forces of the United States on the Rio Grande, at the breaking out of the war with Mexico, was unsuccessful. While thus engaged, he was assigned by Governor Trias to the command of the garrison at Chihuahua and served for several months in that capacity. Upon his return to New Mexico he was detailed on the general staff of the Governor and Commanding General of the department for duty at headquarters, and thus served until the near approach of the Army of the West under General Kearny, in August, 1846, made his presence in the field necessary.

Volunteers had promptly responded to the call of General Armijo, which, with the dragoons and garrison troops in camp at and near Santa Fé, augmented his forces to four thousand men. Most of this force was mounted and all provided with arms and ammunition. With the approach of the troops under General Kearny, Armijo concentrated his command in the Apache Canyon and in the mountains to the southeast of Santa Fé, a location most admirably chosen for purposes of defense. General Armijo had proclaimed at public meetings and elsewhere, when the subject of ways and means was being discussed for repelling the advancing army from the east, that he was willing to sacrifice his life and property in the defense of his country. The troops of Armijo had all gathered at the Apache Canyon, as contemplated, and Captain Vigil was giving his cordial co-operation and support, very properly believing their position impregnable, under a determined stand and intelligent direction.

Word finally came that the American army, fifteen hundred strong, was only five leagues distant. General Armijo immediately summoned a council of the officers of the regular troops. He was told, as he had been previously by a council of the volunteers and citizens, "that they should march at once, meet the enemy and give them battle; which being made known to the troops was received with shouts and acclamations of pleasure." Whereupon Armijo responded that he had resolved to advance; but as soon as the citizens had retired, he ordered the dragoons to countermarch, taking with them the artillery, of which he had three pieces. His object soon being apparent, to the protests of the officers, he responded with gross abuse, telling them, among other things, that they were cowards, and that he would not risk a battle where the only discipline and experience of a large portion of the men was that gained in fighting Indians. He was told that "he knew the character and discipline of his men as well before as after ordering them out! They had all expressed their willingness to fight and it was his duty to lead! If it was not his purpose to engage the enemy, why had he ordered them in the field?"

It was all to no purpose, however. He ordered all, except the dragoons, to return to their homes. The latter were ordered south, following the line of the mountains south of Santa Fé to the valley of the Rio Grande. General Armijo, with a body guard of dragoons, took the advance for Chihuahua. It had been determined, in the event of retreat becoming necessary, that Captain Vigil should accompany General Armijo as far as Socorro. Under the circumstances, he peremptorily declined, not choosing to subject himself and men to the caprice of one who had just proved himself so much of a poltroon, notwithstanding the generally pleasant relations existing between them in the past.

Keenly feeling the disgrace to his country in the conduct of Armijo and the hopelessness of stability under the Mexican government; aggravated by a knowledge of the shameless peculations of those in control of the government, and the chronic oppression which rested upon the masses of the people, Captain Vigil naturally concluded there might be relief for his people in the coming of the army of the United States. He naturally loved liberty for liberty's sake. He realized that the reforms under the Republic of Mexico, so often promised, would never be realized. His familiar intercourse during the generation previous with the Santa Fé trader, with "Americans" fresh from the "States," doubtless contributed to the determination of his course. Pride pointed in one direction; duty in the other. The latter prevailed and he promptly resigned his commission as Captain, to submit to what was not only best for his people, but to the then inevitable. His first act, following his resignation, was to consult with his friends and counsel non-resistance and to prepare a proclamation or address to the people assuring safety in person and recommending a yielding to the forces of the United States. This proclamation was signed by the Secretary and acting governor and published. The present effect was to allay fears and the staying of any power for evil which otherwise might have been possible under the lead of some of the ambitious men at that time living at the capital. There is small doubt that the occupation of the Capital by General Kearny, without the loss of life in bloody conflict was largely due to the sagacious foresight and patriotic action of Captain Vigil.

There is also some significance in the fact that Juan Bautista Vigil y Alarid, a cousin of Donaciano's, the last Secretary under the Mexican government, and after the flight of Armijo, the last executive, formally turned over the city to General Kearny, took the oath of allegiance to the government of the United States and continued to act as secretary up to the formal promulgation of the civil government, under the code of laws prepared by General Kearny, on September 22, 1846, and the appointment of civil officials.

Charles Bent, an American merchant, who for many years had been familiar with the country, the people and their language, his wife a native of the country, was very properly selected for chief executive. Next in rank was the Secretary of the Territory. For this office Donaciano Vigil was selected, as not only having given the highest evidence of his friendship for the United States government, but as combining the qualities of natural love for liberty, popularity among the masses of the people, and ability. His perfect familiarity with the country, the people and its resources made him of the highest possible advantage in council and to General Kearny and his successors.

His subtleness in discovering conspiracy became proverbial, and brought down on his devoted head mob violence and a necessity for guarding his movements. For a time a guard was regularly detailed for service at his office, and for nearly two years his friends would not permit him to appear on the street without an eye to surroundings. The plot of December, 1846, for an uprising against the new government was by him discovered, and, as a consequence, at the time defeated. In like manner other plots were discovered and defeated. In this he was materially aided by the "common people," who remained from the first his steadfast friends. Nothing seriously detrimental to the new government was ever attempted during the time he was connected with the Territorial government but what he was advised of the movement in advance. The people, in contradistinction to the leaders and their immediate friends, were specially interested in the permanent establishment of the new order of things. Under the new they had everything to gain; with the old there was nothing to hope for.

In January, 1847, disturbance seemed imminent at Taos; the malcontents had succeeded in stirring up discontent and dissensions among the Pueblo Indians and the more ignorant and vicious classes in remote districts. Governor Bent thought to allay the growing storm by appearing in person among those with whom he had lived for years, never doubting that his personal influence would be equal to any emergency.

His friends sought to prevail upon him not to go to Taos until the troops could be sent with him. Secretary Vigil advised him that his undertaking was rash, and begged him not to think of it. Governor Bent persisted, however, and the result was a verification of their worst fears. The sad intelligence soon returned of his assassination, and that the storm of insurrection had come and was rapidly spreading. The regular troops that could be spared from Santa Fé, with a considerable force of volunteers, immediately took up the line of march to the seat of war. The troops were met near Cañada by the insurgent force, where, after a battle lasting all day, they were defeated and driven to Embudo, and from that place to Taos, where a stand was made for a time, but were finally given a crushing defeat.

Secretary Vigil, by virtue of his office, succeeded Governor Bent, and a few months later was appointed governor, as appears from the following order:

"Headquarters Ninth Military Department,
"Santa Fé, December 17, 1847.

"General Orders No. 10.

"Lieutenant Governor Donaciano Vigil is hereby appointed Civil Governor of the Territory of New Mexico.

"By order of Brig. Gen. S. Price.

"W. E. PRINCE,
"A. D. C. and A. A. Adj't Gen."

The appointment was confirmed at Washington, and Governor Vigil remained the chief executive of New Mexico until the office was merged into that of the Department Commander, following the cessation of hostilities. Among the first acts as governor was the issuing of a proclamation deprecating the assassination of Governor Bent, and bidding for the apprehension of the chief conspirators.

It was contemplated in the proclamations of General Kearny that New Mexico should have a Legislative Assembly, and, in accordance with this idea, in response to repeated petitions from many sources, in the summer of 1847, Governor Vigil issued a proclamation for an election. Members were elected and the first deliberative body convened in New Mexico, under the United States government, met at Santa Fé on the 6th day of December, 1847, on which date Governor Vigil delivered his first message.

This message, coming as it did from a native of the country, can not be regarded as otherwise than memorable. It is a document that will ever be read with interest, particularly for its comprehensive and ethical spirit.

Not the least feature is that contemplating "freedom from revolutions and internal dissensions, the security of person and property" and the prosperity that must follow.

Among the subjects treated which will be appreciated by those familiar with the gross irregularities ingrained in society and the entire administration under the Mexican government, he calls attention to the necessity of limiting and defining the powers of prefects and the holding of these officials to a stricter accountability in the handling of public funds; the necessity for some provision of law to prevent the defrauding of the revenue and also the defrauding of the Pueblo Indians; that cemeteries should be left to local control, open to all and to optional religious ceremonials at burials, and a more equitable distribution of the water for irrigation, whereby the poor man, with his small tract, should be placed on an equality with the rich man and his broad acres.

A large portion of the message is devoted to education; to the almost entire absence of schools, of their imperative necessity among a free people, and advocating such legislation as would secure free schools for the masses. On this subject Governor Vigil said: "In the contemplation of the institutions of a free people by those who do not enjoy the same benefits they perceive, as by instinct, that they, too, have rights, and they meditate over it until they assert them, value and enjoy them. It is only through the diffusion of knowledge that a people are enabled to follow the example of those nations whose wise policy shows itself in the higher intelligence and happiness of its people. The world generally is progressive, and how can we avail ourselves of the advancement unless the people are educated?"

Governor Vigil was found on the side of the people as against the imperious exactions and oppressions of the priests, as well as against those of the politicians, both of whom were alike resting as an incubus upon the country in 1846, rock-rooted and moss-grown, in contradistinction of the most sacred rights and privileges of humanity, by the authority and prestige of nearly three centuries of church and state combined. Not only his voice, but his pen, were frequently brought to this service, as sundry pamphlets and newspaper articles still extant attest. He found no fault with the people for their unfortunate surroundings. He regarded the situation as the result of a vicious system, for which they were not responsible, and which was their misfortune.

He had an abiding faith that, with enlarged powers, with education, as free men, they would relegate this system to the rear and, in the end, entirely free themselves from their oppressors. He freely sought to impress upon his people their duties, under the enlarged powers coming with the government of the United States, together with the right of free discussion. He had no concern for that sentiment which is expressed in "there are many things which, however well they may be known, must never be mentioned," when applied adversely either to the state or to the material interests of society. He believed with the old reformers that the best safeguard of a free people under a free government was free speech and free discussion. On this account, in all his acts as an official, he was constantly grappling with and laying bare whatever affected human rights adversely; confronting alike all leaders, whatever their cast or profession, whenever their influence was cast in derogation of liberty, either in the person or the conscience.

Governor Vigil lived to see his hopes and predictions largely consummated. The population of New Mexico more than doubled from the time of the coming of Kearny until his death. Educational facilities were extended. The nomadic Indian tribes were no longer a terror to the border settlers. Mail routes and telegraph lines stretched in every direction, and the railroad had already touched the northern boundary line of the Territory. The old "Santa Fé Trail" had passed into history.

On the 11th day of October, 1848, Governor Vigil was succeeded by Lieutenant Colonel Washington, as civil and military governor and commandant of the department. By request, Governor Vigil accepted a re-appointment as Secretary of the Territory, and in this capacity continued to serve the Territory with the same interest and efficiency as in the past, and until the formal organization of the Territory on the 3rd day of March, 1851.

A convention had been called to consider the form of government desirable, and whether with or without slavery. This convention met at Santa Fé the day following the inauguration of Governor Washington. The late governor had been elected a member of this convention from Santa Fé. Here, again, when the now well known fact is considered that the acquisition of New Mexico and California had as a special object with some of the statesmen of the day the formation of several additional slave states, the power and influence of Governor Vigil was felt for the good of the entire people. In the committee to draft a memorial to congress, of which he was a member, he proved to be the controlling spirit, securing the insertion in and adoption of a report declaring distinctly in favor of a "Territorial civil government," and that "We do not desire to have domestic slavery within our borders." The report of the committee was adopted and finally signed by every member of the convention. He was also opposed to the peonage system.

When Chief Justice Grafton Baker was about holding the first district court at Santa Fé under the organic act, it was the intention to use the Castrensa or military chapel, then located on the south side of the plaza, for a court room. This was an act wherein Governor Vigil felt that the rights or ancient usages of the church and of the people were being unnecessarily trampled upon. It came to the attention of the court on the empaneling of the grand jury. Governor Vigil, being one of the number summoned, objected to being sworn, for the reason that "the court was being held in a place consecrated to sacred objects; that the forefathers of himself and many others present were there buried; that with all due respect to the civil authority he protested against the use of the chapel for civil purposes, and begged to be excused from serving the court where he could not help feeling that he was treading upon the ashes of his ancestors." His protest and request were deemed reasonable and were respected, and a room in the old palace was assigned for the use of the court thereafter.

With the establishment of the diocese of Santa Fé in 1850 and the coming of Bishop J. B. Lamy, with the radical changes following, also came in time formidable opposition from the old clergy and their adherents, in one instance, at least, resulting in riot and violence. Here the good offices of Governor Vigil were again made manifest in allaying asperities, counseling moderation and in a final yielding to the new episcopate authority. Thus was Donaciano Vigil—ever aiming to be just, whatever the interest affected, whether that of the people, the government, of religion or of the clergy.

Under the organic act he was elected repeatedly to the Legislative Assembly, and was a member, respectively, for the House, first session (1851-1852); to the Council of the seventh, eighth, thirteenth and fourteenth sessions, the last being in 1864-65.

In legislative matters Governor Vigil was as much the "watchdog," so to speak, as could be imagined. He was dreaded in the partisan or factional caucus, and, as a consequence, was sometimes left out when some sort of legislative jobbery was contemplated. A politician of the predatory sort once said of Governor Vigil: "Oh! He is a nice, clever old gentleman, but rather impracticable from my point of view. I always noticed, when he was a member of the assembly, that when any matter of 'special importance' was under consideration at any of the 'juntas,' that he was liable to be left out." The "old gentleman" could not have received a higher compliment. He was known to be fair and honest. In politics, up to 1855, he had generally been with the Democratic party. After that time he took no really active part in politics, but always remained a firm friend of the Union and the government. At no time in his official career can he be said to have been a partisan.

In May, 1853, he, with Samuel Ellison, was commissioned by Governor William Carr Lane to proceed to the Navajo country to procure certain captives, and incidentally secure, if possible, the return of certain stock that had been stolen. This commission was very successful, securing the restoration to their friends of a number of women and children, although at first the Indians maintained a very defiant attitude. His last official position was that of school director in San Miguel county, under the school law of 1871-'72. While the infirmities of age made it quite impossible to be very active, he retained a lively interest in public schools to the very last. He was always watchful of the course of legislation in educational matters.

During the war of the rebellion he was a staunch, uncompromising Union man. In person he was tall and stately, a powerful frame, and very dignified. He was very cheerful in conversation and was always courteous and kind. At sight he impressed others as being a person of no ordinary character. He was very liberal in his charities; for months at a time, while Secretary and Governor, he dispensed the larger portion of his salary to the poor, although himself a very poor man. All the old residents agree as to his uniform integrity, courtesy and high sense of honor.

In 1849 Governor Vigil was asked by Colonel John Munroe, at the time commander of the ninth military department, what were his feelings toward the Mexican government, when resigning his commission and recommending his people to submit to the forces of the

United States. Governor Vigil replied: "I felt very much as a son would feel towards a father who had given him little or no attention in his youthful days, except as he exacted his hard earnings, and left him to shift for himself when in trouble."

Governor Vigil died at the residence of his son, Epifanio, in the city of Santa Fé, on Saturday, the 11th day of August, 1877, at 6:45 a. m., aged 75 years. A combination of asthma and hernia, which had troubled him, more or less, for many years, doubtless was the immediate cause of his death. He retained his faculties to the last, expressed resignation to his fate and expired without a struggle or convulsion.

There are no two opinions as to his high character, patriotism and sagacity. His power and influence were that of the man, not of wealth or family. All joined in paying tribute to his memory. The response to the proclamation of the governor, announcing his death, and calling a meeting at the legislative hall to pay the honors due at the obsequies of the illustrious deceased, was responded to promptly and generally, but particularly by those who had longest known him. The old citizens, the civil and military officers, the merchants, the native and eastern population, everybody, turned out on short notice. It was by far the largest and most distinguished gathering ever witnessed in New Mexico. It was the hearty acknowledgment and tribute of man's best nature to a late distinguished citizen, officer and true man. His remains lay in state, draped with the flag of his adopted country, in the old Palace, just where he had been almost uninterruptedly for half a century, intimately and honorably associated with the affairs of New Mexico. A military guard was in attendance, detailed from the military headquarters of the district, and flags were at half staff at the executive office, the post and at military headquarters. The obsequies were held at the cathedral and an immense concourse of friends, military and civil officers and citizens generally followed the remains to the grave.

The history of the career of Donaciano Vigil, the firm friend of liberty and humanity, belongs to the people of New Mexico. His is a record of which the people may be proud; a record which all lovers of free government will the more delight to honor as time elapses and his distinguished merits are best understood. It is a record which the native son of New Mexico should ever try to emulate.

A very large public meeting was held in Santa Fé, on the day of the death of Governor Vigil, called by the proclamation of the governor. This meeting adopted resolutions, prepared by Hon. Stephen B. Elkins, which show the esteem in which the late governor was held by the people with whom he had lived for seventy-five years; the resolutions follow:

"WHEREAS, The people of New Mexico, being desirous of recording the high appreciation of the great worth of Donaciano Vigil, as a citizen and official, and bearing testimony to his many virtues; therefore, be it

"*Resolved,* That the people of New Mexico have received, with deepest regret, the sad intelligence of the death of Governor Donaciano Vigil, who, for more than fifty years, was a distinguished and worthy citizen of the Territory.

"*Resolved,* That it is with sorrow we part with the deceased, distinguished for his administrative ability, his perfect integrity, just in the exercise of his prerogatives, when governor of the Territory; respected by all, beloved for his kindness of heart, his memory will continue green with his friends and the people, as one who was the type of a perfect gentleman.

"*Resolved,* That while we bow our heads in humble submission to the unerring will of Providence in severing a tie so closely welded by long years of intimacy with the deceased, in a frontier Territory, so incident with danger and severe trials during many years of his life, we tender our sincere sympathy and condolence to his family, assuring them that the entire community shares with them in their great loss; be it further

"*Resolved,* That a copy of these resolutions, with the proceedings of the meeting, be furnished the family of the deceased, and published in all of the papers of the Territory."

Willard P. Hall.

WILLARD PREBLE HALL.

Willard Preble Hall was born at Harper's Ferry, Virginia, May 9, 1820. He was of Puritan descent, his ancestors having emigrated to Massachusetts from England in 1634. In his ancestral lines, both paternal and maternal, were many of the eminent judges, lawyers and divines of England. His father was a man of remarkable mechanical and scientific attainments, and a celebrated inventor. His preliminary education was had at Baltimore, Maryland, and he graduated from Yale college in the class of 1839—the same class in which were William M. Evarts and several other eminent men.

In 1840, he came to Missouri and studied law with his brother, Judge William A. Hall, of Randolph county. In 1841, he moved to Platte county, and settled at Sparta, the county seat. A glimpse of him as he was then is given by an old resident of Platte City, with whom he stopped over night on his trip from Randolph to Sparta. He described him as a pale, delicate youth, dressed in blue jeans, mounted on a pony, with a pair of leather saddle bags, containing his wardrobe and library. In 1843, he moved to Saint Joseph, which was his home during the remainder of his life.

He stepped into immediate prominence in his profession and in politics. In 1843, he was appointed circuit attorney, succeeding a very capable officer. General Doniphan, speaking of him at this period, says: "He succeeded at once. System and order and logical arrangement were natural with him. He had the criminal law, and especially the statutes of the state, at his fingers' ends, and could refer readily to them in a moment's time. Plain and simple in his manners as a child, naturally frank and easy with everyone, he soon became a favorite, and from his youthful appearance, even a pet with his older friends. He was a very efficient and a very conscientious officer. He prevented grand juries from presenting anything that could not be sustained, and prosecuted, with great energy, those he believed guilty.

In 1844, he was one of the candidates on the Democratic electoral ticket, and canvassed western Missouri north of the Missouri river on behalf of Polk and Dallas, and the annexation of Texas. Doniphan was the Whig candidate for the same office, and was always his antagonist in this canvass. To those who knew what northwest Missouri was in those days, and what Doniphan was in his prime, it would be unnecessary, to those who did not know them it would be impossible, to explain what it meant for this stripling of twenty-four years to meet that matchless orator before a people who loved and honored him as Doniphan was loved and honored in northwest Missouri. How well he maintained himself in the contest is best shown by the fact that he won the unqualified praise and admiration of Doniphan, and as the result was made the nominee of his party for Congress, in 1846, over the heads of many able veterans of his party.

The great issue in the canvass of 1844 was the question of the annexation of Texas. In his canvass for congress in the spring of 1846 Mr. Hall was taunted with the fact that the policy of annexation which he had advocated had plunged the country into war with Mexico. Possibly, in the heat of debate, he had made some pledges; but at any rate, he made proof of his good faith in his principles by volunteering as a private for service in the war. His company formed a part of Doniphan's command in his great expedition across the plains and through New Mexico, conquering the country as he went, until he joined the army of General Taylor in Old Mexico; a military feat which stands in history comparable alone with the retreat of the ten thousand Greeks recorded by Xenophon in the Anabasis. While the command was at Fort Leavenworth, preparing for its march, people from all parts of Hall's district came to the fort, bringing horses and mules and cattle, and other supplies for the army, and there they saw their young candidate, clad in the garb and performing the menial services of a private soldier, unloading the stores from the boats and placing them in wagons. When they returned to their homes, the story of his conduct was told all over the district, and the hearts of the people were touched to such an extent that, although he appeared no more in the canvass, when the election came on in August, he was chosen to congress by a majority of three thousand out of less than ten thousand votes.

After the conquest of New Mexico it became necessary to establish a government over that territory, and for that purpose to frame a code of laws adapted to its condition. General Kearny, the commander, detailed private Hall from the ranks to do the work in connection with Doniphan. Together they prepared the code which General Kearny afterwards proclaimed as the established military law of the territory, and which was afterwards again adopted as the Territorial code, and remained for forty-five years the fundamental law of the Territory. No one who knew Hall and Doniphan, and the capacity of the former and the disinclination of the latter for this kind of work, will doubt that much the greater part of the labor was done by Hall. And Doniphan often said that the work was mainly Hall's. It was certainly a most remarkable duty to which this private soldier was detailed, to write laws that were to govern the conquered country. The code made a small volume, and on the 115 scanty pages is printed in both English and Spanish this entire body of laws, and it would be impossible to find anywhere so complete and perfect a system of laws in many times the space covered here. Here we have a bill of rights announcing the great principles of civil and religious liberty, which are repeated over in all our constitutions, and have passed through the hands of the greatest statesmen of Europe and America; but here we find them, amended and strengthened in expression, more complete and more beautiful than anywhere else. Examine this book and mark the evidences it contains of ripened and mature scholarship and statesmanship, and then—remembering that it was prepared, in a few days' time, amid the turmoil of camp, by a youth of barely twenty-six years, whose short, active life had been passed on this far Western Border, much of it in the saddle, in the midst of legal and political conflicts —to thus determine with what equipment of native ability, of acquired scholarship and experience, this young man set out on his career.

Colonel Hughes, in his history of the Doniphan Expedition, tells us that one day as they were engaged in preparing this code in Santa Fé, General Doniphan entered the room and announced to Hall the fact of his election to Congress. This was in August, 1846. He was immediately relieved from further duty as a soldier, but voluntarily accompanied Colonel Phillip St. George Cooke to California, returned to Missouri the next spring, and took his seat in Congress the following winter.

He was twice re-elected to Congress and then declined further election. He acquired a high reputation in Congress as a working member.

At the end of his congressional service he returned to Saint Joseph and remained there in practice until 1861. In the winter of 1861 the Governor of Missouri and the legislature, which was in session, were both strongly in favor of seceding and joining the Southern Confederacy, and for this purpose an act was passed, calling an election to be held in February of that year to choose delegates to a State convention, the purpose of which, as stated in the act, was "To consider the then existing relations between the Government of the United States, the people and the government of the different states, and the government and people of the State of Missouri, and to adopt such measures for vindicating the sovereignty of the state, and the protection of its institutions, as shall appear to them to be demanded."

Mr. Hall was elected to that convention as a Union man. In early life he had belonged to the extreme Southern wing of the Democratic party, but in 1861 his views had materially changed, and the great issue of that day found no stronger Union man in Missouri or elsewhere than Willard P. Hall. The convention met in due time, and instead of passing an ordinance of secession, as it was expected to do, resolved almost unanimously that Missouri had no just cause for secession.

On July 30, the offices of Governor and Lieutenant Governor were, by ordinance of the convention, declared vacant, and, on July 31, Hamilton R. Gamble was chosen Provisional Governor and Willard P. Hall, Lieutenant Governor. It was then only intended that this government should be provisional and temporary until an election could be held, which was ordered for the following October. But the condition of affairs continued to be so disturbed that an election was impracticable, and this provisional government remained in control during the entire war in Missouri. Governor Gamble was in feeble health most of the time, and often absent from the state for weeks and months, and died early in 1864. He was succeeded by Mr. Hall as governor. The burdens of the administration, therefore, were thrown very heavily upon Hall's shoulders during the entire period.

This provisional government was instituted to maintain law and order. All the criminal and disorderly elements of society, which became so numerous and so defiant in war, knew it for their enemy and fought it with a rage and hatred that was not exceeded by that of the secessionists. It stood for civil government and law, entitled and bound to maintain its rightful superiority over the military power, and thus it was a constant check and curb on the military officers who operated in the state, aroused their jealousy and met a very general opposition from them. It was almost destitute of financial resources. It had many active foes and few active friends, but those few were a host indeed, the ablest, truest and best men who ever lived in Missouri; and over and above all, it had the great weight of the countenance and confidence and support of Abraham Lincoln. It carried the flag of the State and the Nation. It was the ark of public safety in Missouri. With Gamble and Hall as navigators, it found its way through the storms and tempests of those terrible years, and brought its priceless cargo safe to shore. But, at the close, Gamble, worn out, lay dead in his grave, and Hall looked back on the weary waste he had passed over, the long succession of days and months and years of toil and vexation, wrong and abuse, and bitterness of soul, unrelieved by any evidence of gratitude or appreciation on the part of the great majority of the people.

In January, 1865, he was succeeded as governor by Thomas C. Fletcher.

The statesmanship, fortitude and self-sacrificing devotion of Gamble and Hall, during this period, entitle their names to a record in letters of gold on the fairest page of the history of the State. He turned away from official life and from public affairs to devote his remaining life to the profession he loved so well and for which he was so eminently fitted. For nearly twenty years he followed it, practicing in all the State and Federal courts.

He was a remarkably fine and accurate general scholar, and he kept his classical learning, his Greek and Latin, so fresh that he was able to fit his son for Yale college. His manners were frank and simple, always precisely the same, whether greeting a supreme judge, a president, a cabinet minister, or one of his fellows at the bar. In this simplicity of demeanor and address there was recognized a dignity which was the more impressive the better he was known.[65]

He died November 3, 1882.

[65]This account of the life of Willard P. Hall is condensed from a paper read by John C. Gage before the Kansas City Bar Association, February 8, 1896.

General Diego Archuleta.

DIEGO ARCHULETA.

Diego Archuleta was born in the county of Rio Arriba, New Mexico, on the 27th day of March, 1814, at Plaza Alcalde. He received a portion of his education in the public school and with Fr. Antonio Jose Martinez. He journeyed to Durango, when a boy, where he studied eight years, preparing himself for the priesthood. He received the four minor orders requisite for that purpose, but finally relinquished the idea of becoming a priest, and, in 1840, returned to the Territory of New Mexico and settled in his native county of Rio Arriba. Shortly after his return he was commissioned a captain of militia by the Mexican government, and in the invasion of New Mexico by the Texas-Santa Fé Expedition he commanded a body of troops and assisted in the capture of the Texans. In 1843 he was elected a Deputy to the National Mexican Congress from New Mexico, and served with honor for two years, returning to New Mexico in 1845. While serving as a member of the Congress in Mexico it is said that he prophesied the construction, at no then distant period, of a line of railway from the middle west of the United States of America to the Pacific Coast. In recognition of his distinguished services as an officer of the Mexican army he was decorated with the golden Cross of Honor and presented with a diploma or certificate declaratory of his valiant conduct in preserving the integrity of Mexican territory.

At the time of the coming of the Army of the West under General Kearny he was next in command of the military forces of the Territory of New Mexico to General Manuel Armijo, and was urgent in his demands that the invasion be met with prompt and effective resistance. No resistance, however, was made either by Armijo or Archuleta, the latter being a colonel and second in command. The reasons for this lack of dethrow of the government at Santa Fé under General Armijo were never fully understood by the people of New Mexico. After the war Armijo was tried at the City of Mexico for cowardice and desertion in the face of the enemy; witnesses were summoned from New Mexico for the prosecution, but Armijo was acquitted of the charges against him. The secret history of the causes leading to the flight of Armijo and the dispersing of the troops under his command, at least twenty-four hours before General Kearny reached the Apache Pass, is told by Senator Thomas H. Benton,[66] who states that at the time of the fitting out of the expedition known as the Army of the West, with General Kearny in command, there was a citizen of the United States, long a resident of New Mexico, on a visit of business in the Capitol at Washington, by name James Magoffin, a man of mind, of will, of generous temper, patriotic and rich. Magoffin knew every man in New Mexico and his character, and all the localities, and could be of infinite service to the invading force. Mr. Benton proposed to Magoffin to go with the expedition, to which he agreed. Magoffin was taken before the President and Secretary of War and the arrangements were made. After leaving Bent's Fort, on the Arkansas, Magoffin was sent ahead with a staff officer (Captain Cooke), the latter charged with a mission, Magoffin charged with his own plan, which was

---

[66]Thirty Years' View, Vol. II, pages 682, 683 and 684.

SELLO SEGUNDO

Para los años de mil y mil ochocientos

DOCE REALES.

ochocientos cuarenta cuarenta y uno.

EL INFRASCRITO MINISTRO DE ESTADO
y del Despacho de Guerra y Marina.

Por cuanto en Decreto de 28 de Agosto de 1840, y en uso de la facultad que concede al Gobierno el Congreso Nacional en el de 26 del mismo mes y año, se ha concedido una Cruz de honor á los Generales, Gefes y Oficiales que han combatido en *defensa de la integridad del Territorio nacional, con las modificaciones que el Gobierno tenga á bien determinar, atendidas las circunstancias de los hechos y de los individuos;*

y habiendo acreditado el Ciudadano *Diego Archuleta, Comandante de Escuadron graduado, Capitan de Rurales,* haber concurrido á la campaña de *Nuevo México contra los aventureros de Tejas en 1841, se le concede por sus servicios un escudo de honor al brazo izquierdo con el lema y en la forma q. designa la Suprema Orden de 17 de Diciembre último, y le corresponde conforme á lo dispuesto en el artículo 4.º* por estar comprendido en el expresado primer Decreto; el Exmo. Sr. Presidente ordena que se le expida el presente Diploma, por el cual podrá usar de tan honorífico distintivo, conforme al modelo que existe en la Plana mayor del Ejército y Direcciones respectivas, á donde se tomará razon de este documento que se le otorga como un testimonio de su valor, fidelidad y patriotismo. Dado en México á *veinte. y uno* de *Diciembre* de mil ochocientos cuarenta y *uno. Vigesimo primero* de la Independencia y *Vigesimo* de la Libertad.

Diploma de la Cruz de honor subsistuida en Escudo, que por la Campaña de Nuevo México contra los aventureros de Texas en 1841, se concede al Ciudadano Diego Archuleta Comandante de Escuadron graduado, Capitan de Rurales.

San—

Tesorería Departamental del N.º Mexico.

Rehabilitado pago cuatro pesos cuatro rs. de diferencia de este papel al del que previene el Supremo Decreto de 30 de Abril del año px.º pp.º Santa Fé En.º 3 de 1842.

Bno J Mar[...]

Santa Fé Marzo 23 de 1842.

Entreguese al interesado para que disfrute del honorifico distintivo que se le concede en este diploma.

Manuel [Armijo]

MILITARY OCCUPATION OF NEW MEXICO. 243

to operate upon General Armijo and prevent any resistance to the American advance. This was accomplished. Armijo agreed to make no defense of Apache Pass. But Colonel Archuleta, second in command, was determined to fight, and threats of the assassination of the commander in chief were freely made by officers of his command.[67] It was necessary to make some arrangement with Colonel Archuleta. He was of an entirely different mould from Manuel Armijo, and only accessible to a different class of considerations—those which addressed themselves to ambition and power. Magoffin knew the side upon which to approach him. It so happened that the understanding among all was that Kearny's intentions only covered the conquest of that portion of New Mexico lying east of the Rio Grande. It was represented to Archuleta that Kearny would leave the country to the west of the Bravo untouched. He was advised and recommended by Magoffin to issue a pronunciamento and seize that portion of the country for himself. The idea suited Colonel Archuleta. He knew the strength of the United States and was only too well aware of the weakness of Mexico. He agreed not to fight. The army which had gathered at the defile dispersed, none knowing exactly why. General Kearny occupied the capitol, and the conquest was complete and bloodless.

Colonel Archuleta complied with his part of the contract. Magoffin had been sincere in his representations, but General Kearny had other orders and took possession of the whole country, and moved on with a part of his force to California. Archuleta, deeming

[67]Statement made to writer by Don Nicholas Pino, of Galisteo, N. M.

himself cheated, determined upon a revolt. Colonel Archuleta organized the first conspiracy for the overthrow of the government at Santa Fé under General Sterling Price, who had been left in command by Kearny. This attempt was discovered. Together with other prominent Mexicans, within thirty days after the discovery of the first, he organized another conspiracy, which resulted in the death of Governor Bent and others, but which was put down by the American forces inside two weeks. Archuleta fled, but he was afterwards invited to return to the Territory, and upon taking the oath of allegiance was admitted to the friendship and confidence of the authorities at Santa Fé.

In 1857 Colonel Archuleta was United States Indian agent for the Southern Utes and the Apaches, which position he held for five years. In 1861 he was placed at the head of a regiment of auxiliaries, with the rank of lieutenant-colonel, and was stationed for a time at Fort Union, and again, during the administration of Abraham Lincoln, he was named as Indian agent for the Utes, Apaches and Jicarrillas. In the same year he was commissioned a brigadier general by Governor Henry Connelly; inasmuch as this commission bears the signatures of four of the most distinguished New Mexicans of that period, a reproduction of the same is given. For fourteen years he was a member of the legislative assembly of the Territory of New Mexico. He was a candidate for the Thirty-seventh Congress of the United States, but was defeated by John S. Watts. He was the first man to transport a family carriage across the Great Plains. He was the son of Juan Andres Archuleta, a prominent and wealthy citizen of Rio Arriba, and in 1841 was

Don Diego Archuleta, Santa Fe, N. M., 1884.

Henry Connelly

GOVERNOR AND COMMANDER IN CHIEF
OF THE
TERRITORY OF NEW MEXICO.

GREETING:—

TO *Diego Archuleta*

KNOW YE, That We, reposing special trust and confidence in your patriotism, valor, conduct and fidelity and being duly informed, that you have been duly elected to the office hereinafter named, do commission you *Brigadier General of the first division of — — —* the Militia of the Territory:—You are therefore carefully and diligently to discharge the duties of the office hereby conferred upon you by doing and performing all manner of things thereunto belonging, according to the laws of the United States and of this Territory, and to the Military rule and discipline.

In testimony whereof, I have hereunto set my hand and caused to be affixed the Great Seal of the Territory of New Mexico: Done at Santa Fé, this *seventh* day of *September* A. D., in the year of our Lord one thousand eight hundred and sixty *one* and of the Independence of the United States the eighty *eighth*

Henry Connelly
Gov. N.M.

Registers *Adjutary Office. No 9 the day of September 1861*
R. S. Osburn
Adjutant General N. M. Militia

By the Governor, *Miguel A. Otero*
SECRETARY OF THE TERRITORY.

married to Jesusita Trujillo, and there were seven children of the union. He died at Santa Fé, while a member of the Legislative Assembly of 1884, of heart failure. On the 20th of March, 1884, while engaged in his duties as a member of the legislature, on the floor of the house, he was taken suddenly ill. He was taken to the home of Don Rafael Lopez, where he was stopping, and on the following day rallied considerably, and a very important measure being under consideration in the House, he was assisted to his accustomed seat in order to cast his vote. He remained only long enough to perform this duty and was taken to his apartments, where the utmost care and attention were shown him; every known medical treatment was brought to bear on his case but, despite all efforts, he continued to sink and grow worse until death came to his relief. His death was not altogether unexpected. The House of Representatives met and adjourned after passing appropriate resolutions and designating proper committees to look after the details of the funeral obsequies. The Council also met and passed similar resolutions. His remains were removed to the hall of the Society of St. Francis; thence they were taken to the Church of Our Lady of Guadalupe, where mass was said, when they were again removed to the St. Francis Hall, being finally taken to the Hall of the House of Representatives, where they lay in state until the day of the funeral. On the day of the funeral native and American citizens alike assembled in vast numbers, performing the last honor to the distinguished statesman. The procession which followed the remains to their last resting place in the Catholic cemetery was one of the largest ever seen in the City of Santa Fé. The 22d Infantry Band of the United States Army led the procession, which included the General commanding the District, Brigadier General D. S. Stanley, his staff and other officers of the U. S. Army, stationed at Santa Fé, the members of the legislative assembly, the county commissioners, secret and patriotic societies, it being estimated that over two thousand five hundred people marched in the procession.

Diego Archuleta was an intense patriot and his following was large and enthusiastic. He bitterly opposed the American occupation, but gave in when he saw that further effort was vain and useless. His life was a busy one throughout. He held many offices of honor and trust. He filled them all with ability. His last speech in the House of Representatives was in favor of an amendment to a pending educational bill, which declared for non-sectarian administration of the schools of New Mexico. In making this speech, he said that he was then an old man, that he expected very soon to be called to his Maker, and, when that time came, he would go with the satisfaction of knowing that his vote had been cast in behalf of freedom, in behalf of free, non-sectarian education of the youth of his country. His last vote cast in the House was in favor of the construction of the Capitol building at Santa Fé.

Senator Thomas H. Benton.

THOMAS H. BENTON.

It is not to be expected in these sketches that anything more than the briefest of outlines of the professional life and public services of so celebrated a man as Thomas Hart Benton should appear. He belonged to the classic age of American eloquence and it is hoped that at no distant day some one will appear as his biographer who will be competent to do justice to the memory of one of the greatest of American statesmen. As a logical reasoner, he was inferior to Daniel Webster; as an orator, Henry Clay was his superior, but in depth of mind, and in the power to conceive and execute any great public measure, he was the equal of either, and in some respects the superior of both. Benton loved his country and in all his life as a public servant, in considering any measure pending in the congress of the United States, he strove to ascertain its effect upon the entire nation. He was a great lover of the West. He was a great friend of New Mexico. He was a senator of the Nation and not of a single state. During the days immediately following the Treaty of Guadalupe Hidalgo, Senator Benton did all in his power in the senate of the United States to secure to the people of New Mexico the rights to which they were entitled. At an early period in his career in the senate, Benton took the position that the government should never depend upon the sale of its public lands as a source of revenue, but that the true policy was to aid and encourage immigration by a reduction of the price of the public domain; and, as most of the immigrants were poor, to give them ample time in which to pay for their homes. To this end, he introduced a bill reducing the price to one dollar and twenty-five cents an acre, and, upon certain conditions, to give them pre-emption and settlement rights, so that they could pay for their homes out of the proceeds of their labor. All of the New England states, led by Webster, opposed this policy, as tending to deprive them of a part of their productive population, but Benton was successful and the West has always been grateful to him on that account.

He was very fond of western adventurers and for many years made it a point to entertain all of them who came to his city. At one time he had a personal interview with Kit Carson, who, surrounded with maps and charts, explained to Benton the character and location of what he considered the most desirable route between Independence and Santa Fé. It is not strange, therefore, that a man of his wonderful memory was even more familiar with the western wilds and savage tribes than many who had lived all their lives among them.

Senator Benton was born near Hillsborough, North Carolina, March 14, 1782. In his youth he received a very liberal education. He lived with his mother for a number of years, in the State of Tennessee, and came to Missouri in 1813. In 1820, at the time of the admission of the State of Missouri into the Union, Benton was chosen United States Senator. He continued in the Senate of the United States, by successive elections, for thirty years. He was a man of very strong prejudices. He devoted several years of the latter part of his life to the preparation of two most valuable works, one 'A Thirty Years' View;' the other 'An Abridgment of the Debates in Congress,

From the Foundation of the Government, to 1856.' These works are of great value. Senator Benton died in the City of Washington, April 10, 1858. His remains were brought to St. Louis and were interred in Bellefontaine cemetery. As the casket containing all that was mortal of Missouri's greatest statesman was borne to its last resting place, more than fifty thousand people gazed upon the solemn scene. All business houses were closed; public buildings were draped in mourning and the flags of the city and harbor were at half mast. The State of Missouri has been represented in the Senate of the United States by several great men since Benton's time, but no one approached his mental stature unless possibly Carl Schurz.

Upon the return of the Missouri Mounted Volunteers under Doniphan from Mexico, a great celebration was had in the city of St. Louis, on the 2d day of July, 1847. Among others delivering addresses on that occasion was Senator Benton, whose address was as follows:

"Col. Doniphan, Officers and Men:—I have been appointed to an honorable and pleasant duty—that of making you the congratulations of your fellow-citizens of St. Louis, on your happy return from your long and almost fabulous expedition. You have indeed marched far, and done much, and suffered much, and well entitled yourselves to the applause of your fellow-citizens, as well as the rewards and thanks of your government. A year ago you left home. Going out from the western border of your state, you re-enter it on the east, having made a circuit equal to the fourth of the circumference of the globe, providing for yourselves as you went, and returning with trophies taken from fields, the names of which were unknown to yourselves and your country until revealed by your enterprise, illustrated by your valor, and immortalized by your deeds. History has but few such expeditions to record; and when they occur it is as honorable and useful as it is just and wise to celebrate and commemorate the events which entitle them to renown.

Your march and exploits have been among the most wonderful of the age. At the call of your country you marched a thousand miles to the conquest of New Mexico, as part of the force under General Kearny, and achieved that conquest without the loss of a man or the firing of a gun. That work finished, and New Mexico, itself so distant and so lately the *ultima thule,* the outside boundary of speculation and enterprise, so lately a distant point to be attained, becomes itself a point of departure, a beginning-point for new and far more extended expeditions. You look across the long and lofty chain—the Cordilleras of North America—which divide the Atlantic from the Pacific waters, and you see beyond that ridge a savage tribe which had been long in the habit of depredating upon the province which had just become an American conquest. You, a part only of the subsequent Chihuahua column, under Jackson and Gilpin, march upon them, bring them to terms, and they sign a treaty with Col. Doniphan, in which they bind themselves to cease their depredations on the Mexicans, and to become the friends of the United States. A novel treaty that, signed on the western confines of New Mexico, between parties who had hardly ever heard each others' names before, and to give peace and protection to Mexicans who were hostile to both. This was the meeting and this the parting of the Missouri Volunteers with the numerous and savage tribe of the Navajo Indians, living on the waters of the Gulf of California, and so long the terror and scourge of Sonora, Sinaloa and New Mexico.

This object accomplished, and impatient of inactivity, and without orders (Gen. Kearny having departed for California), you cast about to carve out some new work for yourselves. Chihuahua, a rich and populous city of nearly thirty thousand souls, the seat of government of the State of that name, and formerly the residence of the Captains-General of the internal provinces under the vice-regal government of New Spain, was the captivating object which fixed your attention. It was a far distant city, about as far distant from St. Louis as Moscow is from Paris, and towns and enemies, and a large river, and defiles and mountains, and the desert, whose ominous name portended death to travellers—jornada de los muertos (the journey of the dead)—all lay between you. It was a perilous enterprise, and a discouraging one for a thousand men, badly equipped, to contemplate. No matter. Danger and hardship lent it a charm, and the adventurous march was resolved on, and the execution commenced. First, the ominous desert was passed, its character vindicating its title to its mournful appellation—an arid plain of ninety miles, strewed with bones of animals, perished of hunger and thirst; little hillocks of stone and the solitary cross, erected by pious hands, marking the spot where some Christian had fallen, victim of the savage, of the robber, or of the desert itself—no water, no animal life, no sign of habitation. There the Texas prisoners, driven by the cruel Salazar, had met their direst sufferings, unrelieved, as in other parts of their march in the settled portions of the country, by the compassionate ministrations (for where is it that woman is not compassionate?) of the pitying women. The desert was passed and the place for crossing the river approached. A little arm of the river, Brazito, made out from its side. There the enemy in superior numbers, and confident in cavalry and artillery, undertook to bar the way. Vain pretension! Their discovery, attack and rout were about simultaneous operations. A few minutes did the work. And in this way our Missouri Volunteers of the Chihuahua column spent their Christmas day of the year 1846.

The victory of the Brazito opened the way to the crossing of the river Del Norte, and to admission into the beautiful little town of the Paso del Norte, where a neat cultivation, a comfortable people, and vineyards and a hospitable reception offered the rest and refreshment, which toils and dangers and victory had won.

You rested there until artillery was brought down from Santa Fé, but the pretty town of the Paso del Norte, with all its enjoyments, and they were many, and the greater for the place in which they were found, was not a Capua to the men from Missouri. You moved forward in February, and the battle of Sacramento, one of the military marvels of the age, cleared the road to Chihuahua, which was entered without further resistance. It had been entered once before by a detachment of American troops, but under circumstances how different! In the year 1807, Lieut. Pike and his thirty brave men, taken prisoners on the head of the Rio del Norte, had been marched captives into the city of Chihuahua; in the year 1847, Doniphan and his men entered it as conquerors. The paltry triumph of a Captain-General over a Lieutenant was effaced in the triumphal entrance of a thousand Missourians into the grand and ancient capital of all the internal provinces, and old men, still alive, could remark the grandeur of the American spirit under both events—the proud and lofty bearing of the captive thirty, the mildness and moderation of the conquering thousand.

Chihuahua was taken, and responsible duties, more delicate than those of arms, were to be performed. Many American citizens were there engaged in trade; much American property was there. All this was to be protected, both lives and property, and by peaceful arrangement, for the command was too small to admit of division and of leaving a garrison. Conciliation and negotiation were resorted to, and successfully. Every American interest was provided for and placed under the safeguard, first, of good-will, and next, of guarantees not to be violated with impunity.

Chihuahua gained, it became, like Santa Fé, not the terminating point of a long expedition, but the beginning point of a new one. General Taylor was somewhere, no one knew exactly where, but some seven or eight hundred miles towards the other side of Mexico. You had heard that he had been defeated, that Buena Vista had not been a good prospect to him. Like good Americans, you did not believe a word of it, but, like good soldiers, you thought it best to go and see. A volunteer party of fourteen, headed by Collins, of Boonville, undertake to penetrate to Saltillo, and bring you information of his condition. They set out. Amidst innumerable dangers, they accomplish their purpose and return. You march. A vanguard of one hundred men, led by Lieutenant-Colonel Mitchell, led the way. Then came the main body (if the name is not a burlesque on such a handful) commanded by Col. Doniphan himself.

The whole table-land of Mexico, in all its breadth from west to east, was to be traversed. A numerous and hostile population in towns, treacherous Comanches in the mountains, were to be passed. Everything was to be self-provided—provisions, transportation, fresh horses for remounts, and even the means of victory—and all without a military chest, or even an empty box, in which government gold had ever reposed. All was accomplished. Mexican towns were passed in order and quiet, plundering Comanches were punished, means were obtained from traders to liquidate indispensable contributions, and the wants that could not be supplied were endured like soldiers of veteran service.

I say the Comanches were punished. And here presents itself an episode of novel, extraordinary, and romantic kind—Americans chasing savages for plundering people whom they themselves came to conquer, and forcing the restitution of captives and plundered property. A strange story this to tell in Europe— where backwoods character—Western character—is not yet completely known. But to the facts. In the mesquite forest of the Bolson de Mapima, and in the sierras around the beautiful town and fertile district of Parras, and in all the open country for hundreds of miles round about, the savage Comanches have held dominion ever since the usurper, Santa Ana, disarmed the people, and sally forth from their fastnesses to slaughter men, plunder cattle, and carry off women and children. An exploit of this kind had just been performed on the line of the Missourians' march, not far from Parras, and an advanced party chanced to be in that town at the time the news of the depredation arrived there. It was only fifteen strong. Moved by gratitude for the kind attentions of the people, especially the women, to the sick of General Wool's command, necessarily left in Parras, and unwilling to be outdone by enemies in generosity, the heroic fifteen, upon the spot, volunteered to go back, hunt out the depredators and punish them, without regard to numbers. A grateful Mexican became their guide. On their way they fell in with fifteen more of their comrades, and in a short time seventeen Comanches killed out of sixty-five, eighteen captives restored to their families and three hundred and fifty head of cattle recovered for their owners, was the fruit of this sudden and romantic episode.

Such noble conduct was not without its effect on the minds of the astonished Mexicans. An official document from the prefect of the place to Captain Reid, leader of this detachment, attests the verity of the fact and the gratitude of the Mexicans, and constitutes a trophy of a new kind in the annals of war. Here it is in the original Spanish and I will read it off in English. It is officially dated from the prefecture of the Department of Parras, signed by the prefect, Jose Ignacio Arrabe, and addressed to Capt. Reid, the 18th of May, and says: 'At the first notice that the barbarians, after killing many and taking captives, were returning to their haunts, you generously and bravely offered, with fifteen of your subordinates, to fight them on their crossing by the Pozo, executing this enterprise with celerity, address and bravery worthy of all eulogy, and worthy of the brilliant issue which all celebrate. You recovered many animals and much plundered property, and eighteen captives were restored to liberty and to social enjoyments, their souls overflowing with a lively sentiment of joy and gratitude, which all the inhabitants of this town equally breathe, in favor of their generous deliverers and their valiant chief. The half of the Indians killed in the combat and those which were wounded do not calm the pain which all feel for the wound which your Excellency received defending Christians and civilized beings against the rage and brutality of savages. All desire the speedy re-establishment of your health, and although they know that your own noble soul will be found the best reward of your conduct, they desire also to address you an expression of their gratitude and high esteem. I am honored in being the organ of the public sentiment, and pray you accept it, with the assurance of my most distinguished esteem. God and Liberty.'

This is a trophy of a new kind in war, won by thirty Missourians, and worthy to be held up to the admiration of Christendom.

The long march from Chihuahua to Monterey was made more in the character of protection and deliverance than of conquest and invasion. Armed enemies were not met and peaceful people were not disturbed. You arrived in the month of May in General Taylor's camp, and about in a condition to vindicate, each of you for himself, your lawful title to the double sobriquet of the General, with the addition to it, which the

Colonel of the expedition has supplied, 'ragged as well as rough and ready.' No doubt you all showed title at that time to that third sobriquet; but to see you now, so gayly attired, so princely equipped, one might suppose that you had never for an instant been a stranger to the virtues of soap and water, or the magic ministrations of the blanchisseuse and the elegant transformations of the fashionable tailor: Thanks, perhaps, to the difference between pay in the lump, at the end of service, and the driblets along in the course of it.

You arrived in General Taylor's camp, ragged and rough, as we can well conceive, and ready, as I can quickly show. You reported for duty! You asked for service—such as a march upon San Luis de Potosi, Zacatecas or the "Halls of the Montezumas," or anything in that way that the General should have a mind to. If he was going upon any excursion of that kind, all right. No matter about fatigues that were past, or expirations of service that might accrue; you came to go, and only asked the privilege. That is what I call ready. Unhappily, the conqueror of Palo Alto, Resaca de la Palma, Monterey and Buena Vista was not exactly in the condition that the Lieutenant-General might have intended him to be. He was not at the head of twenty thousand men; he was not at the head of any thousand that would enable him to march, and had to decline the proffered service. Thus the long-marched and well-fought volunteers—the rough, the ready and the ragged—had to turn their faces towards home, still more than two thousand miles distant. But this being mostly by water, you hardly count it in the recital of your march. But this is an unjust omission, and against the precedents as well as unjust. "The Ten

Thousand" counted the voyage on the Black Sea, as well as the march from Babylon, and twenty centuries admit the validity of the count. The present age and posterity will include in the "going out and coming in" of the Missouri volunteers the water voyage as well as the land march, and then the expedition of the One Thousand will exceed that of the Ten by some two thousand miles.

The last nine hundred miles of your land march, from Chihuahua to Matamoras, you made in forty-five days, bringing seventeen pieces of artillery, eleven of which were taken from the Sacramento and Brazito. Your horses, traveling the whole distance without United States provender, were astonished to find themselves regaled, on their arrival on the Rio Grande frontier, with hay, corn and oats from the States. You marched farther than the farthest, fought as well as the best, left order and quiet in your train, and cost less money than any.

You arrive here to-day, absent one year, marching and fighting all the time, bringing trophies of cannon and standards from fields whose names were unknown to you before you set out, and only grieving that you could not have gone farther. Ten pieces of cannon, rolled out of Chihuahua to arrest your march, now roll through the streets of St. Louis to grace your triumphal return. Many standards, all pierced with bullets while waving over the heads of the enemy at the Sacramento, now wave at the head of your column. The black flag, brought to the Brazito to indicate the refusal of that quarter which its bearers so soon needed and received, now takes its place among your trophies, and hangs drooping in their nobler presence. To crown the whole, to make public and private happiness go together, to spare the cypress where the laurel hangs in clusters, this long and perilous march, with all its accidents of field and camp, presents an incredibly small list of comrades lost. Almost all return, and the joy of families resounds intermingled with the applause of the state.

I have said that you made your long expedition without government orders; and so indeed you did. You received no orders from your government, but, without knowing it, you were fulfilling its orders—orders which never reached you. Happy the soldier who executes the command of his government; happier still he who anticipates command and does what is wanted before he is bid. This is your case. You did the right thing at the right time, and what the government intended you to do, and without knowing its intentions. The facts are these: Early in the month of November last the President asked my opinion on the manner of conducting the war. I submitted a plan to him which, in addition to other things, required all the disposable troops in New Mexico, and all the Americans in that quarter who could be engaged for a dashing expedition, to move down through Chihuahua and the State of Durango, and, if necessary, to Zacatecas, and get into communication with General Taylor's right as early as possible in the month of March. In fact, the disposable Missourians in New Mexico were to be one of three columns destined for a combined movement on the City of Mexico, all to be on the table land and ready for the movement in the month of March. The President approved the plan, and the Missourians, being most distant, orders were dispatched to New

Mexico to put them in motion. Mr. Solomon Sublette carried the order, and delivered it to the commanding officer at Santa Fé, Colonel Price, on the 23d day of February, just five days before you fought the marvelous battle of Sacramento.

I well remember what passed between the President and myself at the time he resolved to give this order. It awakened his solicitude for your safety. It was to send a small body of men a great distance into the heart of a hostile country, and upon the contingency of uniting in a combined movement, the means for which had not yet been obtained from Congress. The President made it a question, and very properly, whether it was safe or prudent to start the small Missouri column before the movement of the left and center was assured. I answered that my own rule in public affairs was to do what I thought was right, and leave it with others to do what they thought was right, and that I believed it the proper course for him to follow on the present occasion. On this view he acted. He gave the order to go, without waiting to see whether Congress would furnish the means of executing the combined plan, and, for his consolation, I undertook to guarantee your safety. Let the worst come to the worst, I promised him that you would take care of yourselves. Though the other parts of the plan should fail, though you should become far involved in the advance, and deeply compromised in the enemy's country and without support, still I relied on your courage, skill and enterprise to extricate yourselves from every danger, to make daylight through all the Mexicans that should stand before you, cut your way out, and make good retreat to Taylor's camp. This is what I promised the President in November last, and what you have so manfully fulfilled. And here is a little manuscript volume (the duplicate of it in the hands of the President), from which I will read you a page, to show you that you are the happy soldiers who have done the will of the government without knowing its will:

'The right wing.—To be composed of all the disposable troops in New Mexico; to advance rapidly through the States of Chihuahua and Durango, and towards Zacatecas, and to attain a position about on a line with General Taylor in the month of March, and be ready to push on to the capital. This column to move light, to have no rear, to keep itself mounted from horse in the country, and to join the center column or cut its way out if the main object fails.'

This is what was proposed for you in the month of November last, and what I pledged myself to the President that you would perform, and nobly have you redeemed the pledge.

But this was not the first or the only time that I pledged myself for you. As far back as June, 1846, when a separate expedition to Chihuahua was first projected, I told the President that it was unnecessary; that the Missouri troops under Gen. Kearny would take that place, in addition to the conquest of New Mexico, and that he might order the column under General Wool to deflect to the left and join General Taylor as soon as he pleased. Again, when I received a letter from Lieutenant-Colonel Mitchell, dated in November last, and informing me that he was leaving Santa Fé with one hundred men to open communication with General Wool, I read the letter to the President, and told him that they would do it. And, again, when we heard that Colonel Doniphan, with a thousand men, after curbing the Navajos, was turning down towards the south and threatening the ancient capital of the Captains-General of the internal provinces, I told him they would take it. In short, my confidence in Missouri enterprise, courage and skill was boundless. My promises were boundless. Your performance has been boundless. And now let boundless honor and joy salute, as it does, your return to the soil of your State and to the bosoms of your families."[68]

[68]St. Louis Republican, July 3, 1847.

Carlos Beaubien.

CARLOS BEAUBIEN.

Charles Hipolyte Trotier, Sieur de Beaubien, was the son of Paul Trotier, Sieur de Beaubien and Louise Charlotte Adelaide Durocher, and was born in Canada, at Three Rivers. Several members of his ancestry became prominent in the affairs of Canada and this country. The first representative of the name in Canada was Jules Trotier, who was born in France, at St. Malod'lye au Perche, in 1590, where he was married to Catherine Loyseau. His son, Antoine, Sieur des Ruisseaux, married Catherine Lefebone, of which marriage there was a son, Michael, Sieur de Beaubien, the first of the family to be called Beaubien, Seigneur de la Riviere du Loup. The latter married Agnes Godfroy de Linctot, and, after her death, he married Therese Mouet de Moras. Louis Trotier, Sieur de Beaubien, son of the second marriage, married Marie Louise Robida Manseaux. Of this marriage Charles Hipolyte Trotier, Sieur de Beaubien, was born. He left the Dominion of Canada for the United States during the War of 1812, and came to New Mexico in 1823, in company with a number of French Canadians who were making investigations in New Mexico. Beaubien went directly to Taos, at which place, in 1827, he married Paula Lobato, daughter of one of the most prominent citizens of that region of New Mexico. Of this marriage there were born the following children: Narciso, who was killed during the uprising of 1847, commonly known as the Taos Revolution; Luz, who was the wife of Lucien B. Maxwell; Leonar, who married V. Trujillo; Juanita, who married L. D. J. Clouthier; Teodora, who married Frederick Muller; Petrita, who married Jesus G. Abreu, and Pablo, who married Rebecca Abreu.

In the year 1847 Mr. Beaubien traveled from Taos down to the Cimmaroncita, where he found Lucien B. Maxwell located. A company of cavalry of the United States army was also established there, the post having been built by Lieutenant Wilson, of the army, under orders from General Sterling Price, at that time commanding the military forces in New Mexico and governor of the Territory. It was at this time that Kit Carson constructed a home, about three hundred yards from the site of the military post, the ruins of which are still standing.

Prior to the coming of the American army under General Kearny, a prominent citizen of New Mexico, who was a collector of customs for his government on its northern frontier, the Arkansas, Don Guadalupe Miranda, had asked for a grant of land in northern New Mexico from his government, and this grant was made to Beaubien and Miranda, who had previously agreed to the partnership. After the grant had been made Miranda sold his interest to Beaubien, who, by the purchase, became possessed of over a million acres of land, the value of which at the present day, with its cities, towns and villages, railroads, coal mines and coking plants, approximates fifty millions of dollars. The grant comprised a tract of land larger than three states the size of Rhode Island. The grant was made by Governor Manuel Armijo, with whom Miranda was a great favorite, who was also well disposed toward Beaubien.

Beaubien died in Taos on the 10th day of February, 1864. During his lifetime, socially and in a business way, he was a great favorite. He took an active part in all public matters. He was appointed one of the judges of the Supreme, or Superior Court, by General Kearny, and presided over what was known as the third district, comprising the counties of Taos and Rio Arriba. He was commonly known as "Don Carlos"; was a great friend of Governor Bent, and had great influence among the people of New Mexico, which continued up to the time of his death.

Colonel Christopher (Kit) Carson.

CHRISTOPHER (KIT) CARSON.

Christopher (Kit) Carson, as he was known among Americans, was born in the state of Kentucky in the year 1808. He came to New Mexico about the year 1827, on a hunting and trapping expedition. From that time until the coming of the army of the United States under General Kearny he trapped and hunted from the Arkansas river to the Pacific Coast. He was well known to all the Indian tribes, and none was more familiar with their character, manners and customs. He was familiar with many of the Indian languages. No other white man was trusted by Indians and Mexicans as was Carson. He led the way for Fremont, and performed this service without military aid.

Some time before Fremont's first expedition was begun Carson traveled as far north as the state of Wyoming. On this trip he finally went to California, and returned to Santa Fé by way of Taos. Prior to the discovery of gold in California Carson guided a number of overland parties to the Coast, and during the war with Mexico he was commissioned to carry the mail from Ft. Leavenworth to the Coast.

When General Kearny left Santa Fé for California, and had traveled as far south and west as the Gila river, he met Carson and several companions returning from California. He induced Carson to return to California with him, and Carson participated in all the hardships of the journey.

Colonel Carson joined Kearny's command on the 18th day of October, 1846, and guided the small force to California, reaching that state on the third day of December. A scouting party under Carson's command captured some spies that had been sent out by the Mexican General commanding the enemy's forces, who informed Kearny that the Mexicans intended to attack them before they could join forces with the Americans then in possession of San Diego. Carson advised Kearny to evade this attack, as their horses and men were exhausted from their long march, and take another route. General Kearny, however, chose to attack the enemy without delay, and for that purpose ordered an advance at one o'clock in the morning. His troops were tired and hungry, and came upon the advance guard of the enemy before daylight. This guard slept, fully dressed, with their saddles as pillows and their horses picketed near by. The attacking force consisted of fifteen Americans, under the command of Captain Johnson, with Carson as second officer. The guard drew back into camp, and the party under Johnson and Carson was reinforced by Captain Moore, with twenty-five men. Moore ordered an attack upon the enemy's center, hoping to effect a division and create confusion in the camp. In the charge Carson's horse stumbled and fell, carrying the rider to the ground. There he lay until the entire command passed over him. As soon as they had passed he seized a gun from the hand of one of his men who had been killed, his own having been broken in the fall, mounted and rode on. Many of the men were mounted on mules, which proved unmanageable, and, although the enemy was forced to retreat a short distance, the condition of the Americans was soon discovered, and, turning back, what would have been nearly a bloodless victory was changed into a terrible slaughter. Thirty of the Ameri-

West Pueblo of Taos, N. M.

can force were either killed or severely wounded, and, although the main party of the Americans came up, the Mexicans fought with great courage. General Kearny, although severely wounded, remained at the head of his troops, hoping that two mountain howitzers which were to be brought up would help in forcing the enemy to retreat. But the gunners were shot down and the Mexicans captured the horses attached to one with a lasso. Some fortunate accident or ignorance rendered the Mexicans unable to use the gun, or greater slaughter of the American force would have ensued.

The Americans retreated to a rocky shelter near by, having only three officers left, and waited for the enemy's attack. Both sides were exhausted by the continued fighting, and neither was cheered by the thoughts of a decisive victory. The night was spent in burying the dead and attending the wounded.

The following morning the march toward San Diego was resumed, Carson, with a body of twenty-five men, leading the way. Towards nightfall, as camp was being prepared near a stream of water, the attack by the Mexicans was resumed; the Americans retired to a hill a short distance off. A fierce cannonade from a neighboring hill was begun by the Mexicans, but the battery was silenced by a party of Americans, who stormed and occupied the hill. They were without food, and there was only water sufficient for the men; the condition was desperate, and a council was held to determine what measures had best be pursued. Carson took part in this council, and volunteered to try and pass the enemy's lines and reach San Diego to obtain assistance from Commodore Stockton. Lieutenant Beale, of the United States Navy, volunteered to accompany him. The proposition was accepted by General Kearny, although none believed they would ever reach San Diego.[69]

Carson and Beale left the camp as soon as it was dark. They removed their shoes, in order to insure silence while passing the triple line of sentries which the Mexicans had stationed around the foot of the hill. Several times, as they crept cautiously along, these sentinels could have touched them with their rifles. Their advance was very slow, but finally they cleared the Mexican lines. For a distance of more than two miles they had crawled upon the ground, sometimes each hearing the other's heart beat, so deathly was the stillness. Through the thorny bushes and cactus they trod with shoeless feet. All that night and all of the next day and into the night they continued their journey. At last the challenge of the sentinel at San Diego was heard. They were taken into the presence of Commodore Stockton, their story was told, and at once a force of two hundred men was sent by forced marches to relieve Kearny and his men.

Carson was detained in San Diego, as without proper care there was danger of his losing both of his feet, so severely had they been lacerated. Lieutenant Beale was partially deranged by the hardships of the journey, and did not fully recover his health for more than two years.

Carson and Beale left California together, and crossed the country from San Diego to Santa Fé, bearing despatches for Washington. When they arrived at St. Louis he was entertained by Hon. Thomas H. Benton. Reaching Washington, Mrs. Fremont met him

---

[69]Lieutenant Emory's Account.

Home of Kit Carson, Taos, N. M.

at the station, declaring that her husband's description of him made an introduction unnecessary, and conducted him to her own and her father's house. Carson was lionized while in Washington.

In the spring of 1848 he was again sent to Washington, bearing despatches, and was the guest of Senator Benton. He returned to New Mexico during the summer.

During the following winter, 1849-50, the Indians were more than usually troublesome. On one occasion a party of them had stolen all of the horses belonging to some cavalrymen who were camped near Carson's home. An expedition was immediately organized, consisting of three settlers and the soldiers who had been robbed, under the command of Carson. Carson soon overtook the thieves, twenty well armed and mounted warriors. In the fight which followed five Indians were slain, and, recognizing Carson as the leader, whose prowess they well knew, the balance fled, leaving all of the stolen horses except four in Carson's possession.

In the summer of 1850, at Santa Fé, Carson learned that a number of desperadoes had volunteered to accompany two wealthy men as far as Independence, intending to rob them on the way. He collected a party, and in one hour from the time of receiving the information was following them. He was joined two days later by an officer of the army with a detachment of twenty men, and after several days' hard riding overtook the caravan and arrested the leader of the desperadoes. The owners of the caravan, Messrs. Brevoort and Weatherhead, when informed of the danger which had been theirs, were greatly surprised, and offered Carson a large sum as a reward for his services. This

Carson refused, but later, upon their return from St. Louis, the traders presented Carson with a pair of silver-mounted pistols, suitably inscribed.

The following summer, Carson, returning from a trip to St. Louis, met with what was perhaps the most perilous adventure of his life, subsequent to the close of the war with Mexico. An officer of the United States army had affronted the Cheyenne Indians by whipping one of their chiefs. The Indians were unable to avenge this insult upon the officer himself, but, filled with rage, were lying in wait for other persons traveling over the Santa Fé Trail. It so happened that Carson's party was the next one following. He and his party of fifteen were captured, and at a council of the Indians were sentenced to death. Many years before, while a hunter at Bent's Fort, Carson knew the Cheyennes well, but it seems that the party which had captured him did not recognize him as their old friend. The Indians had spoken in their own tongue, not knowing that their words were understood by the prisoners. Carson addressed them in Cheyenne, told them his name, and reminded them of his old friendship, and, after another council, they were released and immediately left for Rayado.

Carson lived at Fernando de Taos for many years. After he returned from California, and while General Sterling Price was in command at Santa Fé, Carson did all in his power to suppress the rebellious actions of a number of conspirators, among them Diego Archuleta, who sought to overthrow the power of the American government. Carson always believed that the Fr. Antonio Jose Martinez, of Taos, was the chief conspirator of them all, and was fully aware of the strong anti-American sentiments which the priest entertained. Carson seldom made threats, but on one occasion, at Taos, he said that nothing would give him more pleasure than a chance to kill the priest.

After the peace with Mexico Carson built a home on the Rayado, where he lived with his wife and his niece, Teresina Bent, afterwards the wife of Aloys Scheurich. It was while living here that a large party of Comanches, Cheyennes and Arapahoe Indians suddenly appeared before the house. Carson believed from their actions that they were hostile, and, calling his wife and niece into a room in the building, told them that he only had two shots in his pistol, and that the moment the Indians should succeed in entering the door, something he expected to happen immediately, he intended to shoot them both; but the Indians did not make the anticipated assault.

In the year 1854, Carson was appointed Indian agent for the Ute, Apache and Pueblo tribes. He held this office until 1861. In the preceding year Carson accompanied a party of friends on a trip from Taos to the San Juan country, in the northwestern part of New Mexico. While on this journey his horse fell with him, injuring him very badly. He never fully recovered from the effects of this fall, and it is believed that the injuries received were the cause of his death eight years later.

Carson was at Taos when the news reached the Territory that Ft. Sumpter had been fired upon by the Confederates. He immediately began the work of raising a regiment of native soldiers. The regiment was shortly organized, with Ceran St. Vrain as its colonel, and was known as the First New Mexico Cavalry, and was composed of citizens of the counties of Taos, Rio Arriba, Santa Fé and Mora. Carson was Lieutenant Colonel and J. Francisco Chaves the major of the regiment. It was mustered into the service at Ft. Union. St. Vrain soon resigned his colonelcy, and Carson became its commander. The regiment fought in the battle of Valverde, and after that fight a portion of the regiment garrison Ft. Craig for a short time.

In 1863, Carson led an expedition against the Navajo Indians. Several battles were fought, in each of which his command was victorious, the most notable being at Canyon de Chelly, Rito Quemado, near the San Francisco Mountains, and at Mesa La Baca. A portion of his command was mustered out at Albuquerque in 1865, the balance of his regiment afterwards constituting the garrison of Ft. Garland, Colorado, in which locality the Utes were threatening hostilities. Colonel Carson met the chief of the Utes near the present town of Alamosa, where a treaty of peace was successfully negotiated. This portion of Carson's regiment was finally mustered out of service at Santa Fé in the year 1867.

After the civil war Carson lived with Thomas Boggs, near the mouth of the Purgatoire river in Colorado. Here he built a home and established a small ranch. On this property he spent the remainder of his life, which was filled with suffering, and which he believed was caused by the accident received in the San Juan country several years before. His wife died on the 27th day of April, 1868, and Carson passed away on the 23rd day of May of the following year. During the last weeks of his illness he was treated by the government surgeon at Fort Lyon. While he was

Grave of Kit Carson, Taos, N. M.

reclining and smoking a pipe which had been given to him by General Fremont, he was stricken with a severe fit of coughing, expectorated a large quantity of blood, and holding the hand of his intimate friend, Aloys Scheurich, gasped "Good-bye, Compadre," and died.

Colonel Carson died a very poor man; in fact, he left his family almost nothing. He was utterly uneducated and when it was necessary for him to write his name it was with great effort that he accomplished the feat. He never used intoxicating liquor. He had none of the vices of the times in which he lived. He was one of the most generous of men. He was a member of the Catholic Church, having been baptized at the time of his marriage with Josefa Jaramillo. He belonged to the Masonic order and was a member of Bent Lodge, at Taos. There was no better rifleman on the frontier and he was known to have been able to toss a silver dollar thirty or forty feet in the air and strike it with a ball from his rifle before it fell to the ground.

Carson was buried at Ft. Lyon alongside his wife, but, as he had often expressed a desire to be buried at Taos, late in the year 1868 his remains and those of his wife were disinterred and taken to Taos, where they now lie in the cemetery of that place. Only one monument has been erected to the memory of this greatest of all American frontiersmen. This stands in front of the Federal building at Santa Fé and was built by Senator Stephen W. Dorsey.

Carson's word was as good as his bond. The men under him in the army rendered him implicit obedience. Carson was a small man physically, his forehead was large and his eyes expressive. He was possessed of both physical and moral courage and when he believed he was right nothing could intimidate him. He was a man of great intelligence, although uneducated, and often had the officers under him read to him, thus storing away in his retentive mind a wealth of knowledge that few of his time could equal.

Colonel Manuel Antonio Chaves.

MANUEL ANTONIO CHAVES.

It is peculiarly fortunate, in writing of the lives of the Spanish conquerors and the events transpiring in this section of America, that it is possible to trace the course of events with great accuracy, particularly in relation to genealogy. We are indebted to the records of the Catholic fathers for this great privilege. Looking backward for more than two hundred years, the historical biographer is not compelled to indulge in flights of the imagination, but is always safe, having at his command that recorded certainty of dates and persons which prevents those journeys into the regions of tradition and legendary fable so often pursued by many. There is very little of the mist of uncertainty connected with the history of the long line of descendants of those Spaniards who planted the cross of Christianity and civilization in this portion of America; but this fact does not detract from the interest of study or thought. The legendary fables of the Middle Ages are scarcely less interesting than the recitals of recorded facts found in searching the history of the Spanish speaking settlers of New Mexico.

Almost a century before the Pilgrims landed on Plymouth Rock the banner of Santiago had been planted on the walls of Zuni and in the valley of the Rio Grande. Long before Jamestown, in the City of Mexico, already rebuilt on the ruins of Montezuma's capital, 'floating about like corks on water,' were hundreds of unemployed soldiers of fortune, dashing cavaliers, men of rank and position, eager for conquest and exploration. The age was both heroic and romantic and finds no parallel in the history of the world, and each advancing age of our literature brings cumulative evidence of the delight with which the extraordinary events and circumstances surrounding the expeditions of the Spaniards into this country must always be regarded. The progress of these expeditions attracted the attention of the entire Christian world. The adventures of Cortez and Alvarado were the talk of the courts of Europe. The Spanish cavalier thought only of the renown and glory to be won in the infinite wilderness of the new world, just risen above the waves of the Atlantic. The accounts of the historians of the conquest of Mexico inspired a desire for further conquest. The popular literature of the period shows with what power the Spanish imagination had seized upon the thought of the great empire which had come to the crown through the arms of Cortez and his conquering hosts. For more than a century this enthusiasm continued, and those who came were not of the class compelled to leave their native shores, but consisted of representatives of the most wealthy and powerful families; men who cherished noble designs and great hope. Accompanying these cavaliers came the holy fathers, imbued with the strength of a holy purpose, endowed with a moral courage which was sublime.

It is the personnel of these expeditions that gives the charm to the story of the Spanish conquistador. Unlike the conditions which existed when the Atlantic coast was settled by the Anglo-Saxon, the Spanish armies were not recruited from the slums and by-ways of the great cities of the kingdom. In the ranks of their armies were found those who were high-born and nobly bred.

Such were the ancestors of Don Manuel Antonio Chaves, a lineal descendant of one of the Spanish conquistadores, led by DeVargas.

In the year A. D. 1160 the beautiful Spanish city of Chaves was in the hands of the Moors. For many years they had occupied and held it against the constant endeavors of the Spanish king, Don Alonzo Enriquez, to restore it to his crown. It remained for two cousins of the king to subjugate the Moorish occupants. They were Garci Lopez and Ruiz Lopez, who raised an army in Portugal, and besieged the city. These young men were intrepid warriors and, after repeated assaults upon the city's walls, it fell into the hands of these young captains. The city had five gates, and, in the final assault, thousands of the Moors perished by the sword. Information of the downfall of the city was quickly communicated to Don Alonzo, who immediately visited the city, exiled the Moors who had survived, and gave the city to two brothers, who were also made knights of Santiago and ordered to add to their surname that of Chaves. This is the origin of the Chaves family name. On his visit to the city the king was accompanied by his queen and two princesses; all of these were present at the ceremony when knighthood was conferred upon the brothers, at which two fine Andalusian horses and saddles were presented and the golden spurs were placed upon their feet by the royal princesses' own hands.[70]

---

[70]Chaves es familia muy noble y antigua en Espana, cuyó nombre toma de la Villa de Chaves en Portugal, en esta forma: Garci Lopez y Ruiz Lopez, hermanos, ganaron esta villa ano de 1160 a los Moros sin ayuda del Rey, sino por

si los; y por esta misma memorable azana les queda los de
este linage el apelido de Chaves. Esto lo afirmo un letre que
permanece en el arco de la Yglesia mayor de dicha villa; que
dice:
>Dos hermanos con ai guinas
>Sin Rey ganaron a Chaves;
>Donde en Rouxo Cristalina,
>Les hoy dado por mas signas
>En su escudo cinco llaves.

Estos caballeros eran parientes muy cercanos del Rey
Don Alonzo Enriquez. En 1212 el cabeza mayor de la familia
de Chaves tomo parte en la batalla de las Naves de Tolosa,
como lo canto Don Luis Zapasa en su canto famoso:
>Son Chaves cinco llaves relucientes
>En hermoso escudo colorado;
>Su orla con ocho aspas excelentes
>De San Andres el bienaventurad.
>Por los que antiguamente de sus gentes
>Fue el lugar de Baeza conquistado
>Que su esfuerzo fue tal dia
>Y fue de Portugal su antigua guia.

De los caballeros dichos descendio Martin Reymundes de
Chaves, el primero que paso de Portugal a Castilla, antes
del ano de 1280, a servir al Rey Don Fernando IV, y a la
Reina Dona Maria, su madre, la cual ano de 1304, le envio
por su Embajador al Infante Don Enriquez de Castilla y
otros senores que habian ido a Aragon a jurar por Rey a
Don Alonzo de la Cerda, y hal andose en Ariza, hizo tanto
con ellos y estando el dia siguiente para jurar dicho Cerda,
deshizo el trato en la forma que leemos en la cronica del
Rey Fernando.

The foregoing is found in the Royal Archives of Spain,
at Madrid. The head of the Chaves family in Spain to-day
is El Conde de Caudilla, who is stationed in the royal palace,
and whose title is "Mayordomo de la Semana." The Grand
Duchess de Noblejas is his cousin, and in the middle of her
coat-of-arms is found that of the family of Chaves.

Don Fernando de Chaves,[71] whose full name was Fernando Duran de Chaves, and a son, Don Bernardino Duran de Chaves, were officers under Don Diego de Vargas Zapata Lujan Ponce de Leon. Don Bernardino had a child named Diego Antonio de Chaves, whose son, Pedro de Chaves, married Doña Catalina Baca, of Tomé, in Valencia county, New Mexico. A sister of Doña Catalina was the indirect cause of the massacre of nearly all the inhabitants of the town of Tomé by Comanche Indians in later years. Don Pedro de Chaves had a number of children, among whom was Don Julian Chaves, the father of Don Manuel Antonio Chaves.

---

[71]Translation from Diary of Diego de Vargas Zapata Lujan Ponce de Leon. In the New Mexico collection of Archives, now in the possession of the United States Government, Washington, D. C., and which were unhappily loaned to the general government for purposes of translation and chronological arrangement, with the understanding that they would be presently returned to the custody of the Territorial authorities, but which are now most indecently claimed by the general government.

December 1, 1693.

Entry into this town of Santa Fe, by said governor and captain-general:

On the sixteenth day of the month of December, date and year above, I, the said governor and captain-general, about the eleventh hour of said day, made my entry into this town of Santa Fe, and coming in sight of the walled village where the Teguas and Tanos reside, with the squadron on the march and in company of the very illustrious corporation of this town and kingdom, its high sheriff and color-bearing alderman, the captain, Don Bernardino Duran de Chaves, carrying the standard referred to in these acts and under which this land was conquered, we arrived at the square where we found the said natives congregated, the women apart from the men, all unarmed and abstaining from any hostile demonstration, but instead of behaving themselves with great composure, and on proffering to them our greeting, saying 'Praise to Him' several times, they answered 'Forever'; and seeing the approach on foot of the very reverend father custodian, Friar Salvador de San Antonio, and in his train the fifteen monks, priests and reverend father missionaries and the lay brothers of our father, St. Francis, chanting on their march divers psalms, I get down from my horse and my example was followed by the said corporation, corporals and officers of war and by the ensign of the royal standard in company with the said high sheriff and color-bearing alderman, all having gone out with the purpose of receiving the said reverend fathers, who, in union with their very reverend father custodian, came, singing in processional order, and when I made due obeisance as I was passing on my way to the entrance of said village and town, and the same thing was done by my followers, and in the middle of the square a cross had been raised, where all present knelt down and sang psalms and prayers, including the Te Deum, and in conclusion the Litany of Our Lady and the said very reverend father custodian, attuning his voice, sang with such joy and fervor that almost every one without exception was duly moved by the happiness of hearing in such place the praises of our Lord God and His Most Holy Mother. And after he sung the hymn three times, I offered my congratulations to said very reverend father and the rest, telling them that notwithstanding the last year, at the time of my happy contest, I had given possession to the very reverend father, President Friar Francisco Corvera, who was one of the fathers who came at the time as chaplains to said army, which said reverend father President had witnessed and accepted and in this manner and in the name of this order and in favor of his sacred religion would do it again and would grant it to him anew with great pleasure, considering the great resignation with which all, together with their very reverend father, do so heartily and freely agree to employ themselves in the administration of the Holy Sacraments in this said newly conquered kingdom; to which the said very reverend father answered, tendering his thanks for himself and all his order, and that by the use of said grant, invested and given by me, the said governor and captain-general, they had enough for the maintenance of their rights—much more than when they entered immediately in the administration of the missions above mentioned; and then I spoke to said corporation and told them I restored to them possession of their town and that likewise they ought and should give me, the said governor and captain-general, testimonials of having taken the same, entering again therein and of the pacification of said Indians and their submission to the Divine and Humane Majesty; in the same manner, to the said natives in the plaza of said village, I told and repeated what Our Lord, the King had sent me on the news I gave his royal Majesty of their surrender last year, with orders that this kingdom should be re-peopled; that with the information I had given of my having pardoned them and of their obedience which was the cause of said pardon, all his displeasure had vanished and he would call them again his children, and for that reason he had sent many priests in order that they might be Christians as they were, and that likewise he sent me with the soldiers they saw for the purpose of defending them against their enemies; that I came not to ask anything of them, but only for two things: that they should be Christians as they ought, hearing mass and saying their prayers, and their sons and women attending to the catechisms as the Spaniards did; and the second was that they might be safe from the Apaches and friendly with all, and that this was my sole object in coming, and not to ask or take away anything; and the said very reverend custodian assured them of my good heart and the good intentions which animated the Spaniards, which were not as they had supposed; that is I, the said governor and captain-general had come to kill them as they said, he would not have come, and so they should give no credit to anything but what I and their reverend father told them; besides I ordered them that if they had among them any bad and malicious Indian they should tie him up and bring him to me to ascertain the truth about what he said, and in case of falsehood I would order his instant execution, and that in this way we could live as brothers and be very happy; and after this talk we went away again, leaving them their village, to seek a more protected site, the soil being covered with snow, and only about

Manuel Chaves, whose full name was Manuel Antonio Chaves, was born in the town of Atrisco, on the west side of the Rio Grande, opposite the present city of Albuquerque, on the 18th day of October, 1818. His father was Don Julian Chaves, a great grandson of General Fernando de Chaves, the owner of the Atrisco land grant. His mother was Doña Maria de la Luz Garcia de Noriega, a daughter of Captain Francisco Garcia de Noriega. In 1844 he was married to

---

midday I found in the outflows and slopes a table land and mountain susceptible to some repair, and therein I, the said governor and captain-general established my camp, despising the dwelling place, a tower house which had been prepared for my occupation, having in the same a fireplace, which a resident told me belonged to said house and as such to himself; to which I replied he might repair to the same; and in testimony whereof, regarding said entry, I sign my name in company with the very illustrious corporation and corporals and war officers; likewise the two secretaries who were present therein in said town.

 (Seal) Dated Ut Supra.
    DIEGO DE VARGAS ZAPATA
     LUJAN PONCE DE LEON.
    LORENZO DE MADRID.
    FERNANDO DE CHAVES.
    J. DE LEYBA.
    LAZARO DE MESQUIA.
    ROQUE MADRID.
    JOSEPH MIERA.
    XAVIER DE ORTEGA.
     Secretary of the Town Corporation.
    JUAN DE ALMAZAN.
  Before me: ANTONIO DE BALVERDE,
    Secretary of Gov. and War.
I attest the above:
  ALFONZO RAEL DE AGUILAR,
    One of the Secretaries of Gov. and War of the Governor and Captain-General."

Doña Vincenta Labadie, a great grand-daughter of the famous captain, Sebastian Martin. He died at his home, at San Mateo, Valencia county, New Mexico, in 1889, leaving a family of eight children. Manuel Chaves was descended from a long line of intrepid warriors and, by nature, was a leader of men. When very young the family moved from Atrisco to Cebolleta, where he lived until 1831, when he took up his residence in the Villa de Santa Fé. When sixteen years of age he took part in his first Indian campaign against the Navajos. His oldest brother, Don Jose Chaves, organized a company of fifty young men for the campaign and Don Jose was made commander. In those days all the savage tribes were at war and many were the murders committed by them in their merciless raids. Many Mexican children were carried into captivity. The settlers, by way of retaliation and the infliction of punishment upon the Indians, in their campaigns into the Indian country, would also take captive children, bring them to the settlements, where they would either be sold or retained as servants. These captives were always treated with the greatest kindness by the Mexicans.

The expedition, of which Chaves was a member, was composed of picked men, and the hopes of its members for a successful issue ran high, expecting, as they, did, to return, bringing droves of horses and sheep and numerous captives, which last, at this time, were worth five hundred dollars each. A terrible fate, however, awaited them. Having travelled many days, and expecting to find the Navajos scattered all over their country, as was their custom, as they lived in bands, the expedition arrived at the Cañon de Chélly, where thousands of Indians were gathered, holding great feasts and ceremonial dances. The Mexicans were soon discovered by the Indians and, in the terrific battle which ensued, lasting all day, every one of the expedition was either killed or wounded. Only two survived—Manuel Chaves and a civilized Navajo boy, who had accompanied the expedition from Cebolleta, where he had been raised by a prominent Mexican family. Chaves had seven arrow wounds, one arrow having pierced his body through and through; the boy was also wounded in the breast, but not so severely as to prevent his hiding in the rocks of the cañon. When night came the Indians moved to their camps, believing that every one of their enemies had been slain. After much effort Chaves succeeded in finding the dead body of his brother, which, with the aid of the boy, he carried to a nearby arroyo and buried in the sand. Finally the two young men started on their journey to the settlement at Cebolleta; all night and the following day they travelled, arriving on the morning of the second day at a beautiful spring of clear, sweet water, situate where now is located Fort Wingate, New Mexico. They had been without food or water since the beginning of the battle three days before. Chaves removed his clothing and took a bath in the cold water of the pool near the spring, and his wounds bled freely. The Indian boy would not get into the water, fearing that the result would be bad for his wound. Instead, he took some *carnaza* from the inside of his moccasins and attempted to dress the wound in his breast. Starvation seemed to be their lot, when they found some very large cactus, and stripping the thorns, made an excellent meal. That night the pair slept in a grove of trees not far from the spring, and, when daylight came, Chaves, much to his surprise, found the Indian boy dead and his body very badly swollen. Covering the boy's body with brush, Chaves proceeded on his way alone, traveling for two days and nights with no food except cactus. On the morning of the third day he came across some fresh moccasin tracks, which led him to a large rock, which he managed to climb, where, to his great surprise and satisfaction, he found a big hole, full of water. The day following he came to the lovely valley where San Mateo is now located and passed the night under two beautiful oak trees.[72]

The next day he noticed some smoke on top of the San Mateo Mountains, and later found some Mexican shepherds, who prepared a litter and carried him to the town of Cebolleta. He continued living in Cebolleta for several years and became renowned as an Indian fighter, leading many successful expeditions against the savage foes. About 1837, he took up his residence in Santa Fé, where he lived for many years, and where, with the Pinos and other leaders, he figured very prominently in the history of the Capital.

In 1841, when Manuel Armijo was governor of New Mexico, news was brought to Santa Fé that a large party of Americans were traveling through the eastern portion of New Mexico and at the time were in the vicinity of Anton Chico, on the Pecos river.

---

[72]In 1876, Chaves moved from the Pecos river, where he was then living, to San Mateo, and built his home within one hundred feet of the oak trees. Immediately back of these trees he built a family chapel, in which his remains lie buried together with those of his wife and children who have died.

The governor was advised that the men were armed and were not traders similar to those who traveled over the Santa Fé trail from the Missouri river. Armijo very wisely came to the conclusion that they were Texans bent upon asserting the claim of the Texas Republic to all that portion of New Mexico lying east of the Rio Grande. Calling together his military staff, a council was held and it was determined to immediately apprehend the invaders. Diego Archuleta and Manuel Chaves were ordered to organize a force of one hundred men, with instructions to proceed to the camp of the American force and bring them to the capital dead or alive. No time was lost by Chaves in organizing this command, and, well armed, they left the Capital for Anton Chico, and soon learned that the Americans were in camp not far from San Jose, at a place called Cañon Largo, situate in a dense forest. During the night they surrounded the camp of the Americans, and, at daylight the following morning, Chaves posted his men in convenient places and walked into the camp where breakfast was being prepared. He went unarmed. Being familiar with the English language, he saluted them in that tongue and asked for the leader of the party. As he spoke, a fine looking young man came from a tent and announced that he was the commander of the party and that his name was Cooke. Chaves then explained to him that, acting under the orders of the governor of New Mexico, they had come from Santa Fé for the purpose of taking them to the Capital as prisoners, and explained further the belief entertained by Governor Armijo as to their motive in coming to New Mexico. Cooke protested that they were simply traveling as friends on pleasure and hunting, and this being the case, he did not see any good reason for their being molested; that they were well armed, on account of the Indians, and asked what would be done in the event he refused to surrender. Chaves then gave a call and in a moment his men approached the camp from all directions, rifles in hand. Chaves informed Cooke that he and his men would be well treated on the trip to Santa Fé and, after receiving their arms, proceeded at once to the Capital, where, on their arrival, they were turned over to Governor Armijo. The Governor gave the entire party in charge of Captain Damásio Salazar, an officer in the Mexican army. Chaves and Cooke became very friendly during the march to Santa Fé, and, upon application to Governor Armijo, Cooke became the guest of Chaves at his home in Santa Fé until the entire party were ordered sent to the City of Mexico by Armijo, who fully believed that he had captured the advance guard of an army of conquest and occupation from the Republic of Texas. Cooke made many friends in Santa Fé, who parted with him with great regret. Chaves and Archuleta received the cross of honor from the Mexican Government on account of their services in this exploit.

Chaves was a resident of Santa Fé when the army under General Kearny took possession of the city and territory. He was one of the officers under Armijo, in command of the volunteer forces at Apache pass, and was in favor of a defense of the position taken by the Mexican troops in the narrow defile through which the Kearny column was expected to pass.

In December, 1846, rumors were current in certain circles in Santa Fé that a conspiracy was being formed by certain Mexican leaders looking to the overthrow of the government. Some old residents of Santa Fé, who had come from the United States long before the Mexican war, informed General Price, who was in command of the American army at Santa Fé, that there was no doubt that the Americans would be attacked when they least expected it, and that most of them would be killed. Information of the same sort was brought to Donaciano Vigil, the secretary of the Territory, by a woman of shady character named Tules Barcelona. Steps were immediately taken by the military to suppress the outbreak and twelve or fifteen prominent Mexicans were taken into custody, while others, more prominently connected with the affair, made good their escape. Among those arrested by General Price were Manuel Chaves, and his warm friends, Miguel Estanislado Pino and Nicolas Pino. General Price was advised to keep them in prison and all would be well, and also suggested that it would be well to have Manuel Chaves shot, as he was the most dangerous man in the Territory in case of trouble. Chaves and the Pinos were arrested while sitting under the portal in front of the Exchange hotel. Don Miguel E. Pino was the greatest statesman of his day in New Mexico. He was a venerable looking man and was respected and loved by all who knew him. He was kept in the military prison seven days and finally released. Don Nicolas Pino, a younger brother of Don Miguel, was the best looking man in New Mexico. He favored his father, Don Pedro Bauptista Pino, the only man who ever represented New Mexico in the

Spanish Cortes. He was a very large man, over six feet tall and weighed about two hundred and twenty-five pounds. Don Nicolas was kept in jail twenty-two days. Don Manuel Chaves was a small man, five feet seven inches in height and weighed about one hundred and forty pounds. He had steel gray eyes and light brown hair and a florid complexion. One day while Chaves was in prison, General Price sent Captain Angney to talk with him and ascertain whether he had any information of the conspiracy that was said to be forming all over New Mexico for the purpose of killing the Americans, and whether he was in sympathy with the movement and would co-operate with the conspirators if free to do so. Chaves said in reply: 'Captain, be kind enough to take my compliments to General Price and say that he has nothing to fear from me now. When Armijo disbanded the volunteer army at Cañoncito, I gave up all hope of being of any service to my country at this time, and my record as a man will show that I am not at all likely to sympathize with any movement to murder people in cold blood. Tell him also that if the time ever comes when I can be of any service to my own country, General Price will find me in the front ranks."

Enemies of Chaves finally induced General Price to order a court martial for his trial. This court convened in January, 1847, and Chaves, under a strong guard, was taken to Military Headquarters where the court was in session. He was charged with treason against the United States and Captain Angney was detailed to defend him. Captain Angney was a lawyer by profession and his defense of Chaves was masterly.

He contended that inasmuch as the prisoner was not a citizen of the United States there could be no treasonable act on his part, and that in being ready to resist the Americans who had taken possession of the country, was an exhibition of patriotism on his part and worthy of the admiration of all brave men, and that his own country would forever bear the stain of disgrace if it undertook, under any pretext, to shoot a man for endeavoring to defend his country in time of need. Chaves was acquitted and set at liberty. He retired to his home, immediately in the rear of the Guadalupe church in Santa Fé, and, early the following morning, was informed of the breaking out of the revolution at Taos and the killing of Governor Bent and other Americans at that place. Steps were taken at once by General Price to put an end to the revolution and to punish the insurgents. An "Emergency Battalion" was organized in Santa Fé, made up of citizens, with Ceran St. Vrain as captain. Chaves was offered a commission in this battalion by St. Vrain, but declined, and, having taken the oath of allegiance to the United States, marched in the ranks to Taos, an enlisted man. Don Nicolas Pino also enlisted and both took an active part in the battle of Taos. While the battle was in progress Chaves and St. Vrain were fighting side by side, when two Indians came running toward them on horseback, evidently looking for a hand to hand conflict. As they approached, Chaves raised his rifle and fired; St. Vrain expected to shoot the other Indian, but, at the very moment of taking aim, a big Apache Indian jumped from behind some cedars and grabbed St. Vrain's rifle; a fierce struggle followed; St. Vrain called to Chaves to kill the Indian who was coming on horseback, as he would handle the Apache. Chaves had killed the Indian at whom he had fired his first shot and his companion turned and fled. Chaves then ran to the assistance of St. Vrain and struck the Apache a terrific blow on the head with his "Hawkins" rifle. The Indian fell dead across the legs of St. Vrain, who was completely exhausted and in another moment the Indian would have taken his life with an immense knife which he had been trying to use. From that day St. Vrain and Chaves were the greatest of friends.

Chaves was a wonderful shot with the rifle and bow and arrow. No Indian was ever found who could shoot an arrow as far as he. While he lived in Santa Fé many parties of Indians were accustomed to come to the city for the purpose of shooting with him and wagering horses, blankets and buckskin on the result, but they were invariably defeated.

In 1855, the Utes and Apaches of the North went on the war path and many settlers were killed. The military authorities determined to send an army to suppress them. For this purpose a battalion of mounted volunteers was called into service by General Garland, at that time in command of the Department of New Mexico, with headquarters at Santa Fé. Colonel Ceran St. Vrain was placed in command of the battalion and Manuel Chaves was a captain of one of the six companies comprising the command. Alexander McDowell McCook was the Quartermaster of the expedition. He was then a young lieutenant and afterwards became a Major-General during the Civil War. William Craig and Smith H. Simpson were officers in this expedition.

This expedition left Santa Fé and traveled to the north as far as a place known as Saguache, where the Utes and Apaches in great numbers were in camp. Scouts had advised the main body of the Indians of the approach of the troops, and, as the latter came in view, from the forest came the Indian charge, all mounted, wearing war bonnets, and carrying shields and lances. There were hundreds of the painted savages, and the attack turned into a hand-to-hand conflict. A young Apache chief rode to and fro, yelling at the top of his voice, and encouraging his warriors at every hand. This chief, with lance in hand, boldly charged upon Captain Chaves, who killed him with a shot from his unerring rifle; before the Indian had fallen from his horse he was dragged to the ground by Antonio Tapia and scalped with a knife, which afterwards came into the possession of Major Weightman, and was used by him when he killed Felix X. Aubrey in the Exchange hotel, at Santa Fé. The Indians finally turned and fled, having suffered great loss. Following this battle, were fought those of Cochotopa, Poncha Pass, Nepesta, Cerro Blanco and El Rito, in all of which the troops were victorious. [73]In

---

[73]"Company D New Mexico Mounted Volunteers.
Head of San Luis Valley, New Mexico, April 30, 1855.
Col. Fauntleroy.
Sir: I have the pleasure in reporting to you that after I received your order through Lieutenant Magruder, A. A. G., to burn everything that was left by the Utes, I burned a great number of shields, bows and arrows, buck-skins and other things not worth mentioning. In the meantime, I marched up to the mountains and above the camp to the right, close to the Arkansas river, and counted forty bodies of dead Indians within about three miles of the camp where we had the fight. My company found 29 horses and one

the month of July, 1855, the surviving chiefs came to Santa Fé and asked for peace, and, in August of that year, a treaty was signed.

In 1859, the Southern Apaches began the commission of many depredations, and many settlers and travelers were murdered by marauding bands, chiefly under the leadership of the great Apache Chief, Mangas Coloradas.

Colonel Loring, a hero of the Mexican War, was, at that time, in command of the Department of New Mexico. He determined to lead, in person, a campaign against the Apaches. He requested Captain Chaves to raise a company of volunteers to accompany him. This was done by Chaves in five days. The expedition was composed of several companies of regulars and the volunteers, under Captain Chaves. Traveling south, on the Jornado del Muerto, the command crossed the trail of a very large band of Indians. Colonel Loring called a council of his officers to determine upon the best plan of pursuit. Many opinions were expressed, and finally Loring asked Chaves what, in his judgment, was the best plan. "Colonel," said Chaves, "I am a soldier, and came here to obey orders, but now that I am asked my opinion, I think there is only one way, and that is to follow them Indian fashion, traveling day and night, make no fires, and eating what we can without cooking. They know we are on their trail, and unless we move rapidly they

---

mule. I do not doubt that the Indians that got away will die in a very short time, as the blood on the trail shows that they could not live long.

I remain your obedient servant,
MANUEL CHAVES,
Captain, N. M. Mounted Volunteers."

will be in Mexico before we get sight of them. If you will allow me to go ahead with my company, I know that I will overtake them." "All right, captain," said Loring, "if you can stand it, we can; go ahead." The pursuit began. Day and night they traveled the dreary, sandy desert wastes. Some of the men, exhausted, fell from their saddles; others fell asleep while riding; officers and men began to grumble, and, finally, Loring halted the command and the men took a night's rest, all but Captain Chaves, his half-brother, Don Romen A. Baca, Don Lorenzo Labadie, his brother-in-law, and Don Jesus Chaves, a close relative. These were all Indian hunters and scouts of experience. When they had made a close examination of the trail, Chaves came to the conclusion that the Indians were only a short distance in advance. Carefully and stealthily each man scouted and searched, and, within two hours, the Indians were located at the bottom of a deep cañon; their fires were so numerous that they could not be counted. Quickly Chaves and his companions returned to camp and requested Colonel Loring to order an immediate advance. The order was given, and before daylight the troops had arrived at the rim of the cañon, where the almost extinguished camp fires of the Indians could be plainly seen. The proper manner of attack was discussed by Loring with his officers, some advising that the command be divided, one part going below, and the other above the Indian camp. Captain Chaves stated that if this plan was pursued, before the bottom of the cañon could possibly be reached by the troops, the Indians would be far away; that the only way was to dash down the precipitous walls of the cañon, on foot, thus giving the enemy a complete surprise and kill or capture them before they could run away. Some of the officers opposed Chaves' plan as being too dangerous, a Captain Butler saying that it was a barbarous proposition, when Loring ordered Butler to take his company and go below and find a place for easy descent into the cañon. Turning to Captain Chaves, he said: "Now, Captain, I will go down the precipice with you." And down they went, spreading consternation and dismay in the ranks of the Indians; a great slaughter followed; Indian after Indian fell by the bullets that were fairly rained upon them. Colonel Loring only had one arm, having lost the other in the Mexican war, but with pistol in hand he was always in the lead. Many Indians were captured, among others the chief himself, the famous, bloodthirsty warrior, Mangas Coloradas. Chief Mangas was a very old man, with white hair, and was captured as he came out of his tent, rifle in hand. The troops were now in hot pursuit of the Indians who had fled down the cañon. Captain Chaves left a man named Johnson, a volunteer, with others, behind, to guard the captives. When they returned they found that Johnson had killed the chief, saying that he had done so while Mangas was endeavoring to escape.

The year following the return of this expedition witnessed the breaking out of the civil war. When the news of the firing upon Ft. Sumpter reached military headquarters at Santa Fé, Colonel Loring sent for all the officers in the several camps and posts in New Mexico to be present at a conference at Ft. Marcy. The meeting was held in the old Palace at Santa

Fe. He told the officers of the commencement of hostilities and stated that he had called them together that they might decide which side each would take. "For my part, he said, "the South is my home, and I am going to throw up my commission and shall join the Southern army, and each of you can do as you think best." Captain Jewett and several others, from the South, expressed the same sentiments. Colonel Loring called upon his old friend, Captain Chaves, and asked him to join him and promised that he would receive a commission as Colonel in the Southern army. Captain Chaves declined, saying, "Colonel, when I took the oath of allegiance to the United States, I swore to protect the American flag, and if my services are needed I shall give them to the country of my adoption and her flag."

The same year volunteer regiments were raised in New Mexico, and Captain Chaves received a commission as Lieutenant Colonel of the 2d Regiment, New Mexico Volunteer Infantry. Miguel E. Pino was colonel of the regiment. Colonel Chaves, with a portion of the regiment was ordered to Ft. Fauntleroy, now Ft. Wingate, where he remained in command until February, 1862, when the entire regiment, under Colonel Pino, proceeded to Valverde and took part in that battle on the 21st day of that month. After the battle of Valverde, Chaves and a portion of his regiment followed the Confederate forces north, and took part in the battle of Glorieta, some of his men aiding in the destruction of the Confederate wagon train at Cañoncito. After the war was over, Colonel Chaves returned to his home to find that the Navajos had stolen all his sheep, cattle and horses and left him penniless.

After Colonel Chaves had been mustered out of the army, the Navajos made a descent upon the valley of the Rio Grande in the county of Socorro, killing many people and driving off great herds of cattle, horses and sheep. They also carried into captivity a son of Matias Contreras, a very prominent citizen of Socorro county, who is still alive. Colonel Chaves was notified of the raid and Contreras asked his aid in recovering possession of his son. Chaves started with eight picked men and joined Contreras and Tomas Baca, of Socorro, and took up the trail of the Indians. After traveling about one hundred miles they came upon the Indians, who numbered over one hundred warriors. Chaves and his companions were mounted on mules, and as the Indians saw them coming they turned to give them battle. Chaves and his men dismounted and tied their animals to trees. From behind the trees also Chaves and his intrepid companions fought. At first the Indians directed all their efforts to the killing of the mules, picking them off one by one. The fight lasted all afternoon until dark, at which time every man had been killed by the Indians except Chaves, Contreras and Baca. Baca's leg had been broken by a rifle ball, and that night Chaves and Contreras carried him as best they could, until they found a sheltered place, where they expected the battle would be renewed in the morning. The Indians, however, left during the night. When this fight began Colonel Chaves had 183 bullets and plenty of powder; when night came he had just three bullets left. According to Colonel Chaves and his companions, over fifteen savages fell that day by Chaves' rifle. During the entire fight he walked from one tree to another, firing the guns of his companions, while they loaded his for him. One of the young men who lost his life in this battle was Jose Maria Chaves. All day he fought, was wounded half a dozen times, and finally fell with a bullet through his head. Colonel Chaves was not even wounded, although two bullets passed through his hat. The three friends left the scene of battle for the Rio Grande, and on the way met Captain Roman A. Baca, with a party of men, who had come out, believing that Colonel Chaves and his companions had all been killed. Colonel Chaves said many times that this was the hardest battle he ever fought.

Colonel Loring, after the close of the civil war, went to Egypt, where he was an officer under the Khedive. On his return to the United States, he wrote a volume of personal memoirs, in which he tells most graphically of his campaigns and services to his country in New Mexico and the Southwest. He writes most highly of his friend, Colonel Manuel Chaves, and says that, had "Chaves lived in the Middle Ages, he would have been a second Cid Campeador."

General Nicolas Pino.

NICOLAS PINO.

There were many valiant cavaliers accompanying the Re-Conquistador, Captain General Diego de Vargas Zapata Lujan Ponce de Leon, to the Kingdom of New Mexico in the year 1693, not the least of whom was Captain Nicolas Ortiz Niño Ladron de Guevarra. He was a most adventurous spirit, whom a restless love of enterprise induced to join the expedition under the great Spanish captain. The life of Ortiz is as brilliant and exciting as a fairy tale, and his remarkable adventures served to develop a bold and courageous character.

While yet a boy he had won the favor of his king by winning from the Moors the city of Guevarra, by which exploit he secured from his royal master the addition to his name, "Niño Ladron de Guevarra."

When the expedition under De Vargas sailed from Spain for the New World, having in view the re-conquest of New Mexico, Captain Nicolas Ortiz Niño Ladron de Guevarra brought with him his wife and family. His wife was named Maria Ana Garcia Coronado. There were several children, of whom the eldest was also Nicolas Ortiz Niño Ladron de Gueverra. The latter married Doña Juana Baca, and of the marriage there were three children, Nicolas Ortiz Niño Ladron de Guevarra, Third, Francisco and Toribio Ortiz Niño Ladron de Guevarra. The eldest married Doña Gertrudis Paiz Hurtado, of which marriage there were two children, Juan Antonio and Antonio Jose. The last named married Doña Rosa de Bustamente, the daughter of Don Pedro de Bustamente, Governor

MILITARY OCCUPATION OF NEW MEXICO. 311

of the Province of New Mexico, of which union there were five children, among them a daughter, Ana Gertrudis Ortiz Niño Ladron de Guevarra, who became the wife of Juan Domingo Baca. There were twelve children of this marriage, one of whom, Ana Maria, married Pedro Bautista Pino in the latter part of the eighteenth century.

Don Pedro Bautista Pino was probably the greatest statesman ever born in New Mexico under Spanish rule. He was the only representative to the Spanish Cortes ever sent from New Mexico. He went to Spain in 1810, and made a report to the King, written at Cadiz, November 12, 1811, which report is, for all purposes, a history of New Mexico up to that time. In his capacity as representative in the Spanish Cortes, he accomplished little, and after his return to New Mexico, a statement of his services abroad was embodied in a charming couplet, as follows:

"Don Pedro Pino fue;
Don Pedro Pino vino."

Don Pedro Bautista Pino was the father of Facundo Pino, Miguel E. Pino and Nicolas Pino, each one of whom was prominent in the affairs of New Mexico at the time of the coming of the Army of the West under General Kearny.

There are hundreds of descendants of Nicolas Ortiz Niño Ladron de Guevarra living in New Mexico to-day. Some of these, whose names will appear later in this narrative, were active in the political affairs of New Mexico at the time of the American conquest.

The Pinos were of the most influential residents of the Territory. All of them, time and again, held important positions, either by election or appointment, under the Mexican government. They were all of military spirit and were among the best educated men of the Territory. Indian campaigners, every one of them, each with a record of courage and daring unsurpassed by any of the great Indian fighters of that period.

When the news reached Santa Fé of the invasion of Mexican territory by the American army, the Pinos immediately responded to the call issued by Governor Armijo for volunteers, to resist, with all the means at their disposal, the American advance. They at once began raising companies and procuring arms and ammunition. Meeting at Santa Fé with Don Tomas Ortiz, Don Diego Archuleta, the Trujillos from Rio Arriba, and other patriots, they gave counsel to General Armijo and helped to concentrate the Mexican forces at the Apache Pass. Not one of them favored the abandonment of the Mexican position in the Apache Pass, and each viewed with manifest disgust the action of General Armijo in sending the volunteers to their homes and his own flight to the south. When the city was taken by Kearny, not one of the Pinos took the oath of allegiance to the American government, they, with others, considering themselves still citizens of the Mexican republic, loyal to its interests, although at the time practically under the control of the United States.

After the departure of General Kearny for California and Colonel Doniphan for Chihuahua, with their commands, and some time after the coming of General Sterling Price with the Second Missouri Mounted Volunteers, a number of Mexican patriots, unwilling, without an effective blow, to see their country conquered, never consenting to follow in the footsteps of others, prominent in the affairs of the time, who had subscribed their allegiance to the United States, and believing that the overthrow of the American forces was possible, began to hold meetings at which were discussed several plans for the accomplishment of this object.

These meetings were held at a house on the south side of the public plaza, near the place where then was located the military church, La Castrenza.

The 19th of December, 1846, at midnight, was the time first appointed for the commencement of the revolt, which was to be simultaneous all over the department. In the meantime each one of the conspirators had a particular part of the Territory assigned to his charge, to the end that the people of the whole territory might be enlisted. Only the most influential men, those whose ambition induced them to seek preferment, were to be made acquainted with the plan.

Those who were cognizant of this plan to overthrow the government, as has been ascertained from statements made by some of those arrested at the time, as well as from others who afterwards, when it was plain that their life and liberty were no longer at stake, freely made known the names of those who were thus engaged, were Don Tomas Ortiz, Don Diego Archuleta, Don Domingo C. De Baca, Don Miguel E. Pino, Don Nicolas Pino, Don Manuel Chaves, Don Santiago Armijo, Don Augustin Duran, Don Pablo Dominguez, Don Jose Maria Sanches, Don Antonio Maria Trujillo, Don Santiago Martinez, Don Pascual Martinez, Don Vicente Martinez, Don Antonio Ortiz, of Arroyo Seco, Don Facundo Pino, Fr. Antonio Jose Martinez, Fr.

Leyba and the Vicario, Juan Felipe Ortiz. All of the foregoing were related, either by blood or marriage. The Vicario, Juan Felipe Ortiz, and Tomas Ortiz were brothers, and were direct descendants of Captain Francisco Ortiz Niño Ladron de Guevarra. One can fairly estimate the far-reaching influence of this combination of patriots when it is known that the Vicario, Ortiz, was at the head of the Church, next to the Bishop, whose seat was in the city of Durango. Exercising very little less influence was the Fr. Antonio Jose Martinez, of Taos, acknowledged by all to have been one of the strongest men intellectually in the priesthood and living in New Mexico at that time. The American military officers, as well as the civil officials, were never able to prove conclusively that any one of these churchmen was actually present and participating in the formation of the plan to overthrow the government, but, in later years, Don Diego Archuleta and the Pinos did not hesitate to say so.

The plan fell through, however, owing to information in regard to it having been communicated to Donaciano Vigil, Secretary of the Territory, by a woman of shady reputation, by the name of Tules Barcelona, who was the proprietress of one of the largest gambling houses in the Capital, and who was on familiar terms with one of the principal revolutionists. Donaciano Vigil immediately made known to General Price what had been told him, and a number of arrests by Price's officers immediately followed. Among those arrested was Don Nicolas Pino. Don Jose Maria Sanches and Don Augustin Duran were also among those apprehended. Ortiz, Baca and Archuleta made good their escape.

When brought before General Price and his officers, in the main room of the Old Palace, Don Jose Maria Sanches made confession of his part in the conspiracy and told of the meetings and the action taken. He said: "Don Diego Archuleta was the leader at the meetings and made the motion for the nomination of a governor and a commanding general. He nominated Tomas Ortiz for the first office and himself for the second. This motion was carried and was signed by every one present."

This writing was hid above the ceiling in the house of the mother of one of the Pinos. At the meeting the entire plan of assault was determined upon and the 19th of December fixed as the day. Afterwards, owing to the fact that a sufficient number outside of the city of Santa Fé had not been fully notified, the day for the uprising was postponed until Christmas eve.

The manner in which Tomas Ortiz made his escape from Santa Fé, after the conspiracy had been detected, is told by close relatives.

Don Clemente Ortiz, now living in Santa Fé (1909), seventy-eight years of age, says: "I am a first cousin of Tomas Ortiz, the leader of the revolution of 1846. Many times I heard from him the story of the revolution. I also heard it from Don Miguel E. Pino. One day in December, 1846, Don Donaciano Vigil called to Don Augustin Duran, who was passing along the portal of the Old Palace, and said to him, 'What is the news?' 'I know nothing,' said Duran. 'Yes, you do,' replied Vigil. 'There is a conspiracy being organized against the Americans. A meeting was held last night by the leaders at the house of Manuel Pino. I know all about it. Another will be held to-night at La Castrenza (Military Chapel). It is intended to start a revolt against the Americans and to capture all the officers from the commanding general down. Emissaries have been sent out to all the nearest points demanding that the people come to Santa Fé and take part in the uprising. The night of the 24th of December is the time when it will happen. The people will all be advised that when the third bell rings for the midnight mass (Misa del Gallo) the men will leave the chapel and arm for the outbreak."

Duran and others were arrested by the military the same day and Duran also confessed at the hearing before the military officers.

General Price stationed his soldiers all over town and at the home of every one of the known revolutionists.

"One evening about dark, I told my father, Antonio Matias Ortiz, that soldiers were guarding our house. My father commanded the servants to lock the doors and fasten the windows. In the morning I heard some one calling at the door and went out to see who it was. A soldier asked me, 'Is Mr. Ortiz here?' and I answered 'Yes.' I then went into the house and told my father that the soldiers wanted him. My father put on his hat and cloak and went out, when the soldiers ordered him to march to headquarters. He was taken to the headquarters of General Price, which were located right where the new parochial school is situate in Santa Fé at this time. As the soldiers approached the headquarters, they met Captain Angney, an officer under General Price, who recognizing Don Antonio Matias Ortiz, told them to release him, as he was not the Ortiz they wanted. This same Captain Angney afterwards married Isabel Conklin, a sister-in-law of Clemente Ortiz and a daughter of Don Santiago Conklin, a prominent resident of Santa Fé at that time. Captain Angney had his own headquarters at the house of Francisco Baca y Ferrus. His home quarters were at the home of Domingo C. De Baca, one of the conspirators; this building is the one now owned by and in which lives Eugene A. Fiske and is just west of the residence of the Vicar-General.

"The Vicario, Juan Felipe Ortiz, many times asked my father, Antonio Matias Ortiz, to join the conspiracy, but he refused to do so. Don Miguel E. Pino also told me, at the time I was serving as a volunteer at the government post at Galisteo, in 1856 and 1857, at the home of Don Nicolas Pino, that the plan of the conspiracy, as drafted and signed by all the conspirators, was taken by Don Miguel E. Pino and hidden at the house of his mother, Doña Ana Maria Baca, who was the wife of Don Pedro Bautista Pino. It was hidden in the ceiling. It was never found. As to the manner of the escape of his cousin, Tomas Ortiz, Don Clemente says that after Don Tomas arrived at Galisteo, from Santa Fé, he rode by way of the Estancia valley through Manzano and Abo, across the Gallinas mountains to the junction of the Rio Bonito and Ruidoso, at or near the present site of Ft. Stanton, thence to the ford of the Rio Grande, known as the Ponce de Leon ford, and thence to Chihuahua.

Doña Isabel Cabeza de Baca, widow of Don Jose D. Sena, in her life time, in discussing the facts relative to the conspiracy of December, 1846, told of the escape of Tomas Ortiz from Santa Fé. Mrs. Sena was the daughter of Domingo C. de Baca, one of the conspirators, and her mother was Josefa Ortiz, a sister of Don Tomas Ortiz, the leader of the conspiracy.

Mrs. Sena says that the soldiers came to the house of the Vicario, Juan Felipe Ortiz, looking for his brother, Don Tomas. They decided to make a search of the store-room (dispensa), where they believed Tomas was hiding; when they entered the room the women all fled except Ana Maria Ortiz, who was watching some toast (costales de biscocho); in this store-room there was also a large supply of provisions, which that night was sent to Galisteo on pack mules, awaiting the coming of Don Tomas. Ana Maria Ortiz was the wife of Eugenio Archuleta, a brother of Don Diego Archuleta. During the time that the soldiers were thus searching the house, Don Tomas was hiding on a balcony facing the garden of the Vicar-General. When the soldiers left, he was taken from the balcony and dressed in the garb of a servant girl, and from his place on the balcony was lifted with ropes to the roof of the chapel on the right-hand side of the cathedral; he was then lowered into the garden and taken by Pedro Trujillo to the house of his mistress, a woman named Peregrina, who lived on the Arroyo Sais, above where the arroyo crosses Palace Avenue in Santa Fé. Trujillo carried Tomas Ortiz on his back and passed over a trail leading to the rear of where is now located St. Vincent's sanitorium. On the way to the arroyo where Doña Peregrina lived, Trujillo was met by a squad of soldiers, who asked him whom he was carrying, and he told them it was his daughter, who was very sick. They finally reached the house of Doña Peregrina.

Meanwhile preparations had been made for two horses, the fleetest of any in Santa Fé; these were stationed on the bank of the Santa Fé river, about two hundred yards from the house of Peregrina; after taking Ortiz to the house, Trujillo went to the river, where the horses had been brought. Shortly Ortiz came out, dressed as a servant girl and carrying a tinaja (water jar) on his head, evidently going to the river for water. As he was proceeding down the arroyo he was met by some soldiers on foot, who asked if "she" knew where lived a woman named Peregrina, and if so, whether Tomas Ortiz was at her house. Ortiz replied "yes," and pointing out the house, said, "Ortiz is there in the kitchen now." The soldiers then proceeded to the house, and Ortiz, picking up his skirts and throwing them over his shoulder, ran down the arroyo toward the river. As he did so, two Mexican women, standing near a small adobe house, shouted to the soldiers, "Haya va Tomas Ortiz, Gringos pendejos!" Ortiz reached the river, where with his friend, Trujillo, he mounted his horse and was soon lost to sight on his way to Galisteo, where he joined with Don Francisco Ortiz y Tafoya, who had been sent to Galisteo by the Vicario with fresh horses, money and provisions for his flight to Chihuahua.

Don Miguel E. Pino and Don Nicolas Pino did not take any part in the revolutionary movement afterwards. They had nothing to do with the outbreak at Taos, and Don Nicolas, after he was released from prison in Santa Fé, having been arrested while sitting in front of the old Exchange hotel, took the oath of allegiance to the United States and, when the news of the death of Governor Bent reached Santa Fé, enlisted in Captain St. Vrain's company of volunteers, and, with his friend, Don Manuel Chaves, went to Taos and took an active part in the attack upon and defeat of the insurgents at that place.

After the treaty of peace with Mexico, Don Nicolas Pino and his brothers were among the most loyal of the citizens of New Mexico to their adopted government. All of the brothers held many positions of trust under American rule, both military and civil. Don Miguel and Don Nicolas were both officers and in command of substantial bodies of volunteers during the war of the rebellion. Until their death there was no session of the legislative assembly but what some one of the Pinos was a member, either of the house or council. Don Facundo Pino was president of the council several times. He was president of the legislative council in 1861, at the time of the breaking out of the war. Don Diego Archuleta was president of the same body during the war, the sessions being the Thirteenth and Fourteenth. Don Miguel E. Pino was president of the council in 1865, and after the war was over, and again in 1866, Don Nicolas Pino was president of the council in 1869, and was a member of that body in 1873 and in 1878.

The first legislative assembly of the Territory of New Mexico convened at Santa Fé on the second day of June and again on the first day of December, 1851. The president of the council at the first session was Fr. Antonio Jose Martinez, and of the second session, Juan Felipe Ortiz. Both of these very distinguished New Mexicans, who only four short years before had sought the overthrow of the American power, were now among its most loyal supporters. Don Juan

Felipe Ortiz was the president of the council of the second legislative assembly, and his brother and co-conspirator, Tomas Ortiz, was clerk of that body. In 1853, Tomas Ortiz was elected a member of the legislative council from Santa Fé county and served with distinction.

Don Nicolas Pino survived all his brothers. He died in November, 1896, and is buried in the village cemetery at Galisteo. All of the Pinos were of noble mold. They were of a brave and chivalrous class. They fought the battles of frontier days and lived to see the changes which American progress and civilization have wrought. Don Nicolas was in his 77th year when he passed away. He was a man of large means. He was charitable and kind, as he was gallant and brave.

"How sleep the brave, who sink to rest,
By all their country's wishes blest!
When Spring, with dewy fingers cold,
Returns to deck their hallowed mold,
She there shall dress a sweeter sod
Than Fancy's feet have ever trod.
By fairy hands their knell is rung,
By forms unseen their dirge is sung,
There honor comes, a pilgrim grey,
To bless the turf that wraps their clay,
And Freedom shall awhile repair
To dwell, a weeping hermit, there."

David Waldo.
From a Photograph in the Possession of His Daughter, Mrs. Lula Waldo Sloan.

DAVID WALDO.

David Waldo was the Captain of "A" Company of the First Missouri Mounted Volunteers. The company was organized at Independence, Mo., and marched from that place to Fort Leavenworth, arriving on the 6th day of June, 1846, where it was mustered into service for one year on that day. The company participated in all the events of the march to Santa Fé and Chihuahua, and was mustered for discharge at New Orleans, La., on June 22, 1847.

The Lieutenants were: First, John Reid; second, David I. Clayton and Henry I. Chiles. John S. Webb was First Sergeant.

Captain Waldo was the son of Jedediah and Polly (Porter) Waldo, and was born at Clarksburg, Virginia, April 30, 1802. In his early youth he was engaged in rafting logs down the Ohio river. He came to Missouri in the year 1826, and went into the logging business on the Gasconade, floating the logs into the Missouri, thence to St. Louis. The revenue from this business sufficed to carry him through a complete medical course at Transylvania University, Lexington, Ky. After receiving his degree in medicine, he returned to the Gasconade country, where he lived for a short time, moving later to Osceola, in St. Clair county, and afterwards to Independence, Jackson county, Missouri.

He did not long continue in the practice of his profession, and soon after coming to Independence began trading over the Santa Fé Trail, and was engaged in mercantile business in Chihuahua and Taos, Mexico, as early as 1831. At the commencement of hostilities with Mexico, Captain Waldo had already amassed a large fortune in business. For sixteen years he had again and again traversed the old Trail, and knew all the people of New Mexico of consequence, socially and in a business way. To him was largely due the appointment of Charles Bent as governor of New Mexico by General Kearny. It is well known that General Kearny consulted Captain Waldo in the making of all the civil appointments, prior to his departure for California. Captain Waldo was a master of the Spanish language, and of most pronounced scholarly attainments. He was essentially a man of affairs, and, of all the officers under Kearny and Doniphan, was best acquainted with the citizens of New Mexico. Old diaries and records show him to have been identified with the business life of the Territory for years prior to, as well as after, the conquest. He assisted in the preparation of the code of laws promulgated by General Kearny and translated the code into the Spanish language. Whenever any papers or documents fell into the hands of Doniphan, they were always given to Captain Waldo for translation. He was a great friend of William Gilpin, the major of Doniphan's regiment. It was Captain Waldo who, in 1843, loaned Gilpin a part of the money necessary for his expenses, when Gilpin started overland and alone on an expedition from Independence, Mo., to the mouth of the Columbia river. Captain Waldo accompanied him as far on the trail as Lone Elm, where Gilpin fell in with the party under John C. Fremont.

During the march to Santa Fé and Chihuahua Captain Waldo remained the steadfast friend of Gilpin, and did his utmost to secure his election as Lieutenant Colonel of the regiment, upon the resignation of Lieutenant Colonel Ruff. The latter was a West Pointer and was not popular with the men. Gilpin was also a graduate of the military academy, and largely on this account was defeated in the election.

After Kearny's command had been at Santa Fé about a month, Captain Waldo and Captain Stephenson, with their companies, under command of Major Gilpin, were dispatched to the town of Abiquiu, on the Chama river, for the purpose of keeping the Indians in check in that part of the Territory. Abiquiu, for many years, had been an outpost against the Apache and Ute Indians. Later on Captain Waldo and his troop took part in the campaign against the Navajos, resulting in a treaty of peace with that powerful tribe.

Shortly before the battle of Brazito Captain Waldo was severely injured by a fall from his horse, but this did not prevent his active participation in the battle on Christmas day.

Shortly after Doniphan's command reached El Paso, a proclamation by Don Angel Trias, governor of Chihuahua, fell into the hands of the Americans and was translated by Captain Waldo, as follows:

"Soldiers: The sacrilegious invaders of Mexico are approaching the city of El Paso, an important part of the state, where the enemy intend establishing their winter quarters, and even pretend that they will advance further into our territory. It is entirely necessary that you go; you, defenders of the honor and glory of the Republic; that you give a lesson to these pirates.

"The state calculated much upon the aid that would be given by the valiant and war-worn citizens of the Pass, but treason has sown there distrust and the patriotic people, by disgraceful mutiny, retreated at thirty leagues distance from a small force under the command of General Kearny, when they might have taken him and his force prisoners at discretion. Subordination and discipline were wanting.

"You go to re-establish the character of those Mexicans, and to chastise the enemy, if he should dare to touch the soil of the state; the state ennobled by the blood of the fathers of our independence. I confide in your courage, and, alone, I recommend to you obedience to your commanders and the most perfect discipline.

"All Chihuahua burns with the desire to go with you, because they are all Mexicans, possessed of the warmest enthusiasm and the purest patriotism. They will march to join you at the first signal; the circumstances of the war demand re-enforcements; they shall be forwarded, let it cost the state what it may. To the people of Chihuahua no sacrifice is reckoned when the honor of the Republic is at stake.

"The enthusiasm with which you march, and the sanctity of your noble cause are sure evidences of victory. Yes, you are led by the God of Battles, and your brows shall be crowned with laurels. Thus trust your friend and companion,
"ANGEL TRIAS.
"Chihuahua, November 9, 1846."

At the battle of Sacramento, on February 28, 1847, Captain Waldo, at the head of his troop, dismounted, stormed a most formidable line of redoubts on the enemy's left, defended by several pieces of cannon and a great number of resolute and well-armed men. It was Captain Waldo's command that took possession of the battery on Sacramento Hill, which had been keeping up a cross-fire on the American right during the entire engagement. The fact that the Mexican batteries were compelled to fire plungingly upon the American advance accounts for the small damage inflicted upon the storming parties. This was particularly true of the Mexican battery placed on the brow of the hill.

When the force under Doniphan began making preparations for the evacuation of the city of Chihuahua the American merchants who had been engaged in business in that city were alarmed for fear the departure of the American army would leave them and their property entirely without protection. Just what arrangements were made by Doniphan looking to the safeguard of American interests in Chihuahua are related in a letter from Colonel Doniphan to Captain Waldo, after the return of the regiment to Missouri. The letter is as follows:

"Liberty 10 Jan 48

"Capt D. Waldo

"Dr. Sir.

"I anticipated being in your town to-day and therefore did not answer your favors as I knew it would be more satisfactorily and fully done verbally. In relation to the treaty or agreement made by the merchants of Chihuahua with the Government of that state I can only speak from memory—the agreement had not been consummated when I left the City— (Felix Mesceira not having returned) who had gone as agent for them to the temporal state Government. I first proposed to make a treaty for the merchants with the authorities at the request of Dr. Conelly, McManus, Glasgows &c & Dr. Conelly went to Parral & commissioners came up with him but the merchants by that time had come to the conclusion that a tremendous meeting & sundry resolutions would force me to stay there as long there was a shirt-tail full of goods in the City—when Collins came back from Genl. Taylor and they found I was ordered south they then began to relent & were solely grieved that they had objected to my making a treaty for them. They then desired me to do so—I refused but told them they might stipulate for their safety by making my immediate withdrawal with our forces from the State of Chihuahua & the payment of New Mexican duties the basis of the treaty on the American side. I gave Dr. Conelly a written statement & directed him to send it by Mesceira to the state authorities in which I stated that if a treaty was made that I would leave with our forces in a few days—that I would use my influence to prevent Genl. Wool or any detachment of his army from marching on Chihuahua—and the Mexicans having heard that some reinforcements were coming from New Mexico I was to leave a written order with Dr. Conelly directing such force not to occupy Chihuahua but to pass through as speedily as convenient. This I think was the whole of it—Dr. Conelly promised if Mesceira returned he would send the agreement to me for my approval—they never did so & I do not know what it was—further than my own guaranty.

"I regret that the Govt has been so simple as to send any troops there—surely no good & much harm may come of it & if I had known of such intention in time I would have protested against it.

"I regret to learn that Gilpin's Battalion has made so bad a beginning—I am gratified that he was absent & that no blame can attach to him—I hope they may have a better end—but there is little to hope from the Dutch in that sort of service.

"I send you a discharge for W. P. Johnson it is not very full—I thought it best to write it on the same paper with Genl. Kearny's & it would be all the better explained as I presume his object is his pay perquisites & land scrip, all of which he will get.

"Yrs respectfully,

"(Signed) A. W. DONIPHAN."

Captain Waldo was a man of sturdy character. In his business relations he was very exact. Of all the distinguished men in Colonel Doniphan's command, none suffered a severer personal loss, growing out of the events of the American Occupation of New Mexico than did Captain Waldo. For more than fifteen years prior to the coming of the Army of the West, had been associated with him, as well also in trading for himself, a younger brother, Lawrence L. Waldo, the father of Henry L. Waldo, of Las Vegas, New Mexico. The younger Waldo was of most exemplary habits, kind and courteous, the gentleman in all his social and business life, really loved by all who knew him. His friendship for the Mexicans and Indians was marked, and, like Governor Bent, he had every confidence in their loyalty to and personal regard for himself. Of the Americans remaining at

Santa Fé after the departure of Doniphan for Chihuahua, there was no single individual who better understood the Mexican character, or was in better position to ascertain the true sentiment of the Mexican people toward the American government. He was well aware of the discontent that prevailed among the ambitious leaders, who were convinced that General Armijo had been recreant to his trust, as the executive and commanding general of the Territory, in not giving the American army battle at the Apache Pass. The discovery of the conspirary of December, 1846, and the flight of the known leaders from the capital seemed to have lulled the officers of the army into a feeling of security, but, as a matter of fact, the discovery and arrest of a number of those most prominently identified with the attempt to overthrow the government only served to whet the desire of the people for some sort of protest against the manner in which the conquest had been achieved.

Leaving Santa Fé, in company with some other prominent traders, on his way to Independence, all unaware that the revolution had actually broken out, feeling secure personally on account of his many years' association with the Mexican people, just as his caravan was approaching the town of Mora, on the 19th day of January, 1847, he was shot from ambush and instantly killed.

Six days prior to his death, in a letter written from Santa Fé to Captain Waldo, then with his command at El Paso, awaiting the coming of artillery from Santa Fé to accompany the march on Chihuahua, he said: "It seems that a general mistake has been made by all that were acquainted with the *gente* of this Territory in regard to their willingness to be subject to the rule of the United States. It is satisfactorily ascertained that not one in ten is *agusto*, and, as far as I can judge, and I am well acquainted with the eastern side of the mountains, not one in one hundred is content." His estimate was only too true. Even those who had taken the oath of allegiance at Las Vegas joined the ranks of the insurgents.

On the first of February his death was avenged by Captain Morin and his men, in the complete demolition of the town of Mora. The insurgents fled to the neighboring mountains. Their loss was twenty-five killed and seventeen taken prisoners. The bodies of the Americans who had been assassinated were taken to Las Vegas and interred in the cemetery west of the old town on the right bank of the Gallinas river. Captain Waldo did not receive news of the death of his brother until the 16th day of February, when he was en route to Chihuahua, just twelve days before the battle of Sacramento.

A newspaper, the Reveille, published in Missouri at the time, gives the following account of the massacre of Governor Bent and others in the revolution at Taos and Mora:

"Mr. Thomas Caldwell, whose arrival at Independence was noticed yesterday, came down last evening on the steamer Bertrand, and to him we are indebted for later and more authentic information from Santa Fé. The accounts published yesterday, as copied from the Expositor extra, we are requested to state, are in many particulars incorrect, and were not obtained from Mr. C., but merely from rumor at Independence after his arrival.

"Mr. C., as stated yesterday, left El Paso on the 12th of January, and Santa Fé on the 3d of February. The massacre of Governor Bent, the Lees and others was perpetrated at Taos on the 18th of January, and immediately runners were sent out by the Mexicans to the different towns in the province, calling upon the inhabitants to assist in the murder of the Americans. On the 19th, the night after the murder of Bent and his companions, at Taos, Mr, Romulus Culver, of Clinton county; L. L. Waldo, a brother of the Doctor, and Benjamin Pruett, of Jackson county, together with five others, were killed at Mora, a town of some 2,000 inhabitants, and situated seventy-five miles from Santa Fé. After this outrage the insurgents, to the number of 2,000, collected at a small town called La Cañada, some twenty-five miles from Santa Fé. Col. Price, hearing of this, immediately went in person, at the head of 350 men, and drove them from their position, killing thirty-six of their number.

"This engagement occurred between the 20th and 28th of January, and was followed by another between Price and the insurgents, at Embudo, a small town in the pass of the mountains. It was understood that Price had again succeeded in driving them before him, but their loss in this latter engagement was not known. About the time of the battles between Col. Price and the insurgents at La Cañada and Embudo, Captain Hendly, of the Ray county volunteers, who was on the east side of the mountains, in charge of a party of graziers, hearing of the massacre at Taos and Mora, immediately repaired with about 90 men to the latter place, where he met with a large body of the enemy, and an engagement ensued, in which Capt. H. lost his life. After his fall, his men, under command of their Lieutenant, fell back on Vegas, and reported to Santa Fé the condition of things, and the probability of a well-appointed force being able to defeat the enemy at Mora. On receipt of this intelligence at Santa Fé, Capt. Morin, of Platte, with some 200 men, was despatched to Mora, and on his arrival the inhabitants fled, leaving everything to the mercy of the Americans. The town was burnt, and everything possible for the enemy to subsist upon was destroyed.

"Capt. St. Vrain, of Fort St. Vrain, headed fifty volunteers from among the clerks, attaches, teamsters, etc., of Santa Fé, accompanied Col. Price on his march against the Taos rabble. During the fight de Tafolla, who had on Gov. Bent's coat and shirt, was captured. None of the Armijos were among the rabble; they appeared to be all 'greasers,' that is, loafers. Col. St. Vrain killed a Mexican, one, Jesus. Among them one, Cortez, of Mora valley, was prominent. None of the St. Louis volunteers were with Price save a detachment of Capt. Fischer's artillery. The guns were mounted at Fort Marcy, and under command of Capt. Fischer. Donaciano Vigil, Secretary of State under Bent, was now acting Governor of Santa Fé.

"A great deal of sickness prevailed in town, but chiefly among the teamsters, broken down as they were. There were from three to five deaths per day. Albert G. Wilson, sutler of Price's regiment, had died. Col. Mitchell, Capt. Hudson, Adj. Walker,

Lieut. Elliott, and others well known, were all well. The troops had been discontented, but principally from inactivity.

"Mr. Charles Town, well known in St. Louis, was the only American who escaped the massacre. His father-in-law (a Mexican) gave him a good mule, and he brought the news of the disaster to Santa Fé. It has been stated that Bent was killed at noonday; this is not so; he was killed at night. It has also been rumored privately that Frank Blair was killed. This is another mistake. He was, at the time, in the mountains with Geo. Bent. Mr. Caldwell met Major Clark 120 miles below Santa Fé. At El Paso he left Col. Doniphan and command, all well. The Glasgows and the rest of the traders were well, but losing, from their necessarily heavy expenses. McGoffin was only detained at Chihuahua. Col. Doniphan would, beyond doubt, march on Chihuahua, but was not likely to be taken by surprise, as he was exercising great caution. The Santa Fé theatrical corps had gone south on a rather different campaign. Mr. C. met Lieut. Simpson at 110 mile creek—that number of miles from Independence. He had with him two wagons and ten men, conducting a heavy mail. There was snow falling on the plains from the 16th of February to the 10th of March, almost uninterruptedly. The mail which Mr. C. had charge of, he was obliged to leave on the Arkansas, and it probably would be detained ten or twelve days behind him. Mr. Sol. Sublette had not arrived at Santa Fé, and the presumption is that his despatches must have taken him, by the way of Bent's Fort, to California. Capt. Murphy had arrived at Santa Fé with the government funds."

Captain Waldo and his troop took part in the great parade in the city of St. Louis on July 2, 1847, after the return from the war. He was also prominent in the festivities occurring at Independence upon the return of his company to their homes.

In 1849, March 27th, Captain Waldo was married at Independence, Missouri, to Eliza Jane, daughter of Edward and Margaret (Glasgow) Norris, of Culpeper, Virginia, of which marriage there were five children, David and William Waldo, now deceased, Mrs. Minnie Waldo Hill, Mrs. Lula Waldo Sloan and Mrs. William Hinkle, all of whom are now living in Jackson county, Mo.

After the war with Mexico, Captain Waldo continued trading and freighting over the old Santa Fé Trail, also to Utah and the Platte river country, and was very successful in all his business enterprises. He died at Independence May 20, 1878.

Governor William Gilpin.

WILLIAM GILPIN.

William Gilpin was the eighth and youngest child of Joshua Gilpin, and was a direct descendant of the De Guylpyns who invaded Britain with William the Conqueror. His ancestor in America was Joseph Gilpin, a Quaker, who came to America in 1696 and settled on the Brandywine, in what is now Delaware county, Pennsylvania, at which place William Gilpin was born on the 4th day of October, 1822. During the Revolutionary War his ancestors took no part requiring service in the army. A brother of William Gilpin, Henry, was Attorney General of the United States, appointed by Andrew Jackson. In his youth William Gilpin attended school in England, but returned to America and graduated from the University of Pennsylvania. He had as tutor Nathaniel Hawthorne. After his graduation from the University Gilpin entered the United States Military Academy, where he was taught by Montgomery Blair and George G. Meade. Upon leaving the academy Gilpin was commissioned a Second Lieutenant in the Second Dragoons and was on recruiting service in Missouri for the Seminole War, in which, later on, he was an active participant. After the war was concluded, he made application to lead an exploring expedition to the head waters of the Columbia river, but was denied permission, whereupon he tendered his resignation from the army, which was accepted.

Gilpin moved to St. Louis, Missouri, where he was the editor of a newspaper, which espoused the cause of Senator Benton, the latter always remaining a great friend of Gilpin. In 1840 Gilpin was clerk of the House of Representatives of the State of Missouri and in the following year moved to Independence, where he lived for twenty years. Gilpin was an optimist in every sense of the word; he had unbounded confidence in the future greatness of the West and exerted great influence over others along the same lines. He foretold the present city of Kansas City and prophesied the construction of the Missouri Pacific and Union Pacific railways.

Gilpin never relinquished the idea of his exploring expedition to the Columbia river and, in 1843, sold his law library and other effects for the purpose of raising money to gratify his desire to make the expedition. He set out on this trip alone, having been accompanied a short distance along the Santa Fé Trail by his personal friend, David Waldo. At a point about thirty miles from Independence he fell in with the party under General Fremont. This meeting occurred on the 31st day of May, 1843. This meeting is described in Chronicles of the Builders of the Commonwealth, as follows:[74]

"He went into camp the first evening, out about thirty miles, at a spot called the Lone Elm, David Waldo, the man who had loaned him the money, accompanying him thus far. He found encamped in this vicinity a few men whom he did not at first recognize, but to his surprise they proved to be the party of Fremont. This immortal pathfinder asked Gilpin where he was going, and was told. He expressed astonishment and said, 'Why, even with my whole

---

[74]Bancroft, Chronicles of the Builders of the Commonwealth, page 522.

force, I do not consider myself safe from massacre to-morrow; now if you are determined to go on, throw your pack into one of my charettes, turn your mule into my band, and let me have the re-enforcement of your horse and rifle.' This arrangement was highly satisfactory to Gilpin, as it afforded him companionship and protection for a long distance."

The expedition reached the Coast in the fall. Here Gilpin remained for some time, learning all he could of the country and its resources. He made a report to Washington, in March, 1846, which was printed as a Senate document.

When the war with Mexico was begun he obtained permission from President Polk to raise a regiment, but, upon reaching Independence, he ascertained that a company had already been raised and had gone to Ft. Leavenworth to be mustered into the service. He at once left for Ft. Leavenworth and there found six companies of the 1st Regiment Missouri Volunteers. Company A of this regiment was composed of friends of Gilpin, who anxiously awaited his coming. Kearny was present and, as he did not feel kindly toward Gilpin, determined he should have no command in the regiment. Gilpin knew he would be elected one of the officers of the regiment if he could once get admitted to the company. He found in the Jackson county company a boy whose mother had claimed his discharge on account of his youth. Gilpin paid the boy eighty-five dollars for his place in the ranks. Otherwise he could not have enlisted, as the company was already at its maximum. Gilpin trained and drilled this company from the day he enlisted until the regimental election for officers was held. Colonel

Doniphan was chosen to command the regiment. The latter desired Gilpin for lieutenant colonel, but a graduate of West Point, named Ruff, was elected by two votes. Gilpin was then elected major.

After his election he was told that Kearny wished to see him in his office. He obeyed the summons and Kearny said: "I have received from the President an appointment for you as lieutenant colonel of the Third Regiment, and I suppose this is followed by a life service if you choose. Had you better not withdraw now and avail yourself of this appointment?" Gilpin refused to accept it and marched with the regiment to New Mexico and Chihuahua.

Upon his return from the Mexican war he was taken ill, and while confined to his bed was visited by Governor Edwards of the state of Missouri, who told him that, at the request of President Polk, he had come to ask that he raise a regiment of volunteers for the purpose of opening the Santa Fé Trail and maintaining it, as the country west was infested with hostile Indians. Gilpin, after much argument, accepted and raised a battalion, which was mustered into service at Ft. Leavenworth. Gilpin started west with his army on the 4th day of October, 1847. He followed the Trail, which led to Bent's Fort. Here he spent the winter, drilling his battalion, and sometimes holding council with Indian chiefs. The following spring an active campaign was instituted and, from the middle of July to the end of August, nine battles were fought and two hundred and fifty-three scalps of Indian warriors were taken. This battalion was known as "Gilpin's Battalion, Missouri Mounted Volunteers."

This force, under Gilpin, crossed the Raton mountains on the 10th of March, 1848, descended the Canadian through the country of the Apaches and Comanches during the spring, and fought many fights with the Pawnees on the Middle Arkansas and on the Kaw rivers, until the expiration of the term of service, when peace was declared with Mexico. The marches made exceeded three thousand miles.

When the election of 1860 was held, it is said that William Gilpin was the only man living in Jackson county, Missouri, who voted for Abraham Lincoln. He was one of the men who attended President Lincoln, from Illinois to Washington, for his inauguration, and it was upon this occasion that, under Senator Lane, of Kansas, and Cassius M. Clay, of Kentucky, he helped to guard the White House, sleeping in that edifice each night.

Gilpin was appointed Governor of the Territory of Colorado by Lincoln and served for two years, 1861-1863.

Gilpin was a great student. He wrote several valuable books. He predicted that a railway would be built around the earth by way of Behring Strait.

Gilpin was a tall man, spare built, and weighed in the neighborhood of one hundred and sixty pounds. He made a large fortune by prudent investment in lands in Colorado. He was a typical American citizen. He led the way. He believed in the future of the Great West, when such men as Daniel Webster declared that everything west of the Missouri was a worthless area, a region of savages and wild beasts, deserts of shifting sands and whirlwinds of dust, of cactus and prairie dogs. Gilpin was right. Webster and all New England at that time believed that it was worse than useless to reclaim these deserts or harness the waterpower of the rivers in the mountains. "What use have we for such a country?" said the great Webster. "I will never vote one cent from the public treasury to place the Pacific Coast one inch nearer to Boston than it now is."

Gilpin's ideas as to the great plains and the country to the west to the Pacific Coast are best understood by quoting from an address delivered by him in Cole county, Missouri, shortly after the return of the First Missouri Mounted Volunteer Cavalry from the War with Mexico, in which he said, in closing:

"Fellow Countrymen and Ladies—The soldiers of the first requisition from Missouri, excepting those who sleep forever beneath the shadows of the Sierra Madre, have returned to receive the greetings of their friends and kindred. We bring with us the spoil of the enemy as trophies of our victories.

"These assemblies, these crowds of fair women and brave men, these complimentary festivals and flattering words, resounding in our ears from every village and from every cabin, are the gratifying rewards of our efforts and our deeds.

"Thus are our long-suspended hopes and painful anxieties consummated by a deep and gratifying sense of triumph. So have we performed our task, and such is our munificent reward.

"Suffer me to say, as one elevated by their own suffrages to an important command among them, as well to my fellow soldiers as to those here present who have sons or brothers or friends among them, that I found among the men at all times the most admirable discipline, the most prompt and spontaneous obedience; at all times a modest, unassuming bravery, which met thirst and cold and starvation and exhausting night marches with songs and gayety and merriment.

"They displayed on the field, and in the hour of battle, a quiet anxiety for the charge, and then plunged down upon the enemy with a fiery fury which overwhelmed them with defeat and stung them with despair. These qualities they adorned with moderation after victory and clemency to the vanquished.

"But the career of your soldiers, so happily begun, closes not here. May they not yet devote their young energies to a country which they ardently love and which thus generously illustrates its love for them?

"War has been to our progressive nation the fruitful season of generating new offspring to our confederation.

"During the Revolution, little armies, issuing from the Alleghanies, passed over Kentucky, the Northwest Territory, and Tennessee. These new countries had been reconnoitered and admired. With hardy frames, confirmed health, and recruited year by year of peace, these soldiers returned to occupy the choice spots which had been their bivouac and camping grounds. From the campaigns of war grew settlements of peace, and populous states displaced the wilderness. Another war came, with another generation; armies penetrated Michigan, upper Illinois and into Mississippi. The great Mississippi, crossed at many points, ceased to be a barrier, and the steamboat appeared, plowing its yellow flow. Five great states and 2,-000,000 of people emblazon its western bank.

"And now again have come another generation and another war. Your little armies have scaled the eternal barriers of the mother mountain of the New World, and buried for a time in the mazes of its manifold peaks and ridges, have debouched at many points upon the briny beach of the Pacific.

"Passing round by the great oceans, a military marine simultaneously strikes the shore and lends them aid. Thus is the wilderness reconnoitered in war, its geography illustrated and its conquerors disciplined.

"Your soldiers, resting for a time at home, will sally forth again, and, wielding the weapons of husbandry, give to you new roads that will nurture commerce and a sisterhood of maritime states on the new-found ocean."

Colonel John W. Reid.
From a Photograph by Thompson, Kansas City, Mo.

JOHN W. REID.

John W. Reid was born at Lynchburg, Virginia, June 14, 1820. His ancestors fought in the Revolutionary War. One of them was the founder of Liberty Hall Academy, now Washington and Lee University. In 1841 he moved to the state of Missouri, and settled in Saline county, where he taught school and studied law. In the year 1846 he was admitted to the bar and practiced for a few months in the early part of the year. When the war with Mexico broke out he raised a company in Saline county and was commissioned its captain and served with distinction in Colonel Doniphan's regiment.

After the conquest of the Territory of New Mexico, and while Doniphan's command was preparing to march on Chihuahua, an order came from General Kearny to Doniphan to proceed to the subjugation of the Navajo tribe of Indians, bands of whom had been raiding in the valley of the Rio Grande. Colonel Doniphan was ordered to effect amicable arrangements with the Navajos, if possible.

While at the Pueblo of Laguna, situate on the line of the Atchison, Topeka and Santa Fe Railway, a short distance west of the city of Albuquerque, a chief of the Navajos, named Sandoval, was sent by Lieutenant Colonel Jackson to see the principal men of his tribe and ascertain if they were of a disposition to make a treaty with the Americans. After an absence of ten days or two weeks Sandoval returned and reported that he had seen all the head men of the Navajo nation, and that they were mostly for peace, but they were unwilling to trust themselves among the New Mexicans, unless they should be furnished with an escort of "white men" whose protection would ensure their safety. And, further, that before coming into the American camp they wished to see some of the "white men" among them, that they might talk with them and learn what was desired.[75]

Captain Reid immediately applied to Colonel Jackson for permission, with a small body of troops, to go to the Navajo country and learn for himself whether or not the Navajos desired peace or war. Reid's request was granted, and on the 20th day of October, 1846, he, with thirty volunteers, accompanied by Lieutenants De Courcey and Wells, set out for the Navajo country.

The New Mexicans were amazed at his temerity. To enter the country of this great nation, noted for its fighting men, who had for many years robbed and plundered the citizens of the valleys, with less than an army, was, to the mind of the native, little less than annihilation. Sandoval accompanied the expedition as guide. The expedition, in its march, encountered difficulties of the most appalling nature. It passed over great mountains. Precipices and yawning chasms often left but a narrow passage, where a misstep would plunge horse and rider hundreds of feet to the foot of the cañon walls.[76]

The expedition traveled five days with trifling intermission and camped for a rest near a beautiful spring of water, in a locality where grass was abundant for their horses. Here Sandoval brought to them about forty warriors, together with some of their

[75-76]Hughes' Doniphan's Expedition.

women. At first the Indians showed signs of fear, whereupon Captain Reid, leaving his men in the valley, rode to the top of the hill, along with Sandoval, stopped and saluted the Indians in a friendly manner. Presently, after some conversation with Sandoval, the Indians approached and rode down to the camp, where Indians and Americans passed the night together, the utmost confidence apparently prevailing.

The following day, at the request of the Indians, the expedition moved on to a point some thirty miles distant, where they were advised there was to be a grand junta of Indians and a celebration. The Indians were very anxious to have the captain and his handful of men as guests, and notified him "that most of their people had never seen a white man, but having heard much of the power and wisdom of the Americans, and of the progress of the army in New Mexico, were very anxious to see and entertain them." Captain Reid agreed to their proposal and, following the Indians, the expedition proceeded to the place designated, where they found more than five hundred warriors and women congregated. The Indians received them with the greatest professions of friendship, and made them presents of sheep and other meats which were highly acceptable. Camp was made, when it was immediately filled with Indians, eagerly gratifying their curiosity. The feasting and dancing continued until late at night, during which the captain and his men mixed in the crowd, to the great enjoyment and satisfaction of the Navajos.[77]

The following day the captain proposed a "grand talk," but was informed by the Indians that the head

---
[77] Hughes' Doniphan's Expedition.

chiefs of the nation were not present, and said that with one day's march further into the country, opportunity would be given to talk with the big chiefs, who were men of great knowledge and experience.

Captain Reid, after consultation with the two officers and some of his men, concluded to accompany the Indians. Afterwards, in a letter written describing the perils that surrounded him at the time, Captain Reid said:[78]

"This was the most critical situation in which I ever found myself placed,—with only thirty men, in the very center of a people, the most savage and proverbially treacherous of any on the continent. Many of them were not very friendly. Being completely in their power, we, of course, had to play the game to the best advantage. As there was no pasturage near the camp, we had to send out our horses. Our numbers were too few to divide or even altogether to think of protecting the horses, if the Indians were disposed to take them. So I even made a virtue of necessity and, putting great confidence in the honesty of their intentions, I gave my horses in charge of one of the chiefs of these notorious horse stealers. He took them out some five miles to graze, and we, after taking supper, again joined in the dance, which was kept up until next morning. Our men happened to take the right course to please the Indians, participating in all their sports and exchanging liveries with them. They seemed to be equally delighted to see themselves clothed in the vesture obtained from us, and to see our men adopting their costumes. The emboldened confidence and freedom with which we mixed among

---

[78] Hughes' Doniphan's Expedition.

them seemed to win upon their feelings and make them disposed to grant whatever we asked. They taxed their powers of performance in all their games to amuse us and make the time pass agreeably, notwithstanding our imminently precarious situation.

"We had not arrived at the place of our camp before we were met by all the head men of the nation. The chief of all, Narbona, being very sick, was nevertheless mounted on horseback and brought in. He slept in my camp all night. Narbona, who was probably seventy years old, being held in great reverence by his tribe for the warlike exploits of his youth and manhood, was now a mere skeleton of a man, being completely prostrated by rheumatism, the only disease, though a very common one, in this country. Conformably to a custom of the chief men of his tribe, he wore his finger nails very long, probably one and a half inches—formidable weapons! He appeared to be a mild, amiable man, and, though he had been a warrior himself, was very anxious before his death to secure for his people a peace with all their old enemies, as well as with us, the new men, as he called us.

"Upon the evening after our arrival we held a grand talk, in which all the old men participated. Most of them seemed disposed for peace, but some opposed it, as being contrary to the honor of the Navajos, as well as their interest, to make peace with Mexicans, though they were willing to do so with us. The peace party, however, prevailed, and by fair words and promises of protection I succeeded in obtaining a promise from the principal men that they would overtake me at the Agua Fria, a place some forty miles from Jackson's camp, from whence we would go together to Santa Fé and conclude the final treaty. The night passed off in a variety of diversions and in the morning, notwithstanding the most urgent desire on the part of our entertainers that we would stay, I thought it prudent to return, as we were running short of provisions. Our horses were forthcoming without a single exception, and as soon as we caught them we turned our faces towards camp. Although this expedition was one of much hazard, yet it turned out to be one of much pleasurable excitement, and attended with no loss or harm. The country through which we traveled is amongst the finest portions of Mexico, decidedly the best for the growth of stock and presenting more interest and variety in its features than any over which I traveled. It is, however, very destitute of water, so much so as to make it dangerous for those to travel without a guide. On this account, more than by its mountain fastnesses, it is impregnable to invasion. The people who inhabit it, and who were the object of our visit, are in many respects singular and unlike other of the aboriginal inhabitants of this continent. Their habits are very similar to those of the Tartars. They are entirely a pastoral people, their flocks constituting their sole wealth; but little addicted to the chase and never indulging in it, except when the game may be taken on horseback. Their weapons of war are the spear or lance, the bow, the lasso, in the use of all which they are not excelled. They may be said literally to live on horseback. Of these animals they possess immense droves and of a stock the same originally with the Mexican horse, yet wonderfully improved. They pay great attention to the breeding of their horses and think scarcely less of them than do the Arabians. They also possess many mules, but they are generally the proceeds of their marauding expeditions against the Mexicans. Indeed, the whole of New Mexico is subject to the devastating incursions of these lords of the mountains."

The expedition, conducted by Captain Reid, effected its return to the place from which they had started without any serious molestation or any considerable difficulty. The chiefs started, according to promise, to overtake the captain at Agua Fria, but were induced to turn back by a miscreant Navajo, who assured them that if they ventured to Santa Fé they would all be killed. Having had so many evidences of the bad faith of the Mexicans, they were naturally suspicious and therefore abandoned their purpose.

Later on, at the Bear Spring, a treaty with the Navajos was executed by Colonel Doniphan, all of the principal chiefs of the tribe being present and signing the document.

At the Battle of the Brazito, on Christmas day, 1846, Captain Reid again distinguished himself. The American left was charged by the Mexican cavalry, when Captain Reid with only sixteen mounted men (the rest of his command being on foot) charged upon them, broke through their ranks, hewed them to pieces with their sabres and thereby contributed materially in throwing the enemy's right wing into confusion.[79]

In the battle of Sacramento, Captain Reid, at the head of his troop, charged the enemy, entrenched at

---

[79]Report of Col. Doniphan, March 4, 1847—from Chihuahua to Brig. Gen. R. Jones, Adjutant General U. S. A., Washington, D. C.

the top of the hill, in a most brilliant manner. Major Gilpin in his report of the battle says: "The onset was commenced by a charge at full gallop of Captain Reid's cavalry, accompanied by the howitzers of our battery, upon the round fort in front. These coming upon the gully beneath the Mexican works, the howitzers turned off to the left and passing around the head of the gully unlimbered close under the Mexican muskets and commenced firing shells and grape. The horsemen, some leaping over and others riding around the gully, charged up the slope supporting the howitzers, but, being few in number and coming suddenly upon the dense masses of the enemy, thronged up in their breastworks, and, assailing them with a thick hail of bullets, they obliqued to the left along the slope under the trenches, seeking intervals between the redoubts through which to charge and firing their carbines into the redoubts as they passed in front of them."[80]

In further commendation of the conduct of the officers and men in this battle, Major Gilpin says: "Should you design to place the achievements of our officers and men under the eye of the President, allow me to recommend them as having conquered for themselves, at Brazito and Sacramento, a glory equal to those who fought at Palo Alto, Resaca de la Palma and Monterey."

After the army under Colonel Doniphan had evacuated the city of Chihuahua, and had taken up its march to join General Zachary Taylor, Captain Reid, with a handful of men, being at Parras, ascertained

---

[80]Report of Major Gilpin to Col. Doniphan, Chihuahua. March 2, 1847.

that a band of Comanches had just made a descent from the mountains upon the city, and killed eight or ten of the citizens, carried off nineteen boys and girls into captivity and driven off three hundred mules and two hundred horses. Besides this they had robbed houses of money, blankets and the sacred household gods. They besought Captain Reid to interfere in their behalf; that although they were considered enemies to the Americans, it did not become the magnanimity of the American soldiers to see them robbed and murdered by a lawless band of savages. Captain Reid undertook to recover the innocent captives and chastise the brutal savages. It so happened that Lieutenant Pope Gordon had been sent in advance of the American army, for the purpose of securing water for the men and horses at El Poso. It was just at this time that Reid was joined by Gordon and his small force. The Indians soon appeared, coming from a cañon to the south of the hacienda. They had all their spoils and captives with them. It was their intention also to take water at El Poso. Captain Reid concealed his men in the hacienda. When the Indians had come within a half mile of the hacienda, a charge was made upon them, which was most gallantly accomplished. The Indians fought with desperation. Captain Reid, in a daring charge, received two severe wounds, one in the face and the other in the shoulder, both from steel-pointed arrows. None of Captain Reid's command was killed, but the Indians lost seventeen killed and not less than twenty-five wounded; all the animals and captive boys and girls were retaken and restored to their friends and relatives. A letter of thanks was given to Captain Reid and his men after this battle by the mayor of the city of Parras, which is most complimentary in its terms and which was read to the people at the celebration given at St. Louis, Missouri, on the return of the regiment from the war, by Senator Thomas H. Benton.

In the year 1849 Captain Reid settled at Independence, Missouri, and was there engaged in the practice of the law until 1853, when he was elected to the state legislature, and was re-elected in 1855. He was the author of the Constitutional amendment under which the state of Missouri was not permitted to incur an indebtedness exceeding thirty millions of dollars. In 1855, together with C. H. Hardin and Thomas C. Richardson, he was appointed member of a commission to revise the laws of the state. Captain Reid was very prominent in the border troubles between Missouri and Kansas prior to the Civil War, and commanded the Missouri forces that burned Osawatomie, in Kansas. In 1858 he was a candidate for Congress, but was defeated. In 1860 he was again a candidate, and was elected and served during the portion of the extra session of 1861 and later resigned. He spent a year in the military prison at St. Louis, at the end of which time he was released on his parole and agreement to take no further part in the war. Toward the close of the war he went to Liberty, Missouri, and lived there about two years. In 1865 he removed to Kansas City and commenced the practice of the law, in partnership with William B. Napton. This partnership only lasted about a year, when he retired from the practice of law, and devoted his entire time to his own real estate interests, which became very important after the panic of 1873. Besides giving his attention to his own private affairs, he devoted much time to the upbuilding of Kansas City, and his labors in this direction were of great value.

To him Kansas City is largely indebted for its present greatness. Captain Reid was a soldier and a brave one. In his profession he was always highly honored by the bar, of which he was a member, and by the community in which he lived. He was twice married, first to a Mrs. Flournoy, and second to Miss Sallie Magraw, of Independence, Missouri, whose father, M. F. Magraw, was a pioneer Santa Fe trader.

He died November 23, 1881.

General Sterling Price.

STERLING PRICE.

Major General Sterling Price claimed descent from Lord Baltimore. He was born in Prince Edward county, Virginia, September 14, 1809. Very little is known of his early life. He attended the schools in the county where he was raised, and graduated, at the age of nineteen, from Hampden-Sidney College. He came to the state of Missouri in 1830, and settled in Chariton county, where he lived until the breaking out of the war between the states.

General Price was a man of fine character. He was elected to the legislature, and in the year 1842 was Speaker of the House of Representatives. He was elected to the Congress of the United States in 1844. He resigned his seat in Congress to accept a commission in the army. He raised the 2nd Regiment of Missouri Mounted Volunteer Cavalry, which was mustered into the service in August, 1846. He was its Colonel and marched with his regiment to Santa Fé, where he assumed command of the Territory after the departure of General Kearny for California and Colonel Doniphan for Chihuahua. He suppressed the rebellion of the Indians and Mexicans in January, 1847, an account of which is given elsewhere in this volume. He was commissioned a Brigadier General, July 20, 1847. He returned to Missouri after the treaty of Guadalupe Hidalgo, and in 1852 was elected Governor of the State of Missouri, which office he filled capably for four years.

Prior to the breaking out of the war between the states, General Price was a strong Union man; he earnestly advocated the preservation of the Union, and was elected a delegate to the convention called by the state legislature as a Union advocate. He was elected president of the convention. General Price did all in his power to prevent secession by his state, and did all that he could to maintain its policy of neutrality. He was made commander of the state guards, but the course of events made it necessary for him to finally join the confederate armies. He was made a Major-General, and his services were rendered principally in Missouri and Arkansas. He led the Confederate army with great skill at the battles of Wilson Creek and Pea Ridge. On the 20th day of September, 1862, he fought the battle of Iuka, and later on was in the battle of Corinth. General Price and his Missourians were the idols of the army. In 1864 he again invaded Missouri, but the campaign was one of disaster, and he retreated into Arkansas.

Physically, General Price was a fine specimen of manhood; he was over six feet in height and straight as an Indian. He was dignified, graceful and gentle and in every way a gentleman.

When the war between the states was at an end General Price went to Mexico, where he sought service with the Emperor Maximilian. He returned to Missouri and engaged in the commission business in St. Louis, and died September 29, 1867.

General Price was a soldier in every sense of the word. He was a great general. He was a strict disciplinarian, but the care of his soldiers was always his first consideration. He was very companionable, and was beloved by all his men. In Missouri he was known as "Old Pap Price," and to-day the memory of the man is sacred in some parts of the state. He treated the captives from the Union army with great tenderness and consideration. Those Union men who had been captured by his army, upon their return to the Union ranks, were loud in their praises of General Price. He was always solicitous as to the sick, and it made no difference to him whether the soldier was a confederate or a federal. As was said of him, "He was more than their commander; he was their personal friend; Old Pap Price was their father indeed." His own troops not only loved him, but were devoted to him. His figure in the battle-field, clothed in a common brown linen coat, with his white hair streaming in the wind, was the signal for wild and never-ending cheers so long as he was in sight, and there was not one of his soldiers, it was said, but who was willing to die if he could only fall within sight of his commander.

ANTONIO JOSE OTERO.

Antonio Jose Otero was a native of Valencia county, New Mexico, having been born in the Plaza of Valencia on the 13th day of March, 1809. He was the son of Vicente Otero. His mother's name, before marriage, was Gertrudes Chaves. His grandfather was Don Pedro Otero, who came to Santa Fé about the year of American Independence, and afterwards moved to Valencia. Judge Otero lived at Peralta, in the county of Valencia, when the American army under General Kearny took possession of the Territory, and was thirty-five years of age when invested with the judicial ermine by General Kearny. He was married to Francisca Chaves, and left him surviving Manuel Rito, Teresa, Adolfo, Meliton S., Mariana and Virginia Otero. He died on the 19th day of November, 1870, at Peralta, his home.

Judge Otero presided over the third circuit court, which comprised all of the territory south of Santa Fé and all of what is now the Territory of Arizona. William Henrie and Celso Cullar Medina were clerks of his court. Some of the records may be found in the office of the probate clerk of Valencia county.

He was a man of enlarged views and commanding influence, and was held in high esteem by those who enjoyed his personal acquaintance. He readily accepted the situation when the conquest came, and was always recognized as most loyal to American ideas and institutions. He received a portion of his education at Laguna, New Mexico, where he was taught by Fr. Penol, a Franciscan friar. He also studied with Fr. Antonio Jose Martinez, of Taos. He was endowed by nature with fine intellectual powers, all of which were developed and strengthened by discipline which enabled him to comprehend readily and accurately the important questions demanding his attention in after years. He was a very cautious man, rarely giving expression to an opinion until, upon reflection, the matter under consideration was clearly and definitely fixed in his mind. It is a matter of more than passing notice that Judge Otero, born and reared under the Spanish and Mexican governments, whose laws and customs were so different from those of the United States, growing to manhood in a portion of the world at that time far removed from all the influences of modern thought and civilization, residing in a locality whose inhabitants were engaged six months in every year in wars with hostile Indians, could so well fill his place upon the bench.

While sitting as a member of the Superior Court he delivered the only opinion coming from that court which has been preserved. This opinion was delivered in the month of January, 1848, in the case of Joab Houghton, administrator of Juan A. Archuleta vs. Manuel Armijo, and was an action of debt. The plaintiff at the time was Chief Justice of the court of which Judge Otero was a member, and the defendant was the ex-governor and commander-in-chief under Mexican rule. In his opinion, the court says:

"The appellant files his motion for dismissal of the appeal on the ground that there is no affidavit, as required by the statute. This would certainly be good cause for the dismissal if the court regarded the case as being before it by the common mode of appeal. There seems to be an obscurity in the law as it exists at present, which the court feels bound to follow as far only as the dictates of justice would warrant. In the strict letter of the statute there is but one mode of appeal, and the want of an affidavit would be good cause for a dismissal; but in another section of the statute it appears to recognize a difference in an appeal and a writ of error. The court, believing that the ends of justice will be attained by bringing the merits of the appeal before it, overrules the motion of the plaintiff."

It will be seen by this opinion, or at least by its wording, that the court found it necessary to follow an "obscurity in the law," to the end that substantial justice might be done to all concerned.

Judge Otero was the only man of Spanish or Mexican origin who ever sat upon the Supreme Bench in New Mexico. He was a representative of his race, faithful to his friends, his country and his God, and no better eulogy could be pronounced, no monument or statue of bronze or marble could equal in value the record he left his people—a just and upright judge.

Governor Henry Connelly.

HENRY CONNELLY.

Henry Connelly was of Irish descent, his forefathers having been citizens of the County Armagh, Ireland. About the year 1689 the Connellys came to America and settled where now is built the city of Charleston, South Carolina. His ancestors in America were heroes of the Revolution, fighting in the patriot armies of Washington, Greene, Morgan, Gates, Lincoln and Pinckney. After the Revolution some of the Connellys moved west into Kentucky, Dr. Henry Connelly's father settling in Nelson county of that state about the year 1789. Henry Connelly was educated in the county schools. Afterwards he attended the Medical school of the Transylvania University at Lexington, Kentucky, being among the first to graduate from that institution. Dr. Henry Connelly graduated in 1828 and soon left Kentucky for Missouri and settled in Liberty, Clay county, of that state. In the same year he left the state for Chihuahua, Mexico. Here he was employed as a clerk and later on purchased the establishment. He was in business in the city of Chihuahua for many years and had for a partner Edward J. Glasgow, who had been in business at Mazatlan. He was married in Mexico, in the town of Jesus Maria, in the year 1838. There were three children born of this marriage, one of whom, Peter, is now living in Kansas City, Missouri.

Prior to the breaking out of the war with Mexico, Dr. Connelly brought his children to Missouri and returned to Chihuahua. His wife died a few years afterward.

Dr. Connelly was in Santa Fé at the time that General Kearny reached Bent's Fort on the Arkansas and acted as agent for Governor Armijo at the time that Captain Cooke arrived in the capital. Prior to Doniphan's capture of the city of Chihuahua, about the time of the battle of Brazito, Dr. Connelly was arrested by the Mexican authorities and taken to Chihuahua and confined, but was subsequently released. He remained in Chihuahua until the close of the war, leaving that city for Santa Fé some time in 1848, and going to the city of Santa Fé, in which place he resided up to the time of his death. He also had a home at Peralta, Valencia county, where he married Dolores Perea, widow of Jose Chaves, the father of Colonel J. Francisco Chaves, from whom the author received most of the information contained in this sketch. Dr. Connelly was engaged in merchandizing in New Mexico from the time that he came from Chihuahua and had houses in several towns in the Territory.

Dr. Connelly was governor of New Mexico during the war between the states and was reappointed by President Lincoln in 1864. He was succeeded by General R. B. Mitchell, soon after the accession of Johnson to the presidency. To Governor Connelly, more than to any one else, was due the fact that the Confederacy secured no permanent foothold in New Mexico. Socially he was a man of refinement and great intelligence. His good work for the people of New Mexico will some day be perpetuated by a suitable monument to his memory. He died at Santa Fé in July, 1866.

General Francis Preston Blair, Jr.

FRANCIS PRESTON BLAIR, JR.

The ancestors of Francis Preston Blair, Jr., came to America from Ireland in 1735, his great-grandfather having been John Blair, a Presbyterian clergyman. He was born in Lexington, Kentucky, February 19, 1821, and died at St. Louis, Mo., July 11, 1875. He received his early education in the public schools of the city of his birth, and attended Princeton College, from which he was graduated in 1841. He studied law in the office of Lewis Marshall, and later entered upon the practice of his profession at St. Louis, Mo., having formed a partnership with his brother, Montgomery Blair. He came to the far West in 1845, a health seeker, and was at Bent's Fort on the Arkansas when General Kearny and the Army of the West reached that point in July, 1846. He joined the column and came with Kearny to Santa Fé, where he aided General Doniphan, Willard P. Hall and Dr. David Waldo in the preparation of what is known as Kearny's Code. Kearny appointed him United States Attorney, and it was Blair who drew the indictments for treason found against the conspirators who brought on the Taos revolution, in 1847. He returned to Missouri in that year, General Price, the military commander at Santa Fé, having abolished the office of attorney general, to which Blair had been appointed. Upon his return to Missouri, Blair journeyed to Woodford county, Kentucky, where he was married to a Miss Alexander. He returned to St. Louis and resumed the practice of his profession. Blair was never an abolitionist, but was elected to the Missouri Legislature as a Free-Soiler in 1852 and again in 1854. He was a great friend of Senator Thomas H. Benton and supported his son-in-law, Fremont, for President in 1856. In this year he was elected a member of Congress. At the following election he was defeated, but again elected in 1860 and was Chairman of the House Committee on Military Affairs. Blair was a strong Union man and used his great influence in his state to prevent its seceding from the Union. He was particularly active in the city of St. Louis, and it was under his leadership that men were drilled night and day preparatory for the great struggle which Blair knew was coming. General Lyon was in command of this force and through Blair's foresight, in the organization of this army, made it possible for Lyon to capture Camp Jackson.

Some time after the battle of Wilson Creek, Blair was commissioned a Major-General in the Federal army and participated in the Vicksburg campaign, where he commanded the Second Division of Sherman's Corps. He was at this time a member of Congress and was re-elected. Two years later he was in command of the Seventeenth Army Corps and marched with Sherman to Atlanta and the sea. In 1866, after the assassination of President Lincoln, he was made a commissioner of the Union Pacific Railroad. In 1868, he was nominated by the Democratic party for Vice-President, with Horatio Seymour, of New York, as the candidate for President. He was a Senator of the United States from 1871 to 1873, having been appointed to the position upon the acceptance of the resignation of Senator Charles D. Drake, who became chairman of the Court of Claims.

Blair was a strong Union man, but after the war he did everything within his power to assist the Confederate soldier in securing the rights of American citizenship. General Blair's position during the administration of the reconstruction plans following the close of the war was a very dangerous one, but it was very largely through his courage and espousal of their cause that they were finally restored to their civil rights. General Blair was subjected to a great many annoyances and indignities growing out of his efforts to restore the ex-Confederate soldier to his civil rights. He canvassed the state of Missouri, speaking in many places, and, upon several occasions, was assailed and interrupted by persons in his audience who did not understand General Blair's patriotic and unselfish motives and his love for equal rights to all.

Upon one occasion[81] he was addressing a meeting of the citizens of Audrain county. His mission was one of peace and in the interest of a re-constructed Union and the restoration of the ballot to the Confederate soldiers of the state. There were present at the meeting a number of ex-Union soldiers who did not agree with the sentiments being expressed by General Blair, and some of them threatened to take him from the speaker's stand. The crowd of citizens present was very large and filled a large grove of forest trees in which the stand had been placed. Marked attention was being given to every word uttered by the speaker, and just as General Blair was beginning to warm to his subject, a large, stalwart man in the audience, clad in the faded blue uniform of a Union soldier, in the midst of others similarly

---

[81]St. Louis Globe-Democrat, February 19, 1899.

dressed, cried out: "He's a d—d rebel! Let us take him down!" and moved toward the stand in a threatening manner. The audience stood mute, but Blair never flinched. Waving his hand to the audience, he said: "Keep your seats; there's no danger." At the same moment he placed two large revolvers on the stand in front of him and denounced the leader of the threatening mob as a coward and telling him to come ahead and take him down, as he was ready for him. The leader and his friends made no further effort to disturb General Blair, who continued to address the meeting for more than two hours, amid demonstrations of great applause.

General Blair had many such experiences in other portions of the state. At a meeting held in Louisiana, Pike county, an immense crowd was present to hear him. No sooner had he been introduced to the audience, and before he had uttered a word, he unbuckled his belt and placed it, with two large revolvers, upon the table in front of him. Then he said: "Fellow Citizens of Pike County—I have an interesting item of news to tell you before I make my speech. I understand that I am to be killed here to-day. As I have recently come out of four years of that business, I think the killing had better be attended to before the speaking begins." The General paused for a moment. No hostile demonstration was made, and he proceeded with his address. Very soon, however, a large, rough appearing man in the audience arose and shouted: "He's nothing but a rebel! Take him out!" The audience was visibly excited and rose to its feet. But Blair was unmoved, and pointing his finger at the author of the disturbance, said: "Well, come and take me out." But the man made no further move, knowing that Blair intended to use his weapons if any assault was made upon him. He was not interrupted from that time on.

General Blair did not know the meaning of the word fear. Many times was he put to the test under circumstances calculated to unnerve the stoutest heart. Upon one occasion, when it was almost death for a public man to declare himself opposed to the institution of slavery, he made an appointment to address the people of Ironton, Missouri, and it was announced that, if he attempted to do so, he would be mobbed. When General Blair reached the town, it was learned that an armed mob had assembled in the court house to prevent his speaking. When he arose to deliver his address, the few friends he had present were greatly alarmed, but their fears were soon dissipated when they saw his calm demeanor and heard him declare that any man who had come to the meeting armed, with the intention to use violence against him, was too great a coward to attempt it. For nearly two hours he spoke without interruption, and afterwards received the congratulations of many present, who entertained opposite views upon the slavery question. He delivered addresses in nearly every part of the state of Missouri, and, outside of a few rotten eggs that were thrown at him in the night time, he never met with any pronounced resistance.

He was a very brave man, but it has been said, by men who served in his corps, that he never went into battle without ample preparation, and that he always consulted freely with his subordinates before taking any important step. He was without fear and still he was not impetuous. He did not possess a military education, but there were few better soldiers in the army. Both Generals Grant and Sherman had an exalted opinion of his military services, and upon several occasions made reference in the most complimentary terms to his military genius.

General Blair was a politician, and in him were combined more of the elements of political success than most public men have enjoyed. His knowledge of men was great. He was whole-souled and generous, utterly unselfish and kept himself poor in his efforts to assist his friends. No better evidence of his spotless integrity can be found than in the fact that, although he had it in his power to become immensely wealthy, he died without a cent.

Many of the people in Missouri criticised General Blair for his course in espousing the cause of the ex-Confederates, after the close of the war. But this criticism only made Blair the stronger in his determination to see them restored to full civil rights. It was his belief that the only method of restoring harmony and good feeling was to extend to them the hand of fellowship and persuade them that their interest was in the Union and not out of it. The position thus taken and maintained by him was fully appreciated by those whom it was intended to benefit. Shortly after his death, at a meeting of ex-Confederates, in the city of St. Louis, the following resolution was passed:

"*Resolved,* That we, the ex-Confederates here assembled, do as deeply mourn his loss, and as heartily acknowledge his high character and great abilities, as can those who never differed with him in the past great struggle. As soldiers who fought against the cause he espoused, we honor and respect the fidelity, high courage and energy he brought to his aid. As citizens of Missouri, we recognize the signal service done his state as one of her senators in the National Council; as Americans we are proud of his manhood; and as men we deplore the loss from among us of one in whom was embodied so much honor, generosity and gentleness. And we remember with gratitude that, as soon as the late civil strife was ended, he was among the first to prove the honesty of his course by welcoming us back as citizens of the Union he had fought to maintain; and that he never thereafter ceased to battle for the restoration and maintenance of our rights under the Constitution."

General Blair died in the fifty-fifth year of his age, and lies buried in Bellefontaine Cemetery, St. Louis, Missouri.

On the day of his funeral the city of St. Louis was black with its emblems of mourning. A great man had fallen. The bar and divers civil societies followed the funeral cortege to the cemetery. The flags of fifty vessels in the harbor were trailing at half-mast, and every possible demonstration of grief was made at the loss of a man whom General Sherman characterized as "one of the truest of patriots, most honest and honorable of men, and one of the most courageous soldiers this country ever produced."

James Magoffin.

JAMES MAGOFFIN.

James Magoffin was of Irish parentage, his father having been born in the County Down, Ireland. His name was Beriah Magoffin, and he was married in Ireland to Jane McAfee. They emigrated to America before 1800 and settled in Harrodsburg, Kentucky, where James Magoffin was born, in the year 1799. He had six brothers and three sisters, one of whom, Beriah Magoffin, was governor of Kentucky. Beriah Magoffin married a daughter of Isaac Shelby, a granddaughter of Isaac Shelby, Sr, who was the first governor of Kentucky.

James Magoffin came to New Mexico and Chihuahua about 1828, and was married in the City of Chihuahua, in the year 1830, to Maria Gertrudes Valdez. He was engaged in the merchandizing business in Chihuahua, and was the American consul in that state. In 1844 he left Chihuahua and went to Independence, Missouri, where he bought a farm. His wife died at Independence the following year. Later in the year, with his two sons, Magoffin went to Washington and there met Senator Thomas H. Benton. He placed his two sons, Samuel and Joséph, in school in Lexington, Kentucky.

Upon the commencement of hostilities in the war with Mexico, Senator Benton sent to Independence, Missouri, for Mr. Magoffin, and he was given a secret commission by the Government of the United States and instructed to go with General Kearny to Santa Fé and pave the way of the Army of the West for the occupation of New Mexico without bloodshed, if possible. Magoffin was a man of mind, of will, of generous temper, patriotic and rich. He knew every man in New Mexico and his character, and all the localities, and was, in the opinion of Benton, of infinite service to the invading army.[82] He agreed to go with the Army of the West, and what he accomplished at Santa Fé, where he proceeded with Capt. Cooke, is mentioned in the sketch of the life of Diego Archuleta.

"Mr. Magoffin, having prepared the way for the entrance of General Kearny into Santa Fé, proceeded to the execution of the remaining part of his mission, which was to do the same by Chihuahua for General Wool, then advancing upon that ancient capital of the Western Internal Provinces on a lower line. He arrived in that city, became suspected, was arrested and confined. He was a social, generous tempered man, a son of Erin, loved company, spoke Spanish fluently, entertained freely, and where it was some cost to entertain—claret, $36.00 a dozen; champagne, $50.00. He became a great favorite with the Mexican officers. One day the military judge advocate entered his quarters and told him that Dr. Connelly, an American, coming from Santa Fé, had been captured near El Paso del Norte, his papers taken, and forwarded to Chihuahua, and placed in his hands to see if there were any that needed government attention; and that he found among the papers a letter addressed to him, Magoffin. He had the letter, unopened, and said he did not know what it might be, but being just ordered to join Santa Ana at San Luis Potosi, and being unwilling that anything should happen after he was gone to a gentleman who had been so agreeable to him, he had

---

[82]Benton's Thirty Years' View, Vol. II, page 682.

brought it to him that he might destroy it if there was anything in it to commit him. Magoffin glanced his eye over the letter. It was an attestation from General Kearny of his services in New Mexico, recommending him to the acknowledgments of the American government in that invasion; that is to say, it was his death warrant if seen by the Mexican authorities. A look was exchanged; the letter went into the fire and Magoffin escaped being shot.

"But he did not escape suspicion. He remained confined until the approach of Doniphan's expedition, and was then sent off to Durango, where he remained a prisoner to the end of the war. Returning to the United States after the peace, he came to Washington in the last days of Mr. Polk's administration and expected remuneration. He had made no terms, asking nothing, and received nothing, and had expended his own money, and that freely, for the public service. The administration had no money applicable to the object. Mr. Benton stated his case in secret session in the Senate, and obtained an appropriation, couched in general terms, of fifty thousand dollars for secret services rendered during the war. The appropriation, granted in the last night of the expiring administration, remained to be applied by the new one, to which the business was unknown, and had to be presented unsupported by a line of writing. Mr. Benton went with Magoffin to President Taylor, who, hearing what he had done, and what information he had gained for General Kearny, instantly expressed the wish that he had had some person to do the same for him, observing that he got no information except at the point of the bayonet. He gave orders to the Secretary of War to attend to the case as if there had been no change in the administration.

"The secretary (Mr. Crawford, of Georgia) higgled, required statements to be filed, almost in the nature of an account, and finally proposed thirty thousand dollars. It barely covered expenses and losses, but having undertaken the service patriotically, Magoffin would not lower its character by standing out for more. The paper which he filed in the war office may furnish some material for history, some insight into the way of making conquests, if ever examined.[83]

"This is the secret history of General Kearny's expedition, and of the insurrection, given because it would not be found in the documents. The history of Doniphan's Expedition will be given for the same reason, and to show that a regiment of citizen volunteers, without a regular officer among them, almost without expense, and hardly with the knowledge of their government, performed actions as brilliant as any that illustrated the American arms in Mexico; and made a march in the enemy's country longer than that of the ten thousand under Xenophon."

His son, Joseph Magoffin, went to El Paso, Texas, in 1856, and is still living in that city.

---

[83]Upon application to the War Department for copies of the Magoffin papers, the following advice was received:

"It is an invariable rule of the Department not to furnish, nor to permit the making of copies of records such as those described within and for the purpose indicated within.

"By order of the Secretary of War.
"HENRY P. McCAIN,
"Adjutant General."

Colonel Richard Hanson Weightman.

RICHARD HANSON WEIGHTMAN.

Richard Hanson Weightman was born in the District of Columbia, was educated at the United States Military Academy at West Point, and, at the beginning of the war with Mexico, lived in St. Louis, Missouri.

When the call was made by the Governor of Missouri for troops, intended to become a part of the Army of the West, under command of General Kearny, the county of St. Louis, which then included the city of St. Louis, was asked to furnish the artillery for the expedition, while the northern river counties were asked to furnish the riflemen.

Major Meriwether Lewis Clark, of St. Louis, a graduate of West Point, and a veteran of the War of 1812 and the Black Hawk War, undertook to raise the two batteries required. Obedient to a call published in the newspapers, many of the first young men of the city volunteered their services, being influenced in some degree by the Santa Fé traders' stories of fabulous wealth to be gained in the Mexican country. The meeting of the recruits was held on May 28, 1846, in the office of a justice of the peace, over a blacksmith's shop on Third street, between Pine and Olive. Here was organized "Battery 'A,' Missouri Light Artillery."[84]

Richard Hanson Weightman was unanimously elected captain. The other officers chosen were: Andrew J. Dorn and Edmund F. Chouteau, first lieutenants, and John O. Simpson, second lieutenant. The

---

[84]St. Louis Weekly Reveille, May 29, 1846.

sergeants were John R. Gratiot, afterwards elected a second lieutenant while marching across the plains; Davis Moore and A. V. Wilson; the corporals, William H. Thorpe, William Clark Kennerley, Clay Taylor, J. R. White and George W. Winston. Each artilleryman was required to furnish himself with a good horse, saddle, clothing, and, in fact, everything except arms. The uniform adopted, which was similar to the fatigue dress of the regular army, consisted of a flat blue cap with red band bearing the artillery emblem, short blue jacket, with red standing collar, and trousers with red stripes, one stripe for the men and two for the officers. As a further distinguishing mark the officers wore a band of gold lace on the collar.[85] The men all procured Spanish saddles of one pattern. The saddle was little more than a skeleton to which were attached the girth and stirrup straps, rendering it cool and light as possible for the horse. A comfortable seat was obtained by placing a Mackinaw blanket above and beneath the saddle; these blankets were also used by the men for cover. Each man had a stout leather belt, supporting a large bowie knife, and many supplied themselves with "revolving pistols," which were then just coming into use.

Stories of Indian massacres and hardships to be encountered on the Great Plains, told by friends and relatives for the purpose of discouraging the young men from going, served only to whet their appetite for adventure. They were also wrought up by the exciting narratives of an old Canadian hunter, Antoine Clement, famous in his day as the only trapper in the West who could approach a grizzly bear on foot with

---

[85]History of Battery "A"—Mo. Hist. Society Collections.

any hope of victory, and Antoine was going with the expedition.

Battery "A" became the *corps d'elite* of the expedition. Everybody wanted to serve under Captain Weightman and become a comrade in arms of the intrepid Antoine. The result was that Battery "B," needed to complete the battalion, suffered for lack of recruits. The other organizations from the vicinity of St. Louis, Captain Fischer's German Troop of Dragoons, the Laclede Rangers under Captain Hudson, and a company of Florissant mounted men, under Captain Edmondson, were all organized and ready to move before Battery "B" was complete with its quota. Finally, to expedite matters, Captain Fischer's troop was converted into a horse battery, which became Battery "B" of Clark's Battalion.

On June 13, 1846, a crowd of citizens assembled on the levee to see the men of Weightman's Battery, one hundred and five strong, embark with their horses and baggage on the steamboat for the trip up the Missouri river. At Fort Leavenworth the command was mustered in the service of the United States, but had to await the arrival of their guns from Pittsburg. Meanwhile the departure every day or so of long trains of transport wagons, with orders to push on as fast as possible, made the men impatient and despondent. Another distressing circumstance was the illness of Captain Weightman, who, it was feared, would have to be left at the Fort.

The long overland journey began on June 30, 1846. The St. Louis Flying Horse Artillery rode out of Fort Leavenworth into the Great West. To each of the eight long brass guns, the two twelve-pound howitzers and to the caissons were hitched four fine dragoon horses. As usual, with horses first put to artillery service, many mishaps arose. On the second day out, while fording a small stream, with steep banks, the drivers quickly tangled up their plunging and kicking animals and might have stopped there forever, had not the cannoneers dismounted and dragged the guns by hand up the muddy banks. Then came the prairies, with grass so high and rank that it reached to the backs of the horses, making progress very slow.

One month after leaving Fort Leavenworth the column arrived at Fort Bent. After leaving Fort Bent and while on the Purgatoire, a Mexican spy was captured and brought into the presence of General Kearny. He looked for immediate punishment and was much surprised when General Kearny took pains to show him his army and equipment and then told him to report to the Governor of New Mexico what he had seen.

While at Fort Bent the battery received a supply of draught mules to fill the places of the many horses that the long march had killed off. Out of the one hundred fine cannon horses originally supplied, not over forty were left after the march across the Great Plains.

When the command reached Las Vegas it was joined by Captain Weightman, who had been left behind at Fort Leavenworth. The men of Battery "A" greeted him with a round of cheers. Now they were keen for the fray. At the Apache Pass, where they expected to meet the enemy, none was found, and, on the 18th of August, the army marched into Santa Fé.

having traveled over eight hundred and fifty miles in six weeks.

Captain Weightman brought with him and delivered to General Kearny, at Las Vegas, his commission as a Brigadier General in the army of the United States. He was a most gallant and capable officer and participated in the battle of Sacramento. He was also a paymaster in the army and was discharged in 1849. When the war with Mexico was over, he came to Santa Fé, where he practiced law and incidentally conducted a small newspaper. He was very active in the politics of the Territory of New Mexico, and was very pronounced in his criticism of the actions of the military authorities during the military occupation of New Mexico. Together with Captain Angney, who had served with him during the war, he inaugurated a great campaign against Hugh N. Smith, who had been sent to Washington to look after the interests of the people, but Smith was successful and was elected delegate to congress from the Territory. In 1850, just prior to the establishment of the territorial form of government, Weightman was elected United States Senator from New Mexico, in an effort, at that time, on the part of the people, to secure statehood for the Territory. He was elected to congress and served two years, 1851-1852.

At the time that he was conducting a newspaper in Santa Fé occurred the altercation between him and Felix X. Aubrey, resulting in the death of the latter. Aubrey had claimed to have discovered a new pass through the mountains to California. Weightman, in his paper, had cast some doubt upon Aubrey's discovery. Shortly afterwards Aubrey returned to Santa Fé, and, meeting Weightman in the Plaza, proceeded with him to the bar of the old Exchange Hotel (Fonda), where they were about to take some brandy, as was the custom of the time. Aubrey raised his glass to his lips, and, putting it down, said, "What has become of your paper?" Weightman answered: "Dead." "What killed it?" asked the other. "Lack of support," was the reply. "The lie it told on me, killed it," said Aubrey. Without a word, Weightman threw a glass of brandy into Aubrey's face, and, while blinded by its effect, stabbed him to death. Major Weightman, in speaking of the affair afterwards to a friend,[86] said that he saw that Aubrey was angry and was drawing his pistol, and that one or the other must be killed, and that he only struck to save his own life.

Major Weightman was always a great friend of the native New Mexicans. He was always on the alert in their defense. While a delegate in Congress, he made an impassioned address in their behalf, the occasion being the contest for his seat in that body by Captain A. W. Reynolds, whom he had defeated before the people. A letter from Major Weightman, in the Spanish language, sent to two very prominent citizens of New Mexico, of date March 20, 1852, from Washington, has been preserved. Messrs. Miguel Pino and Hilario Gonzales were the recipients of this letter. In this letter Major Weightman says: "Since my arrival in the state of Missouri, I have occupied myself in answering the lies of persons who wish to destroy the good will of the people of our Territory, and who are endeavoring in this way to prevent all legislation

---

[86]Kansas Historical Collections—Vol. 9. Account of W. R. Bernard of Westport, Mo.

by congress for our benefit. In answering the falsehoods of these individuals, and in telling the truth, I have spent time which otherwise I should have dedicated to legislative business and in the performance of my duties as your delegate in congress. Now, I am going to give you an account of the operations of our enemies. On my way to Washington I stopped over in the state of Missouri, where I observed, with much displeasure, the miserable efforts that are being made by pernicious persons, residents of New Mexico, to destroy the good name of the inhabitants of New Mexico. Our enemies have acted with a zeal worthy of a better cause, but to attain their detestable ends, they have not hesitated in using all sorts of falsehood. Their first statement was in prejudicing the minds of the people with monstrous tales against the native New Mexicans and equally so against the honest Americans living there, who have declared that they know our people best and have found them to be good, generous and loyal to the Constitution. These men have published in various newspapers slanderous falsehoods stating that the inhabitants of New Mexico harbor hostility and ill-will toward the government and people of the United States, so much so, that it is unsafe for Americans to live among them. They have tried to make the people believe that the death of Burtinett was nothing but assassination, cowardly and diabolical, and that he was killed for no other purpose than that of trying to exercise his privilege of voting, and that William Skinner, while making a friendly visit to Dn. Juan Cristobal Armijo, had lost his life in the midst of cowardly traitors, who had surrounded him in order to kill him. These are samples of the lies they are circulating. Further than this, they are constantly representing that all the New Mexicans are ignorant, vicious and totally unfit for self-government and unworthy of freedom.

"They have slandered our friend, Governor Calhoun, and myself and are saying of us that we are capable only of administering to the atrocious passions of a corrupt and brutal people. Speaking of the clergy, they refer to them in terms more strongly than of the people generally, saying that they are worse than brutes and dishonor their calling.

"To us these slanders are so enormous that it is almost impossible to believe that there are men so depraved as to invent them. They have attacked Governor Calhoun and myself principally, because we have endeavored to faithfully represent the rights and interests of the people of New Mexico, instead of turning traitors and playing the role of ungrateful beings.

"It is impossible to resist the conclusion that they are endeavoring to secure the re-establishment of the repugnant military government, and believing this to be their purpose, I have deemed it my most sacred duty to follow them step by step, in order that I might be able, at all times and in all places, to refute their slanderous falsehoods.

"In the city of St. Louis, on November 13th, I had the opportunity of making a general reply to their accusations and I herewith send you a translation of the article, which was published originally in English, for your satisfaction. The malice of these enemies of New Mexico does not confine itself to the columns of the newspapers in which their statements first appeared.

"They came to Washington and presented false complaints to the President of the United States, in the form of an accusation against Governor Calhoun and myself. Having received this document, which consisted of twenty pages, the President sent for me, placed it in my hands and asked me to answer its contents. In it are repeated the old lies which now and then have been published in the Gazette, at Santa Fé, touching the character of the population of New Mexico, and adding to all this the slanders above referred to.

"I have observed the natural effect of all this in its prejudicing the mind of the President with the idea that the old inhabitants of the Territory are not deserving of being admitted to the exercise of their full rights of citizenship, nor to govern themselves as citizens of this country; and further, that in order to protect the lives of Americans, who are living among such a mob, it was necessary to re-establish the military government.

"And now I must tell you who are the persons signing these slanderous statements. As already stated, I have seen the original statement, the President, himself, having shown it to me and placed it in my hands. The names signed to it are the following: Messrs. Houghton, Reynolds, Collins, McGrorty, Johnson, Tulles and Quinn.

"Such are the persons who occupy themselves in calumniating and slandering the people whom they so recently endeavored to seduce with their adulations; now, in their rage, they have unmasked themselves, and it is an easy matter now to determine who are our enemies and who are our friends. But, even this step does not seem to satisfy them in their frenzy. To one of the representatives in Congress, Mr. Phelps of Missouri, with their continuous appeals, they have finally induced to believe their falsehoods and have succeeded in having him present a memorial to the House of Representatives, on the part of Captain Reynolds, claiming that he is entitled to my seat in congress, the same to which I was elected by favor of the legal voters of New Mexico.

"That memorial contained various injurious allegations against the character of our people and their governor. Mr. Phelps, in his address, read several extracts from the aforesaid document, the one presented to the President. To Mr. Phelps' speech I made reply, as your representative in congress.

"My reply, which has resulted victoriously, inasmuch as it was based upon truth, was made in the House of Representatives on the 15th of March, and I have already sent printed copies to all parts of the United States. I have sent one copy of it to New York, in order that it may be translated into Spanish, and by next mail I shall have the honor and satisfaction of sending you a translated copy. Then the people will be able to judge whether or not I have defended the honor and interests of New Mexico.

* * * * * *

"I will send you by next mail a complete list of the laws that may be passed. I can mention some that have advanced a few steps, but which are as yet uncompleted, viz.: A law granting to the legislature the right to manage, under certain conditions, the money appropriated for the benefit of the Territory; the law extending the regular sessions to sixty instead of forty days. A law authorizing the employment by each House of an interpreter and four clerks; a law authorizing the governor to convene the legislature in an extra session for ninety days. A law authorizing the President to distribute arms and ammunition of war among the inhabitants, that they may defend themselves against the attacks of the savage Indians that surround them.

"Retaining a lasting memory of the fondness, the hospitality and the confidence, which I have received at the hands of my constituents in all parts of the Territory, I avail myself of this opportunity of assuring you that I am

"Your true friend and servant,

"R. H. WEIGHTMAN,

"Delegate from New Mexico."

Many stories are told of Major Weightman and his courage as a citizen and a soldier. Once, during the campaign with Doniphan, word reached him that he was being maligned by Lieutenant Chouteau. He sent for Chouteau and asked him what he meant by such talk. Chouteau said that Weightman had not treated him fairly in some matter, and grew very angry and demanded the satisfaction of a gentleman. Weightman was ready to afford him all the satisfaction desired, but Chouteau, who was carrying his right arm in a sling, having been wounded, asked that the meeting be postponed for a while, else he would be at a disadvantage. "Oh, that's all right," said Weightman, "I'll hold my right hand behind me and we will shoot with our left hands." Fortunately friends interfered and the duel was prevented.

Once, while engaged in practicing law at Santa Fé, Judge Joab Houghton was accused by Weightman of sitting in a case in which the court was personally interested. Judge Houghton responded with a challenge. In the duel that followed, soon afterwards, Weightman alone fired at the word of command. The Judge, who was deaf, ducked his head, after the bullet whizzed by, and shouted, "I didn't hear the command to fire." "All right," said Weightman, holding up his hands, "you have the right to shoot. Fire now." The seconds rushed in and tried to induce Weightman to apologize and to stop the proceedings. "I'll apologize," said Weightman, "as far as being sorry is concerned, but (addressing his opponent), I can't take back what I said, judge, for it was so." The judge was willing to accept that as an apology, but he declared that if Weightman ever again insulted him on the bench, he would shoot next time to kill.

During the war between the States, Major Weightman was in General Price's army, and was in command of a large force of Missourians on Little Blue, east of Independence, Missouri. Thomas B. Catron, of Santa Fé, N. M., at that time a resident of Lexington, Mo., was an officer in Bledsoe's Battery, a part of Weightman's command. At the battle of Wilson's Creek, Mr. Catron held conversation with Weightman a very short time before he was killed. Weightman had personally given orders stationing the battery at a certain point and ordering them to remain in that position until orders to move came from him. It was only a few moments afterwards that Weightman was shot. Planted on another hill was a federal battery, under command of Captain Barkoff, who had been an officer with Weightman in the war with Mexico. This Union battery was silenced by the tremendous fire from Bledsoe's guns and six guns were captured by the Confederate forces.

Writing of the death of Weightman, Edwards says: "The Confederates also lost many valuable officers, one of the noblest and the best being Colonel Richard Hanson Weightman, the hero of Carthage, the idol of his command, peerless soldier, the chivalrous gentleman and the costliest victim the South has yet offered upon the altar of her sacrifices. Amid the low growls of the subsiding battle, amid the slain of his heroic brigade, who had followed him three times to the crest of Bloody Hill, and just as the shrill, impatient cheers of his victorious comrades rang out wildly on the battle breeze, Weightman's devoted spirit passed away from earth, followed by the tears and heartfelt sorrow of the entire army."[87]

General Sterling Price knew Weightman's capabilities as a soldier, and, in his official report to Governor Jackson, of the state of Missouri, of the battle of Wilson's Creek, says: "Among those who fell, mortally wounded upon the battle field, none deserves a dearer place in the memory of Missourians than Richard Hanson Weightman, Colonel commanding the first brigade of the second division of the army. Taking up arms at the very begining of this unhappy contest, he had already done distinguished services at the battle of Rock Creek, where he commanded the state forces after the death of the lamented Holloway; and at Carthage, where he won unfading laurels by the display of extraordinary coolness, courage and skill.

---

[87]Shelby and His Men, page 36.

He fell at the head of his brigade, wounded in three places, and died just as the victorious shouts of our army began to rise upon the air."[88]

---

[88]Official Report—Gen. Price, Aug. 12, 1861, Springfield, Mo., to Gov. Claiborne F. Jackson.